VISUAL QUICKSTART GUIDE

IPHONE SDK3

Duncan Campbell

Peachpit Press

Visual QuickStart Guide
iPhone SDK 3
Duncan Campbell

Peachpit Press

1249 Eighth Street
Berkeley, CA 94710
510/524-2178
510/524-2221 (fax)

Find us on the Web at: www.peachpit.com
To report errors, please send a note to: errata@peachpit.com
Peachpit Press is a division of Pearson Education.
Copyright © 2010 by Duncan Campbell

Editors: Whitney Walker, Rebecca Freed, and Clifford Colby
Production coordinator/compositor: Danielle Foster
Copyeditor: Kim Wimpsett
Proofreader: Rebecca Rider
Indexer: Valerie Perry
Cover design: Peachpit Press

Notice of Rights

Notice of Liability

Trademarks

ISBN-13: 978-0-321-66953-7
ISBN-10: 0-321-66953-3

9 8 7 6 5 4 3 2 1

Printed and bound in the United States of America

Dedication:

This book is dedicated to my parents, who bought me my first computer—and many, many upgrades.

Acknowledgments:

This book is testament to the power of the Internet. The idea started as a conversation (over Twitter) with a colleague in Scotland. The editors and publishers are in the United States, the technical editor is in New Zealand, and I am in Australia. None of us has ever met, and we relied on Twitter, IM, and e-mail to bring this book to fruition.

Thanks to *Clifford Colby*, *Rebecca Freed*, *Kim Wimpsett*, *Rebecca Rider*, *Danielle Foster*, *Valerie Perry*, and everyone else at Peachpit Press who worked so hard to make this book happen.

Special thanks to *Whitney Walker* for her unending patience, hard work, and help: Without you, this book would never have been completed. You are a true professional.

Thanks to *Wesley Joseph* for his last minute Ninja Graphic Design Skills.

Thanks to *James Sugrue* and *Chris Suter* for their technical editing and all-round Cocoa expertise.

Thanks to *Jason Crane* for his support, advice, humor, and IM conversation topics, consisting mainly of exotic chicken recipes and where to purchase expensive coffee-making devices. My bank manager also thanks you.

Cuddles and pets to my dog, *Kip*, who provided me with much-needed breaks from writing. Every hour. Whether I liked it or not.

Finally, the biggest thanks go to my lovely wife, *Sarah*, for calmly putting up with my more-than-usual grumpiness and for always being on hand with a nice glass of red wine.

CONTENTS AT A GLANCE

TABLE OF CONTENTS

INTRODUCTION

Welcome to the exciting, scary, mystical world of iPhone development!

OK, it's not really mystical, but if you are coming to the iPhone from a non-Macintosh development background, things are likely going to seem quite strange, possibly scary, but I hope exciting! Specifically, Xcode and Interface Builder are different from many other integrated development environments (IDEs), Objective-C has a strange syntax, and the Cocoa frameworks can be overwhelming in their size. My hope is that this book will hasten the learning process, and soon you will see that things are not all that different from what you probably already know— they're just done in a different, and maybe even better, way.

This book is geared mainly toward new iPhone developers, but you should have some prior knowledge of a C-based language and be familiar with object-oriented (OO) concepts. It would take a book many times this size to cover all of the iPhone software development kit (SDK), so I focus on some of the more common and interesting subjects you should know about when developing your own iPhone applications.

How to Use This Book

I find that I always learn better by example, so I have created stand-alone applications when demonstrating the concepts in the book. The aim is to give you enough information to get you started coding (and build something useful) and then point you to the relevant place in the documentation for more information. You should be able to jump straight into a chapter and start coding without reading the prior chapters.

This book is a Visual QuickStart Guide, so it's filled with images to walk you through what you'll see on your computer screen as you build your iPhone applications. The interfaces for most of the examples are created directly in code, rather than by using Interface Builder. I feel it's more important that you first learn what's happening under the hood, and this will also make it much easier for you to figure out where to look when things aren't working the way they should be.

Unfortunately, not all of the material I wrote made its way into this book—but all is not lost! The good folks at Peachpit are making the additional chapters available as a free download on their Web site:

www.peachpit.com/iphonesdkvqs

There you'll find material about accessing the iPhone's multimedia capabilities for playing and recording audio, using the iPhone camera for taking pictures and video, accessing the iPod library from your own applications, querying the Address Book, sending e-mail, and more.

The source code for all the examples in the book is available for download by visiting my Web site:

http://objective-d.com/iphonebook/

OK, let's get started....

OBJECTIVE-C AND COCOA

Objective-C is the language most commonly used for iPhone development. It is a superset of ANSI-C, with a Smalltalk-style syntax. If you have programmed in any modern language (such as C++, Java, or even PHP), you should be able to pick up Objective-C relatively quickly.

Cocoa is the collective name given to the frameworks provided by Apple for both OS X and iPhone development. For the purpose of this book, Cocoa will be used to mean the iPhone-specific APIs.

In this chapter, you will get a brief overview of how Objective-C code is structured and how you build your own classes. You'll then learn how memory is managed before learning about some of the more commonly used Cocoa classes. Finally, you'll learn about some of the design patterns used throughout the Cocoa frameworks.

Frameworks

The iPhone OS provides a set of *frameworks* for iPhone development. A framework, such as UIKit, Core Location, Map Kit, Address Book, and Media Player, is simply a collection of classes designed to help you work with a particular technology.

Adding a framework to your projects enables you to work with the classes contained within that framework. Apple groups these frameworks into four main areas of functionality (**Table 1.1**).

To add a framework to your project:

1. In the Groups & Files pane, expand the Targets section, right-click your application target, and select Get Info.

2. Making sure the General tab is selected, click Add (+) at the bottom of the Linked Libraries list, and then add the framework from the available list (**Figure 1.1**).

3. In the header file of your class, import the framework.

   Code Listing 1.1 shows an example of adding a reference to the `CoreAudio` framework to a class.

Table 1.1

iPhone OS Frameworks	
FRAMEWORK	DESCRIPTION
Cocoa Touch	Frameworks for handling all the touch and event-driven programming as well as access to systemwide interface components such as the Address Book browser, mapping, messaging, and most of the user interface components.
Media	The frameworks used to play and record both audio and video as well as provide support for animation and 2D and 3D graphics.
Core Services	Frameworks for accessing many of the iPhone's lower-level features such as files, networking, location services, in-app purchase support, and configuration information such as network availability.
Core OS	Frameworks providing access to the memory, file system, low-level networking, and hardware of the iPhone.

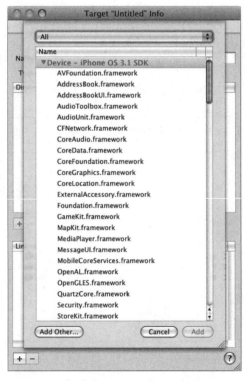

Figure 1.1 Adding a framework to your project.

Code Listing 1.1 Referencing a framework in your code.

```
000                Code
//
//   UntitledViewController.h
//   Untitled
//

#import <UIKit/UIKit.h>
#import <CoreAudio/CoreAudioTypes.h>

@interface UntitledViewController : UIViewController
{
}

@end
```

FRAMEWORKS

Classes

As with regular C, Objective-C separates classes into two files: the header file and the implementation file. The *header* (.h) file is the public interface to your class; it contains declarations for the properties, instance variables, and methods available.

Figure 1.2 shows the main parts of an interface file.

◆ The #import directive, much like the C #include statement, allows you to include header files in your source code. However, #import makes sure the same file is never included more than once.

◆ The @interface line declares your class name and its *superclass*, that is, the parent class from which your class inherits. Any protocols that the class implements are appended to the end within brackets (< and >).

◆ Next, within the braces ({ and }), you define any instance variables used by your class.

◆ Finally, you define the methods and property declarations of your class and then close the implementation file with the @end directive.

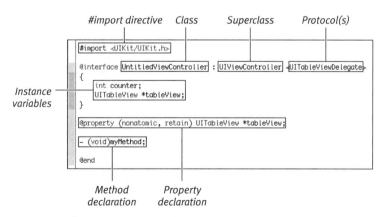

Figure 1.2 The interface file.

CLASSES

The *implementation* (.m) file is where you implement the code for the methods defined in the header file. You can also implement private methods here that won't be visible to anyone using your class.

Figure 1.3 shows the main parts of an implementation file.

◆ Again, the #import directive is used, this time to import the interface declaration.

◆ The @implementation line begins the area where you write the code for your class.

◆ You next use the @synthesize directive to generate the setter and getter methods for the properties of your class. Notice how they can be on the same line, separated by commas.

◆ Finally, you write your code, implementing each of the methods defined in the interface file before again closing the implementation with the @end directive.

Methods

Methods in Objective-C perform an *action* on an object and are surrounded by square brackets:

```
[myObject foo];
```

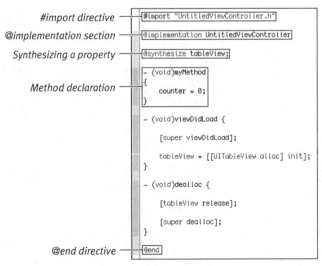

#import directive

@implementation section

Synthesizing a property

Method declaration

@end directive

```
#import "UntitledViewController.h"

@implementation UntitledViewController

@synthesize tableView;

- (void)myMethod
{
    counter = 0;
}

- (void)viewDidLoad {

    [super viewDidLoad];

    tableView = [[UITableView alloc] init];
}

- (void)dealloc {

    [tableView release];

    [super dealloc];
}

@end
```

Figure 1.3 The implementation file.

CLASSES

Here you are calling a method named foo on the object myObject. The process of calling a method is known as *messaging*—the message is the signature of the method including any parameters that are passed.

Objective-C is a verbose language with long and descriptive method and parameter names. The method and parameter names combine to form a *phrase* explaining the action of the method. A variation of camel case notation is used where the first word is usually lowercase, the first letter of each subsequent word is capitalized, and no spaces appear between words:

```
[myObject performSomeAction];
```

This would call the performSomeAction method of myObject.

When passing a value into a method, the parameter name will also often describe the data type if the type is important:

```
[myObject saveInteger:10];
```

This will call the saveInteger method on the myObject object, passing the value 10 to the first parameter.

With multiple parameters, each parameter is named and helps form the phrase describing the purpose of the method. For example, a C function to create a fraction and return the result might look like this:

```
fraction = MakeFraction(10,20);
```

Implemented as an Objective-C method, it might look like this:

```
fraction = [Fraction fractionWith
→ Numerator:10 denominator:20];
```

Here you are calling the fractionWith Numerator:denominator: method on Fraction, passing two parameters, and storing the returned value in the fraction variable.

The syntax for calling and defining methods is very similar. For example, you could define the previous method as follows:

```
-(double)fractionWithNumerator:
→ (int)num denominator:(int)denom;
```

Many classes provide what are known as *class methods*—instead of creating an object and then calling a method on it, you can call a method directly on the class itself.

By convention, class methods (other than +new and +alloc) usually return *autoreleased* objects (see the "Memory Management" section later in this chapter).

When defining class methods, you prefix the method type identifier with a plus (+) sign:

```
+ (MyClass *)classWithInteger:
→ (int)iValue
```

Code Listing 1.2 shows an example of some commonly used class methods.

The shorthand for writing methods is to remove the datatype and parameter name from the method signature, leaving a colon (:) to indicate a parameter. For example, the following method:

```
-(NSString *)appendString:(NSString *)
→ string1 toString:(NSString *)string2
```

could be shortened to the following:

```
appendString:toString:
```

Code Listing 1.2 Some commonly used class methods.

```
 ⊖ ⊖ ⊖                              Code
- (void)viewDidLoad {

    NSString *myString = [NSString stringWithString:@"foobar"];
    NSMutableDictionary *dict = [NSMutableDictionary dictionaryWithObject:nil];
    NSMutableArray *arr = [NSMutableArray arrayWithObject:nil];

    UIButton *myButton = [UIButton buttonWithType:UIButtonTypeRoundedRect];
    UIImage *img = [UIImage imageNamed:@"apple.png"];
    UIFont *font = [UIFont systemFontOfSize:14.0];
}
```

CLASSES

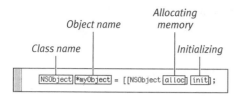

Figure 1.4 Creating an object.

Creating objects

In general, to create an object in Objective-C, you do the following:

◆ Define the type of your object, and give it a name.

◆ Allocate memory with the `alloc` class method.

◆ Initialize the object with an `init` method.

For example:

```
NSObject *myObject;
myObject = [NSObject alloc];
[myObject init];
```

This is normally written as a single statement:

```
NSObject *myObject = [[NSObject alloc]
→ init];
```

Figure 1.4 shows a breakdown of this statement. Notice that there are the same number of square brackets in both examples. This *nesting* of method calls is common in Objective-C, and you will see examples of it throughout this book.

Many classes provide additional *initializer* methods allowing you to perform multiple steps in a single method call. For example, to create an `NSString` and assign it a value, you can use the following:

```
NSString *myString = [[NSString alloc]
→ initWithString:@"some value"];
```

You can also use the class method:

```
NSString *myString = [NSString
→ stringWithString:@"some value"];
```

(`NSString` contains many of these initializer methods, which are discussed in the "Commonly Used Classes" section later in this chapter).

CLASSES

Properties

Properties provide a convenient way for you to get and set instance variables on objects without having to define or use accessor (commonly known as *getter* and *setter*) methods.

◆ For example, if you want to create a new UIView object, you write the following:

```
UIView *myView = [[UIView alloc]
→ init];
```

◆ You can then set the backgroundColor property:

```
myView.backgroundColor = [UIColor
→ redColor];
```

◆ You can also retrieve the value with the same property:

```
UIColor *bgColor =
→ myView.backgroundColor;
```

As already mentioned, properties are defined using the @property keyword defined in the class header (.h) file (**Code Listing 1.3**).

Notice how you can define properties as being readonly and also how the set accessor will be implemented—as a direct assignment (which is the default), as a retain, or as a copy of the object being used for assignment.

In the class implementation (.m) file, using the @synthesize keyword will automatically generate the getter and setter methods (**Code Listing 1.4**).

✔ Tip

■ For more information on properties, refer to the "Declared Properties" section of the *Objective-C 2.0 Programming Language Guide* in the developer documentation.

Code Listing 1.3 Defining properties.

```
@interface UntitledViewController : UIViewController
{
    int counter;
    NSString *username;
    NSString *language;
    NSNumber *age;
}

@property int counter;
@property (copy, readwrite) NSString *username;
@property (readonly, assign) NSString *language;
@property (retain) NSNumber *age;
```

Code Listing 1.4 Synthesizing properties.

```
@implementation UntitledViewController

@synthesize counter;
@synthesize username,language;
@synthesize age;
```

CLASSES

Memory Management

In the "Creating objects" section earlier in this chapter, you created an object:

```
NSObject *myObject = [[NSObject alloc]
→ init];
```

Objective-C uses a process known as *reference counting* for managing memory. When an object is created (in this example by calling the `alloc` method), it contains a reference count—also known as a *retain count*—of one. From then on, each time the object is referenced by anyone (by calling its `retain` method), the reference count *increases* by one. When you are finished with the object, you call its `release` method, which then *decreases* the reference count by one. When the reference count reaches zero, the object's memory is freed from the system.

Objects that aren't released after being retained will leak memory, so it's important to make sure you always release your objects when you are finished with them. Conversely, you need to know when you should retain an object created by someone else; you don't want an object to be released if you are still working with it, and you also don't want to release an object you have not retained.

One useful habit when working with objects is to release them as early as possible. Consider the following code:

```
UILabel *myLabel = [[UILabel alloc]
→ init];
myLabel.text = @"some text";
[myView addSubview:myLabel];
[myLabel release];
```

You first create a label, which will set its retain count to one. After setting the text, you add the label to a view. This will increase the retain count to two (the view calls `retain` on the label when it is added as a subview). You no longer need the label (the view now owns it), so you then release it on the next line. You can now safely forget about managing memory for the label—you balanced your retain/release calls, and the view will release its subviews (and therefore the label) by itself.

This pattern of releasing an object as soon as you are done with it (rather than waiting until later in your code) is a good one to use and helps reduce the likelihood of memory leaks.

Autorelease pools

To make things a little easier to work with, Objective-C provides an *autorelease pool*.

Consider the following example:

```
-(NSString *)makeUserName
{
    NSString *name = [[NSString alloc]
    → initWithString:@"new name"];
    return name;
}
```

Here you have created a new string and are returning it from a method. Unfortunately, someone using this method has no way of knowing that they are supposed to call release on the string being returned, and therefore you'd have a memory leak. You obviously can't call release inside the method because this would set the retain count to zero and you would have nothing to return.

The solution to this situation is to use an autorelease pool:

```
-(NSString *)makeUserName
{
    NSString *name = [[NSString alloc]
    → initWithString:@"new name"];
    return [name autorelease];
}
```

Objects created in the autorelease pool do not need to have the `release` method explicitly called but instead will release themselves at some point in the future—typically when the autorelease pool itself is released.

The disadvantage here, of course, is that while an object exists, it's using memory. If you create a lot of autoreleased objects, you will use up more memory, which may have a detrimental effect on your application's performance. Because of the limited memory resources on the iPhone, it's a good idea to manually manage memory yourself (using `retain`/`release`) whenever possible.

Objects created by calling a class method will generally return an autoreleased object. For example, the following:

```
UIButton *myButton = [UIButton
↪ buttonWithType:UIButtonTypeRounded
↪ Rect];
```

returns an autoreleased object that you don't need to (and should not) release.

Of course, you can still call `retain` and `release` on autoreleased objects if you like, which might be important if you want to hold on to an object. Just make sure you never call `release` without first calling `retain`. Doing so will cause an error and likely crash your application.

Remember this basic rule of thumb: Any time you call the `alloc`, `copy`, or `retain` methods on an object, you must at some point later call the `release` method.

MEMORY MANAGEMENT

If you are creating a lot of autoreleased objects (for example, within a loop), it can often help to create your own autorelease pool at the start of your loop and then free it manually at the end. This gives you the best of both worlds: You don't have to worry about leaking memory with manually created objects, and you can keep your memory usage under control more efficiently by manually releasing the objects in your own pool.

Code Listing 1.5 shows an example of creating and using your own autorelease pool.

✔ Tips

■ In most cases, the Cocoa Touch frameworks use a naming convention to help you decide when you need to release objects: If the method name starts with the word alloc, new, or copy, then you should call release when you are finished with the object.

■ For more information on memory management, refer to the *Memory Management Programming Guide for Cocoa* in the developer documentation.

Code Listing 1.5 Using an autorelease pool.

```
Code

- (void)myMethod
{
    NSString *myString = @"some value";
    for (int i=0; i<9999; ++i)
    {
        NSAutoreleasePool *pool = [[NSAutoreleasePool alloc] init];

        NSString *myString2 = [myString stringByAppendingString:
                                [NSString stringWithFormat:@"%d", myString, i]];

        [pool release];
    }
}
```

Commonly Used Classes

Of the hundreds of classes available in the Cocoa Touch frameworks, you will use a couple of them frequently, even in the simplest of applications.

Strings

Probably the most common class you will use will be NSString. An NSString is *immutable*, meaning that once you have created one, you cannot change it. If you need to alter the contents of an NSString, you should use the NSMutableString class. However, it's much more common to just create a new NSString with the new contents.

◆ Of the many ways to create an NSString, the simplest is probably the following:

```
NSString *myString = @"some string";
```

◆ To create a formatted string, you could use the following code:

```
NSString *myString = [NSString
→ stringWithFormat:@"object =
→ %@",someObject];
```

Some of the more common format specifiers are %d for integer, %f for double, and %@ for objects. (For a complete list of available format specifiers, refer to the "String Format Specifiers" section of the *String Programming Guide for Cocoa* in the developer documentation.)

◆ If you have strings that contain only numbers, you can return numeric values by using:

```
NSString *myString = @"12345";
double doubleString = [myString
→ floatValue];

int intString = [myString intValue];
```

continues on next page

Both of these methods attempt to create numeric values up to the first non-numeric character in the string, so, for example, a string of "123abc" would return 123 for the intValue method.

◆ You can get the length of a string:

```
int stringLength = [myString
→ length];
```

◆ To compare two strings, you can use the following:

```
BOOL areEqual = [string1
→ isEqualToString:string2]
```

This will return TRUE if all the characters in both strings are exactly equal.

◆ To perform a case-insensitive comparison, you can use this:

```
BOOL areEqual = ([string1
→ caseInsensitiveCompare:string2] ==
→ NSOrderedSame);
```

◆ You can also convert the case of a string:

```
NSString *myString = "abcdef";
NSString *upper = [myString
→ uppercaseString];
NSString *lower = [myString
→ lowercaseString];
```

◆ You can easily trim a string of unwanted characters. For example, to remove all whitespace from a string, you could use this:

```
NSString *myString = @"   one two
→ three   ";
NSString *trimmed = [myString string
→ ByTrimmingCharactersInSet:
→ [NSCharacterSet whitespace
→ CharacterSet]];
```

This will give you the string "one two three".

You can create substrings from existing strings in several ways:

◆ For example, to create a new string with the contents "one" from the following string:

```
NSString *numberString = @"one two
→ three";
```

you could use the following code:

```
NSString *aString = [numberString
→ substringToIndex:3];
```

◆ You can use this:

```
NSRange range = NSMakeRange(4,3);
NSString *aString = [numberString
→ substringWithRange:range];
```

to create a new string with the contents `"two"`.

◆ Finally, you can use the following:

```
NSString *aString = [numberString
→ substringFromIndex:8];
```

to create a new string with the contents `"three"`.

◆ You can also create an array containing these three substrings as elements (using the space character as a delimiter) by using this:

```
NSArray *arr = [numberString
→ componentsSeparatedByString:@" "];
```

This will give you the array `{"one","two","three"}`.

◆ To replace substrings in your strings, you can use the following:

```
NSString *aString = [numberString
→ stringByReplacingOccurrencesOf
→ String:@"three" withString:
→ @"four"];
```

This will give you the string `"one two four"`.

continues on next page

COMMONLY USED CLASSES

- You can search for a substring within a string:

```
NSRange foundRange = [numberString
→ rangeOfString:@"two"];
```

This will return the range {4,3} (indicating a match was found at position 4 with a length of 3).

- You can determine whether a string contains a substring:

```
BOOL found = ([numberString
→ rangeOfString:@"two"].location !=
→ NSNotFound);
```

- You can combine strings:

```
NSString *string1 = @"one";
NSString *string2 = [string1
→ stringByAppendingString:@" two"];
```

This will give you the string "one two".

NSString also contains numerous functions for dealing with files. You can read from and write to files, as well as get information such as the file path and extension.

- For example, to read the contents of a file into a string, use the following:

```
NSString *fileContents = [NSString
→ stringWithContentsOfFile:
→ @"myfile.txt"];
```

- You can get the file extension of a file:

```
NSString *fileName = @"myfile.txt";
NSString *fileExtension =
→ [fileName pathExtension];
```

You can also use an NSString to both read and write to a URL.

- For example, to read the contents of a URL into your string, you can use this:

```
NSURL *url = [NSURL URLWithString:
→ @"http://google.com"];
NSString pageContents = [NSString
→ stringWithContentsOfURL:url];
```

Code Listing 1.6 shows some commonly used string methods.

✔ Tip

- For more information on NSString, refer to the *NSString Class Reference* in the developer documentation.

Code Listing 1.6 Some commonly used string methods.

```
- (void)myStringExample
{
    NSString *fileName = @"somefile.txt";
    NSString *fileExtension = [fileName pathExtension];

    NSString *myString = @" one two three ";
    NSString *trimmed = [myString stringByTrimmingCharactersInSet:
                        [NSCharacterSet whitespaceCharacterSet]];

    NSString *string1 = @"some string";
    NSString *string2 = @"some other string";
    NSString *string3 = @"SoMe StRiNg";
    NSString *string4 = @"some other string";

    NSLog(@"%i",[string2 isEqualToString:string4]);
    NSLog(@"%i",[string1 isEqualToString:string3]);
    NSLog(@"%i",([string1 caseInsensitiveCompare:string3] == NSOrderedSame));

    NSString *n = @"12345";
    double d = [n doubleValue];
    int i = [n intValue];
    NSLog(@"%f, %d",d,i);

    NSURL *url = [NSURL URLWithString:@"http://google.com"];
    NSString *pageContents = [NSString stringWithContentsOfURL:url];

    NSString *numberString = @"one two three";
    NSRange foundRange = [numberString rangeOfString:@"two"];
    NSString *oneString = [numberString substringToIndex:3];
    NSString *twoString = [numberString substringWithRange:NSMakeRange(4,3)];
    NSString *threeString = [numberString substringFromIndex:8];

    NSString *repeatString = [numberString
                             stringByReplacingOccurrencesOfString:@"three"
                             withString:@"four"];
    BOOL found = ([numberString rangeOfString:@"two1"].location != NSNotFound);

    NSString *stringa = @"one";
    NSString *stringb = [stringa stringByAppendingString:@" two"];

    NSLog(@"%i - %i",foundRange.location, foundRange.length);
    NSLog(@"%@",repeatString);
    NSLog(@"[%@] [%@] [%@]",oneString,twoString,threeString);
    NSLog(@"%@",[numberString componentsSeparatedByString:@" "]);
}
```

Dates and times

You use the NSDate class to compare dates and calculate date and time intervals between dates:

◆ You can create an NSDate with the current date and time:

```
NSDate *myDate = [NSDate date];
```

◆ You can create an NSDate that represents 24 hours from now:

```
NSTimeInterval secondsPerDay =
↩ 24*60*60;
NSDate *tomorrow = [NSDate
↩ dateWithTimeIntervalSinceNow:
↩ secondsPerDay];
```

◆ You can also create a date from an existing date by using the following:

```
NSTimeInterval secondsPerDay =
↩ 24*60*60;
NSDate *now = [NSDate date];
NSDate *yesterday = [now
↩ addTimeInterval:-secondsPerDay];
```

This will create a date representing this time yesterday.

◆ You can compare whether two dates are exactly equal:

```
BOOL sameDate =
↩ [date1 isEqualToDate:date2];
```

◆ Or, to get which date occurs before or after another date, you can use the following:

```
NSDate *earlierDate =
↩ [date1 earlierDate:date2];
NSDate *laterDate =
↩ [date1 laterDate:date2];
```

◆ You can calculate how many seconds occurred between two dates:

```
NSTimeInterval secondsBetweenDates =
↩ [date2 timeIntervalSinceDate:
↩ date1];
```

◆ Or you can calculate how many seconds occurred between now and a date in the future:

```
NSTimeInterval secondsUntilTomorrow
→ = [tomorrow timeIntervalSinceNow];
```

By using the NSCalendar class, you can create NSDate objects more easily.

◆ For example, to create a date representing June 01, 2010, use the following:

```
NSDateComponents *comp =
→ [[NSDateComponents alloc] init];
[comp setMonth:06];
[comp setDay:01];
[comp setYear:2010];
NSCalendar *myCal = [[NSCalendar
→ alloc] initWithCalendarIdentifier:
→ NSGregorianCalendar];
NSDate *myDate =
→ [myCal dateFromComponents:comp];
```

◆ Similarly, to get the day, month, and year components from an existing date, you could use this:

```
unsigned units = NSMonthCalendarUnit
→ | NSDayCalendarUnit |
NSYearCalendarUnit;
NSDate *now =[NSDate date];
NSCalendar *myCal = [[NSCalendar
→ alloc] initWithCalendarIdentifier:
→ NSGregorianCalendar];
NSDateComponents *comp = [myCal
→ components:units fromDate:now];
NSInteger month = [comp month];
NSInteger day = [comp day];
NSInteger year = [comp year];
```

Calendars also make it a little easier when creating dates from existing dates since you don't have to convert everything to and from seconds.

◆ For example, to rewrite the previous example of creating a date representing tomorrow, use the following:

```
NSDate *now = [NSDate date];
NSDateComponents *comp =
→ [[NSDateComponents alloc] init];
[comp setDay:01];
NSCalendar *myCal = [[NSCalendar
→ alloc] initWithCalendarIdentifier:
→ NSGregorianCalendar];
NSDate *tomorrow = [myCal
→ dateByAddingComponents:comp
→ toDate:now options:0];
```

NSDate in itself is not particularly friendly when you want to present human-readable dates and times to the user. For this, you would normally use an NSDateFormatter.

◆ To get a string representation of the current date using an NSDateFormatter, use the following:

```
NSDate *now = [NSDate date];
NSDateFormatter *formatter =
→ [[NSDateFormatter alloc] init];
[formatter setDateStyle:
→ NSDateFormatterMediumStyle];
NSString *friendlyDate =
→ [formatter stringFromDate:now];
```

◆ To get the current time, you can use the following:

```
NSDate *now = [NSDate date];
NSDateFormatter *formatter =
→ [[NSDateFormatter alloc] init];
[formatter setTimeStyle:
→ NSDateFormatterMediumStyle];
NSString *friendlyTime =
→ [formatter stringFromDate:now];
```

Table 1.2 shows the five predefined formatter styles.

◆ Finally, you can also use the `dateFormat` property of a date formatter to manually set a style:

```
NSDate *now = [NSDate date];
NSDateFormatter *formatter =
→ [[NSDateFormatter alloc] init];
[formatter setDateFormat:
→ @"yyyy-mm-dd"];
NSString *friendlyDate =
→ [formatter stringFromDate:now];
```

✔ Tip

■ See the "Date Formatters" section of the *Data Formatting Programming Guide for Cocoa* in the developer documentation for a complete list of available format strings.

Table 1.2

Predefined NSDateFormatter styles	
STYLE	**DESCRIPTION**
NSDateFormatterNoStyle	The default style if none is specified. No output is produced.
NSDateFormatterShortStyle	A short, numeric-only style: Date: "07/14/10" Time: "12:32pm"
NSDateFormatterMediumStyle	An abbreviated style: Date: "Jun 14, 2010" Time: "12:32pm"
NSDateFormatterLongStyle	A full-text style: Date: "Jun 14, 2010" Time: "12:32:04pm"
NSDateFormatterFullStyle	The longest style: Date: "Tuesday, June 14, 2010 AD" Time: "12:32:42pm GMT"

Arrays

For creating arrays, you use the NSArray class. Similarly to an NSString, an NSArray is immutable; in other words, once you have created one, you cannot alter its contents. Use the NSMutableArray class to create a dynamic area whose contents can be edited.

Arrays represent a collection of objects.

◆ To create an array, you could write the following:
```
NSString *string1 = @"one";
NSString *string2 = @"two";
NSString *string3 = @"three";
NSArray *myArray = [NSArray
→ arrayWithObjects:string1,string2,
→ string3, nil];
```
Notice that the list of objects being added to the array is terminated with nil.

◆ You can also create an array from an existing array:
```
NSArray *myArray2 = [NSArray
→ arrayWithArray:myArray1];
```

◆ You can create an array containing only part of an existing array:
```
NSRange range = NSMakeRange(0,2);
NSArray *subArray = [myArray
→ subarrayWithRange:range];
```
This will create an array containing the first two objects of myArray.

◆ To get the length of an array, use this:
```
int arrayLength = [myArray count];
```

◆ You can access an object at a particular position in the array:
```
NSString *myString = [myArray
→ objectAtIndex:0];
```
Since arrays are zero-based, this will return the first object in the array.

- You can see whether an array contains an object:

```
NSString *string1 = @"one";

NSString *string2 = @"two";

NSArray *myArray = [[NSArray alloc]
→ initWithObjects:string1, string2,
→ nil];

BOOL isInArray = [myArray
containsObject:string1];
```

- You can get the position of an object in the array:

```
int index = [myArray indexOfObject:
→ string1];
```

- You can loop through the values of an array:

```
for (NSString *obj in myArray) {
    NSLog(@"%@",obj);
}
```

- Or, to loop backward through the values of an array:

```
for (NSString *obj in [myArray
→ reverseObjectEnumerator]) {
    NSLog(@"%@",obj);
}
```

- To sort an array of strings:

```
[myArray sortUsingSelector:
→ @selector(localizedCaseInsensitive
→ Compare:)];
```

The @selector keyword here is the name of the method being used to perform the sort.

An NSMutableArray is similar to an NSArray, with the added advantage of being able to modify its contents after creation.

◆ You can add an object to the end of a mutable array:

```
NSString *string1 = @"one";
NSString *string2 = @"two";
NSMutableArray *myArray =
→ [[NSMutableArray alloc]
→ initWithObjects:string1, string2,
→ nil];
NString *string3 = @"three";
[myArray addObject:string3];
```

or to add an object at the beginning:

```
[myArray insertObject:string3
→ atIndex:0];
```

◆ You can replace an object at a particular position in the array:

```
[myArray replaceObjectAtIndex:0
→ withObject:string2];
```

◆ To remove an object:

```
[myArray removeObject:string3];
```

◆ Or, to remove an object at a particular position:

```
[myArray removeObjectAtIndex:0];
```

This will remove the first object.

◆ To remove several objects:

```
NSRange range = NSMakeRange(0,2);
[myArray removeObjectsInRange:
→ range];
```

This will remove the first two objects.

◆ Finally, to remove all the objects in the array:

```
[myArray removeAllObjects];
```

Dictionaries

An NSDictionary is used to store associated key-value pairs. Again, like NSArray, NSDictionary is immutable. Use the NSMutableDictionary class if you need to be able to alter the contents of the dictionary after creation.

Generally, each key-value pair (called an *entry*) consists of an NSString for the key and an NSObject for the value. Keys must be unique within a dictionary; values do not need to be.

NSDictionarys are used extensively throughout the Cocoa frameworks because they provide an efficient and simple way of storing information in an easily retrievable manner. For example, user defaults are stored as dictionaries.

◆ To create a dictionary, you could use the following:

```
NSArray *arr1 = [NSArray arrayWith
→Objects:@"iPhone",@"iPod",nil];
NSArray *arr2 = [NSArray arrayWith
→Objects:@"iMac", @"Mac Pro",
@"Macbook", @"Macbook Pro",nil];
NSDictionary *myDict =
→[[NSDictionary alloc]
→dictionaryWithObjectsAndKeys:arr1,
→@"mobile", arr2, @"computers",
→nil];
```

Notice that like an NSArray, you end the list of objects with nil when creating the dictionary.

◆ To see how many elements are in an dictionary:

```
int dictSize = [myDictionary count];
```

continues on next page

COMMONLY USED CLASSES

◆ To access a value in the dictionary:

```
NSArray *mobile = [myDict
→ objectForKey:@"mobile"];
```

◆ Or, to retrieve the keys for an object, use the following:

```
NSArray *keys = [myDict
→ allKeysForObject:arr1];
```

◆ To retrieve an array of all the values in the dictionary:

```
NSArray *values = [myDict
→ allValues];
```

◆ You can also enumerate through the contents just like an NSArray:

```
for (id key in myDict) {
    NSLog(@"key: %@, value: %@", key,
    → [myDict objectForKey:key]);
}
```

◆ If your dictionary contains only property list objects (NSData, NSDate, NSNumber, NSString, NSArray, or NSDictionary), you can save it to a file:

```
NSString *filePath = [[[NSBundle
→ mainBundle] resourcePath]
→ stringByAppendingPathComponent:
→ @"dict.txt"];

BOOL success = [myDict writeToFile:
→ filePath atomically:YES];
```

◆ Conversely, you can populate a dictionary from a file:

```
NSDictionary *myDict2 =
→ [NSDictionary dictionaryWith
→ ContentsOfFile:filePath];
```

By using an NSMutableDictionary you can add and remove objects after creation.

◆ To add an object to a mutable dictionary you could use this:

```
NSArray *arr1 = [NSArray arrayWith
→ Objects:@"iPhone",@"iPod",nil];
```

```
NSArray *arr2 = [NSArray
→ arrayWithObjects:@"iMac",
→ @"Mac Pro", @"Macbook", @"Macbook
→ Pro",nil];
```

```
NSMutableDictionary *myDict =
→ [[NSMutableDictionary alloc]
→ initWithObjectsAndKeys:arr1,
→ @"mobile", arr2, @"computers",
→ nil];
```

```
NSString *string1 = @"AppleTV";
```

```
[myDict setObject:string1
→ forKey:@"media"];
```

◆ You can also alter an existing object in the dictionary:

```
NSString @string2 = @"airport
→ express";
```

```
[myDict setObject:string2
→ forKey:@"media"];
```

◆ Or, you can remove an object from the dictionary:

```
[myDict removeObjectForKey:@"media"];
```

◆ To remove multiple objects, use the following:

```
NSArray *keyArray = [NSArray
→ arrayWithObjects:@"mobile",
→ @"computers",nil];
```

```
[myDict removeObjectsForKeys:keyArray];
```

◆ Finally, to remove all objects from the dictionary, use the following:

```
[myDict removeAllObjects];
```

Notifications

Notifications provide a handy way for you to pass information between objects in your application without needing a direct reference between them. They are represented by the NSNotification object, which contains a name, an object (often the object posting the notification), and an optional dictionary.

Notifications are posted to a *notification center* whose job is to forward the notification to all *registered observers*—objects that have requested to be told about certain notifications.

◆ To register your object as an observer for a notification, you would write the following:

```
[[NSNotificationCenter
 → defaultCenter] addObserver:self
 → selector:@selector(doSomething:)
 → name:@"myNotification"
 → object:nil];
```

◆ Here you are observing a notification called myNotification.

When the notification is sent to your object (by the notification center), a message is sent to the doSomething: method. By passing nil to the final parameter, you are saying that you want to be told about any notification named myNotification, no matter which object sends it. You could have optionally specified which object you wanted to observe, which might be useful in the situation where multiple notifications have the same name.

◆ To post your own notification to send the dictionary discussed earlier, you can use this:

```
[[NSNotificationCenter
 → defaultCenter] postNotification
 → Name:MY_NOTIFICATION
 → object:myDict];
```

COMMONLY USED CLASSES

◆ You can then access the dictionary being sent:

```
-(void)doSomething:(NSNotification
↪ *)aNote {
    NSDictionary *myDict = [aNote
    ↪ object];
}
```

Code Listing 1.7 shows an example of both posting and receiving a notification. Note that in this example both the sending and receiving objects are in fact the same, which wouldn't normally be the case.

✔ Tips

■ Notice how the notification name has been defined as a variable (`MY_NOTIFICATION`). This is a good practice because the compiler will report a compile-time error if you mistype the notification name.

■ Remember to stop observing notifications by using `removeObserver:` when you are finished with the notification. This is often done in the `dealloc` method.

Code Listing 1.7 Registering for, posting, and receiving a notification.

```
- (void)doSomething:(NSNotification *)aNote
{
    NSDictionary *myDict = [aNote object];
    NSLog(@"%@",myDict);
}

- (void)viewDidLoad {

    NSString *myString = @"some value";
    NSDictionary *myDict = [[NSDictionary alloc]
                    initWithObjectsAndKeys:myString,@"firstObject",nil];

    [[NSNotificationCenter defaultCenter] addObserver:self
     selector:@selector(doSomething:) name:@"myNotification" object:nil];

    [[NSNotificationCenter defaultCenter]
     postNotificationName:@"myNotification"
     object:myDict];
}
```

Timers

Another common task is to have some code run based on some type of timing function. For example, you might be implementing a clock and want the display to update every minute, or you may want to present a message to a user and have it disappear after a certain amount of time.

You can use the NSTimer class to add this type of functionality to your applications. Timers allow you to execute a piece of code after a given amount of time.

◆ The simplest way to create a timer is by using the class method:

```
NSTimer *myTimer = [NSTimer
→ scheduledTimerWithTime
→ Interval:10.0 target:self
→ selector:@selector(myTimerAction:)
→ userInfo:nil repeats:NO];
```

This will create a timer that calls the myTimerAction: method in ten seconds from now. Notice the userInfo parameter: This lets you pass any object you like to your timer method. Passing NO to the repeats parameter means your timer method will be called only once. If you pass YES, the timer would keep repeating every ten seconds.

◆ You then implement your myTimerAction: method:

```
-(void)myTimerAction:(NSTimer *)
→timer
{
   NSLog(@"timer fired!: %@",[timer
     →userInfo]);
}
```

The timer passes itself as a parameter to the method. Notice how you can get the userInfo object you added when creating the time (in this example, nil).

◆ To stop a timer, you call the following:

```
[myTimer invalidate];
```

◆ You can also create a timer that you don't actually want to run until later:

```
myTimer = [[NSTimer timerWith
   →TimeInterval:10.0 target:self
   →selector:@selector(myTimerAction:)
   →userInfo:nil repeats:NO] retain];
```

◆ Then, when you are ready to start the timer, you use the following:

```
[[NSRunLoop mainRunLoop]
   →addTimer:myTimer forMode:
   →NSDefaultRunLoopMode];
```

continues on next page

◆ Another less common way of creating a timer is by using the following:

```
NSTimeInterval *secondsPerDay =
→ 24*60*60;
NSDate *tomorrow = [NSDate
→ dateWithTimeIntervalSinceNow:
→ secondsPerDay];
myTimer = [[NSTimer alloc]
→ initWithFireDate:tomorrow
→ interval:10.0 target:self
→ selector:@selector(myTimerAction:)
→ userInfo:nil repeats:YES];
```

This creates a timer to run tomorrow and repeat every ten seconds.

Again, you need to call addTimer:forMode: to actually start the timer; however, this time you have created a timer that first fires at an exact point in time.

Code Listing 1.8 shows an example of working with a timer.

Code Listing 1.8 Using timers.

```
-(void)myTimerAction:(NSTimer *)timer
{
    NSLog(@"timer fired!: %@",[timer userInfo]);
}

- (void)viewDidLoad {

    NSTimeInterval secondsPerDay = 24*60*60;
    NSDate *tomorrow = [NSDate dateWithTimeIntervalSinceNow:secondsPerDay];
    myTimer = [[NSTimer alloc] initWithFireDate:tomorrow
                                       interval:10.0
                                         target:self
                                       selector:@selector(myTimerAction:)
                                       userInfo:nil repeats:NO];
    [[NSRunLoop mainRunLoop] addTimer:myTimer forMode:NSDefaultRunLoopMode];

    myTimer2 = [NSTimer timerWithTimeInterval:1.0
                                       target:self
                                     selector:@selector(myTimerAction:)
                                     userInfo:nil repeats:NO];
}
```

Design Patterns

When writing applications, you may often find yourself building the same functionality or encountering similar design problems time and time again. *Design patterns* offer a solution to this situation by providing a set of general, reusable, tested solutions to common programming scenarios.

Design patterns are used extensively throughout the iPhone frameworks. If you write an iPhone application, you are using them whether or not you know it. The following are some of the more frequently used design patterns in iPhone development.

Model View Controller

The Model View Controller (MVC) pattern separates an application's data structures (the *model*) from its user interface (the *view*), with a middle layer (the *controller*) providing the "glue" between the two. The controller takes input from the user (via the view), determines what action needs to be performed, and passes this to the model for processing. The controller can also act the other way: passing information from the model to the view to update the user interface.

Breaking your application into distinct components like this reduces dependencies and increases the reusability of the code. It's entirely possible that you could reuse the same model across multiple applications with different views and controllers.

MVC is used everywhere in the iPhone frameworks. You will notice many classes with the word *View* or *Controller* in their names, and almost all the project templates create an MVC-based project.

Delegate

The Delegate pattern is useful as an alternative to subclassing, allowing an object to define a method but assign responsibility for *implementing* that method to a different object (referred to as the *delegate object* or, more commonly, the *delegate*).

Delegates need not implement all (or even any) of the delegate methods for the source object. In that case, the source object's default behavior for the method is often used.

Code Listing 1.9 shows an example of a delegate used for a `UITextField` object. By implementing the `textFieldShould BeginEditing:` delegate method (and in this example, returning `NO`), you can control the appearance of the keyboard.

As with MVC, delegates are frequently used throughout the iPhone frameworks, and you will use them often in your application development.

Code Listing 1.9 Using a delegate.

```
- (BOOL)textFieldShouldBeginEditing:(UITextField *)textField
{
    return NO;
}

- (void)viewDidLoad {

    CGRect rect = CGRectMake(10,10,100,44);

    UITextField *myTextField = [[UITextField alloc] initWithFrame:rect];
    myTextField.delegate = self;

    [self.view addSubview:myTextField];
    [myTextField release];
}
```

Target-action

This pattern is used by most of the controls in the iPhone user interface. When creating a control, you assign the *target* object to send a message to, and you supply the method in that object to call when a particular *action* (for example, tapping a button) occurs. It is your responsibility as the developer to implement the methods for these actions.

Code Listing 1.10 shows an example of using the target-action pattern to handle a UIButton.

Categories

Like delegates, categories provide an alternative to subclassing, allowing you to add new methods to an existing class. The methods then become part of the class definition and are available to all instances (and subclasses) of that class.

Code Listing 1.11 and **Code Listing 1.12** show an example category that adds a new method to the UIImage class. Notice how in both the interface and implementation

Code Listing 1.10 Buttons use the target-action pattern.

```
- (void)buttonTap:(id)sender
{
    NSLog(@"Button tapped");
}

- (void)viewDidLoad {

    CGRect rect = CGRectMake(10,10,100,44);
    UIButton *myButton = [UIButton buttonWithType:UIButtonTypeRoundedRect];
    [myButton setFrame:rect];
    [myButton addTarget:self
                action:@selector(buttonTap:)
        forControlEvents:UIControlEventTouchUpInside];

    [self.view addSubview:myButton];
}
```

Code Listing 1.11 The category header.

```
#import <UIKit/UIKit.h>

@interface UIImage (Additions)

+(UIImage *)newImageFromResource:(NSString *)filename;

@end
```

definitions you use the class name, with the category name in parentheses.

Although you can name your category header and implementation files anything you like, a common convention is to use the original class name with +xxx appended. The xxx describes the additional functionality provided by the category (or, as in the example here, is a generic term indicating additional functionality).

Singletons

You can think of a *singleton* as a global object. There will only ever be one, and it is available to all the classes in your application. Although this pattern is not so frequently used, you will use several important singletons when developing iPhone applications such as UIApplication and UIDevice.

Code Listing 1.13 shows an example of using the UIDevice singleton to check the battery level of an iPhone.

Code Listing 1.12 The category implementation.

```
#import "UIImage+Additions.h"

@implementation UIImage (Additions)

+(UIImage *)newImageFromResource:(NSString *)filename
{
    NSString *imageFile = [[NSString alloc]
                           initWithFormat:@"%@/%@",
                           [[NSBundle mainBundle] resourcePath],
                           filename];
    UIImage *image = [[UIImage alloc]
                      initWithContentsOfFile:imageFile];
    [imageFile release];
    return [image autorelease];
}

@end
```

✔ Tip

■ For more information on the design patterns used in iPhone development, refer to the "Cocoa Design Patterns" section in the *Cocoa Fundamentals Guide* in the developer documentation.

Code Listing 1.13 Using the UIDevice singleton.

```
- (void)viewDidLoad {

    float level = [[UIDevice currentDevice] batteryLevel];
    bool batteryState = [[UIDevice currentDevice] batteryState];

    if (batteryState && level < 0.1)
        NSLog(@"battery almost empty! (%f)",level);

}
```

THE iPHONE DEVELOPERS' TOOLBOX

2

Before you can begin building your own applications for the iPhone, you'll need to register with Apple as a developer and download the iPhone software development kit (SDK). Luckily, both of these steps are easy and completely free—simply visit *http://developer.apple.com*. You'll also find a wealth of information regarding iPhone development, including documentation, tutorials, videos, sample code, and more.

The iPhone SDK includes the Xcode integrated development environment (IDE), iPhone Simulator, Interface Builder, documentation, and a number of other tools you'll need when developing iPhone applications.

About the Xcode IDE

This chapter presents a whirlwind tour of some of the tools you'll use on a daily basis as an iPhone developer. You can find more information on the Apple Developer Connection Web site (*http://developer.apple.com*).

Xcode is part of a suite of development tools used for creating iPhone, iPod touch, and OS X applications. Among others, there are tools for user-interface design, source-code editing and management, integrated debugging, and performance analysis.

When you first launch Xcode, you are presented with a welcome screen (**Figure 2.1**). This screen contains lots of useful information such as links to videos, sample code, RSS feeds, tips and tricks, and documentation. It's well worth your time to go through the tutorials and code and subscribe to the mailing lists and RSS feeds. If you have a question, it's very unlikely you are the first to ask, and the searchable mailing list archives are an excellent place to look for an answer.

If you close this window and choose File > New Project, you'll see the Xcode New Project window where you can choose a template for your project (**Figure 2.2**). As an iPhone developer, you are interested only in the *iPhone OS* section of the list.

Figure 2.1 The Xcode welcome screen.

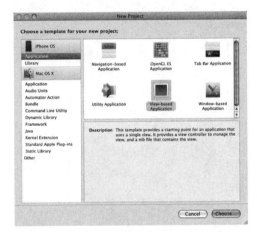

Figure 2.2 Choosing a project template.

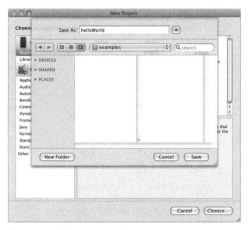

Figure 2.3 Saving your project.

When you select a template type, you'll see a short summary of its use. Xcode automatically creates boilerplate interface (.xib) and code (.h/.m) files for each template. Again, you should spend some time going through each of these templates and familiarizing yourself with them. Most of the examples in this book use the View-based Application template, which is a good one for general use.

Now you'll create a new project and walk through the main parts of the Xcode interface.

To create a new project:

1. Start Xcode.

2. Choose File > New Project.

3. Select the View-based Application template, and save your project as helloWorld (**Figure 2.3**).

Xcode now displays your project in a single window with a number of panes (**Figure 2.4**).

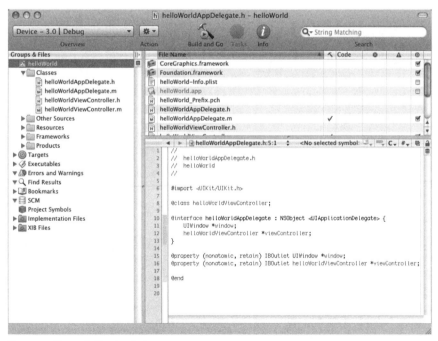

Figure 2.4 The main Xcode window.

About the Groups & Files pane

The Groups & Files pane (**Figure** 2.5) shows the contents and configuration of your project, categorized into either static or smart groups.

Static groups provide a convenient way for you to categorize files and folders. They are used only in the context of an Xcode project, and they do not necessarily reflect any physical folder structure in the file system.

You can create as many static groups as you like, and they can be nested within each other.

By default, Xcode creates the groups described in **Table 2.1**.

The <app>-Info.plist file contains configuration settings about your application. **Table 2.2** lists some of the settings automatically created with your application.

Figure 2.5 The Xcode Groups & Files pane.

Table 2.1

Static groups	
GROUP	**DESCRIPTION**
Classes	Contains the header and implementation files for the classes that are automatically generated for the application type that you selected when you created your project.
Other Sources	Contains the prefix header file used by Xcode to reduce compile time and the main.m file that is the entry point to your application. (It's generally advised that you not touch either of these files unless you know what you are doing.)
Resources	Contains the XIB files containing your application's user interface and the <app>-Info.plist file, which contains your application's settings.
Frameworks	The frameworks used by your application (these may differ based on the template type you chose when creating your project).
Products	Contains the compiled binary representing your application. This is the file that is installed on the simulator and uploaded to Apple for sale in the iTunes App Store. You may notice that if you've never compiled your application or you've never performed a clean (from the Build toolbar), this file will appear with red text. This is how Xcode displays missing files.

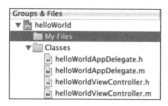

Figure 2.6 Adding a new group.

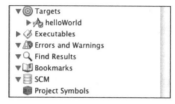

Figure 2.7 The default smart groups.

As a general rule, most developers create their own groups for their code and use the existing Resources folder for files such as graphics, but you can place your code and other project files in any of these groups, move them around, rename or delete them, or create your own. The groups are simply there to make your life as a developer easier when managing your application's code and assets.

To create a new group:

1. Right-click the topmost item in the Groups & Files pane (in this case helloWorld), and choose Add > New Group.

2. Name your group My Files (**Figure 2.6**).

Smart groups are the second type of group (**Figure 2.7**). Again, Xcode automatically creates a number of these groups to categorize various types of information (**Table 2.3**).

Table 2.2

<app>-Info.plist properties	
PROPERTY	**DESCRIPTION**
CFBundleDisplayName	The name your app shows on the iPhone.
CFBundleIconFile	The PNG file containing your application icon.
CFBundleIdentifier	The identifier you set up on the iPhone Developer Program Portal section of the Developer Connection Web site to uniquely identify your application.
CFBundleVersion	The current version of your application. You will update this each time you submit your application to the App Store.
LSRequiresIPhoneOS	Set to true if your application cannot run on an iPod touch.
NSMainNibFile	The initial user interface XIB file, loaded by the call to UIApplicationMain() in the main.m file.

Table 2.3

Smart groups	
GROUP	**DESCRIPTION**
Targets	You will have an entry here for each of your project targets (defined in the next section).
Executables	Contains all of the executables for your project.
Errors and Warnings	Each error or warning your application generates on compile will be listed here.
Find Results	This shows the history of any projectwide searches you have performed.
Bookmarks	This shows all bookmarks for your project.
SCM	If you are using source-code management, this group shows you the status of any files that may have changed under source control. Currently Xcode has support for the CVS, Perforce, and SVN source control systems.

Targets

A *target* is a set of instructions for building a product. These instructions might include such information as which source files to compile or resources to copy, as well as any special instructions for processing them. In most cases, you will be working only with the default target created with your project.

If you expand the helloWorld target (**Figure 2.8**), you'll see folders representing the main steps Xcode will perform when building the sample application: copying files into the application bundle, compiling the source code, and linking against the frameworks in the project.

Right-click the helloWorld target, and choose Get Info (Command+I) to open the Target Info dialog box (**Figure 2.9**). It has five tabs.

◆ **General**—Shows you the libraries and frameworks currently linked against your project, as well as any other dependencies (such as external projects) you may have. You can add other frameworks or linked libraries (such as SQLite) using the Add (+) button in the bottom-left corner (**Figure 2.10**).

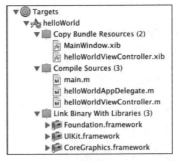

Figure 2.8 The project target group, expanded.

Figure 2.9 The Target Info dialog box.

Figure 2.10 The project's General tab.

Figure 2.11 Build settings for project.

◆ **Build**—Shows you the settings Xcode will use when building your product (**Figure 2.11**). They are grouped into configurations, providing a handy way to apply a range of settings without having to create multiple targets.

By default, Xcode creates *Debug* and *Release* configurations. The *Debug* configuration is what you will generally use in your day-to-day development, allowing you to interact with the application using the debugger, among other things. When you are ready to deploy your application to the iTunes App Store, you would build using the *Release* configuration, creating an optimized, production-ready version of your product.

◆ **Rules**—Specifies how particular file types are processed when your application is compiled. For example, you could pick a certain compiler version to compile your source files.

◆ **Properties**—Shows the contents of the <app>-Info.plist file in a slightly more human-readable form than simply viewing the file itself.

◆ **Comments**—Lets you add your own comments for the project. You can write anything you want here; comments will be stored with the project.

You can find a lot more information on targets and the build system in the *Xcode Build System Guide*.

ABOUT THE XCODE IDE

You may also notice the last two smart groups in the Groups & Files pane, Implementation Files and XIB Files, have the same icon. These are special groups similar to Smart Folders in OS X. If you Control+click the XIB Files folder and choose *Get Info (Command+I)*, you'll be doing a simple match for all files that have the extension .xib (**Figure 2.12**).

To create a smart group:

1. Choose Project > New Smart Group > Simple Regular Expression Smart Group.

2. Change the name to Images and the Using Pattern value to \.(png|gif|jpg|tif)$.

Figure 2.13 shows the completed group definition. You should now see this group at the bottom of your Groups & Files list. Any image files you add to your project will automatically be shown here.

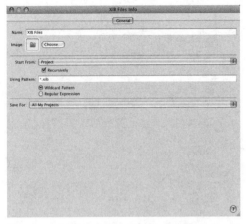

Figure 2.12 Settings for the XIB Files smart group.

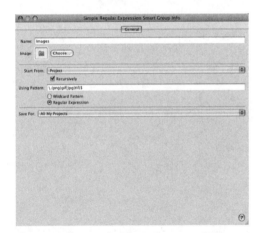

Figure 2.13 The completed smart group settings.

Figure 2.14
The Overview menu showing the current build settings for the application.

About the toolbar

When you first launch Xcode, the default toolbar features the following options:

◆ **Overview**—Shows you the current build settings for your application. This tells you whether you are currently building for the simulator or an actual iPhone, along with which build configuration you are using (**Figure 2.14**).

◆ **Action**—Provides a shortcut to a number of often-used actions.

◆ **Build and Go**—Builds your application and installs and launches it on either the iPhone Simulator or the iPhone (depending on what you've chosen in the Active SDK dialog box, which is accessible via the Overview toolbar menu).

◆ **Tasks**—Allows you to cancel a build in progress.

◆ **Info**—Shows additional information for any item selected in either the Groups & Files pane or the details pane.

◆ **Search**—Allows you to filter the list of items currently shown in the details pane.

Figure 2.15 shows the default toolbar when you first launch Xcode.

Figure 2.15 The default Xcode toolbar.

ABOUT THE XCODE IDE

Although the current toolbar is adequate, there are a couple more items you can add to make it a little more useful. You'll use them later in this chapter.

To update the toolbar:

1. Control+click the toolbar, and choose Customize Toolbar.

2. Drag the Build toolbar item that has the disclosure triangle, and drop it onto the toolbar.

3. In the same way, drag the Debugger and Editor toolbar items, and click Done to close the Customize Toolbar window. Your toolbar should look something like **Figure 2.16**.

About the details pane

The details pane shows a list of files, based on what is currently selected in the Groups & Files pane. For example, if you select multiple groups (**Figure 2.17**), you'll see all files for the groups.

Figure 2.16 The updated toolbar.

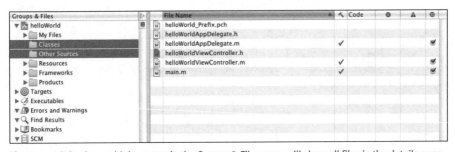

Figure 2.17 Selecting multiple groups in the Groups & Files pane will show all files in the details pane.

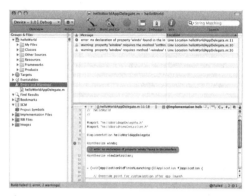

Figure 2.18 Xcode shows detailed information about errors in code.

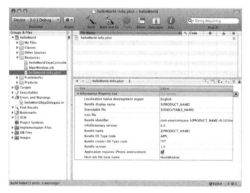

Figure 2.19 Xcode displays property lists as a table of keys and values.

Column headers in the details pane show information such as filename, build errors, and warnings. **Figure 2.18** shows the helloWorld project with a build error and two warnings—notice how Xcode tells you the name and line of the error or warning.

Selecting a file in the details pane opens the file in the editor pane below. Double-clicking or pressing Enter when a file is selected causes it to open in its own editor window.

Depending on the file type, it may display as an image or as a property list (**Figure 2.19**). Read-only files such as frameworks do not show in the editor pane at all.

To see more details about a file, such as its physical location, click the Info toolbar button (or press Command+I).

✔ Tip

■ When you select a property list file, it defaults to displaying as a table of key-value pairs. Although this is useful most of the time, you sometimes want to edit the raw source of the file. You can accomplish this by Control+clicking the property list file in the details pane and choosing Open As.

About the Xcode IDE

About the editor pane

Xcode contains all the features you would expect from a modern editor, such as syntax highlighting, code completion, smart indenting, code folding, multidocument support, unlimited undo and redo, and more.

You can expand the amount of space you have for editing code by clicking the Editor toolbar icon you added earlier (or by pressing Shift+Command+E). This causes the details pane to collapse and provides the full window height for the editor (**Figure 2.20**). Taking this further, if you also hold down the Option key (Option+Shift+Command+E), the Groups & Files pane collapses as well (**Figure 2.21**).

Finally, pressing Option+Command+O causes the current file to open in its own window.

To quickly open files in your project from the keyboard, you can use the Open Quickly dialog box (Shift+Command+D), which lets you start typing to find the filename. Positioning your pointer on a file, variable, or method before invoking this dialog box will default to showing the file containing that variable, method, or name (**Figure 2.22**).

Figure 2.20 Collapse the details pane to increase the area for your code.

Figure 2.21 The editor pane with all other panes collapsed.

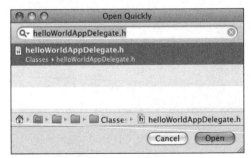

Figure 2.22 Quickly find and open files in your projects.

Figure 2.23 Adding external files to your projects.

When creating new files in Xcode, the default behavior is to put the file in whichever static group is currently selected. If no group is selected, the file is added at the top level of the list—you can of course move your files around within groups at any time after you've added them to the project.

When adding existing files to your projects, you will have the option to copy the items into your project's folder and choose what reference type to use (**Figure 2.23**). It's advisable to always select this option and to use the default reference type. If you were to move your project to a different location or machine at a later date, the file might not exist in the same location. In this situation, Xcode would indicate this by displaying the file in red.

Figure 2.24 The Xcode editor pane with a breakpoint set.

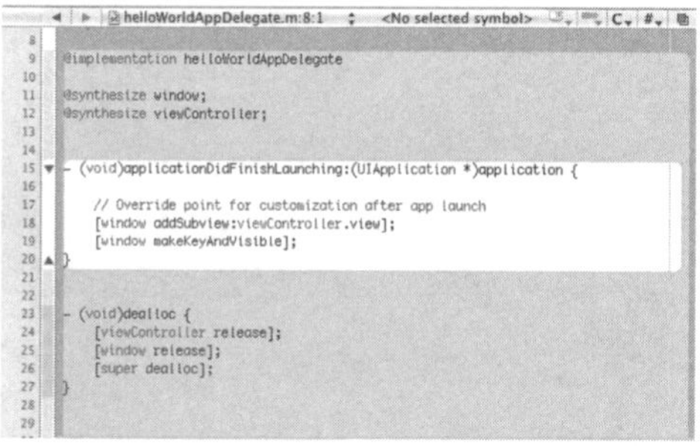

Gutter and focus ribbon

The *gutter* on the left (**Figure 2.24**) shows line numbers, breakpoints, errors, and warnings (you may have to enable line numbers in the Xcode preferences). Clicking in the gutter will add a breakpoint at the current line. Clicking the breakpoint will change it to a light blue color, indicating it has been disabled. To remove the breakpoint, you can either drag the breakpoint off the ribbon or Control+click and choose "Remove breakpoint" (you can also press Command+\ to toggle breakpoints).

Figure 2.25 Highlighting scope makes code more readable.

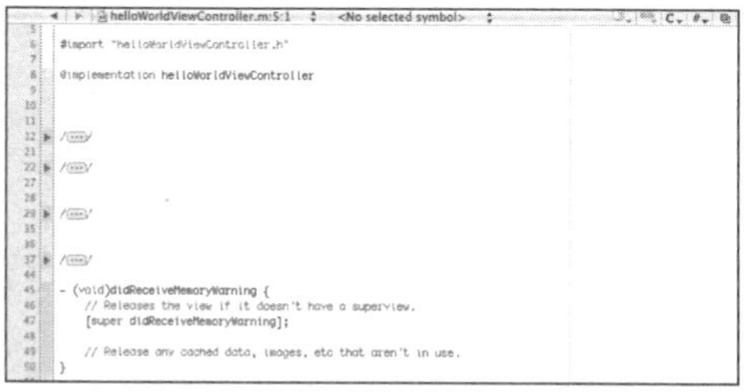

Next to the gutter is the *focus ribbon*. Moving your pointer over a shaded area in the ribbon causes the code for that scope to be highlighted and the rest of your code to be dimmed (**Figure 2.25**).

Clicking in the shaded scope area of the focus ribbon makes your code fold and unfold, replacing your code with a small graphic ellipsis symbol (**Figure 2.26**). Double-clicking the icon unfolds the code.

Figure 2.26 Collapsed code is represented by an ellipsis in the editor window.

This is a great way for you to hide code you'll never read (such as comments at the header of a file) or that you may not change often.

✔ Tips

■ You can also control code folding from the keyboard: Pressing Control+Command+left arrow or Control+Command+right arrow causes the current *scope* to fold or unfold. Pressing Control+Command+up arrow or Control+Command+down arrow causes all methods in the current file to fold or unfold.

■ If you like the scope highlighting effect, you can enable it all the time by choosing Focus Follows Selection from the View > Code-Folding menu. This is a great way to see your code in functional groups.

Find-and-replace operations

Pressing Command+F opens the Single File Find dialog box (**Figure 2.27**), allowing you to perform find-and-replace operations within the current file. Pressing Command+G and Shift+Command+G navigates forward and backward through matches.

Pressing Shift+Command+F brings up the more powerful Project Find window (**Figure 2.28**), which allows you to search through all files within your project and even into frameworks and other projects (although doing so will affect the speed of your searches—the Cocoa frameworks are very large!).

Remember also that Project Find history is also available in the Find Results smart group in the Groups & Files pane.

Bookmarks

Often you'll want to return to a particular line within your source code. Pressing Command+D allows you to bookmark a location. You can then access those bookmarks from the Bookmarks pop-up menu as well as the Bookmarks smart group in the Groups & Files pane.

Figure 2.27 Searching for text within the current file.

Figure 2.28 Searching within the entire project.

```
15    - (void)applicationDidFinishLaunching:(UIApplication *)application {
16
17         // Override point for customization after app launch
18         [window addSubview:viewController.view];
19         [window makeKeyAndVisible];
20         [window convertRect: (CGRect)rect to:window: (UIWindow *)window
21    }
```

Figure 2.29 Code completion shows the parameters of your methods as you type.

Figure 2.30 Xcode presents multiple completion matches as a list.

Jump-to-definition and help

If you Command+double-click any symbol, variable, or method within your code, Xcode opens the relevant file and highlights the definition of that symbol. If more than one definition exists, you'll be presented with a pop-up menu of all the files containing the symbol, allowing you to select which to open. This is extremely useful when browsing the Cocoa header files because you can quickly, for example, jump to the header definition of a class to see its properties and methods.

Similarly, if you Option+double-click, Xcode opens the documentation for that symbol. Again, this is a very quick and easy way of looking up how to use a particular function, class, or method.

✔ Tip

- You can quickly comment or uncomment your code by highlighting a block and pressing Command+/.

Code completion

Objective-C often has very long method names, and the Cocoa frameworks are huge, making it very difficult to remember what to type. This is where code completion comes in: Begin typing a method name, and Xcode will suggest the method it thinks you want based on the context of your code (**Figure 2.29**).

The more you type, the more accurate Xcode's match will become. When the right choice appears, press Tab to have Xcode complete the code for you.

Optionally, if you press the Esc (Escape) key, you will be presented with a list of all matches for the current completion (**Figure 2.30**). You can then navigate the list with the up and down arrow keys and press Enter to choose a match.

If your completion has multiple parameters, Xcode will automatically highlight the first parameter. Once you enter a parameter, you can press Control+/ to move to the next one. Similarly, Shift+Control+/ moves you backward in the parameter list.

Code completion is enabled in the preferences menu, or you can manually invoke it by pressing the Esc key. You can even position the pointer over some existing, already completed code and then press Esc to see a list of other possible completions.

The button at the bottom right of the completion list (**Figure 2.31**) allows you to toggle the sorting of the list between alphabetical and "best-guess" results.

About the navigation bar

Above the content pane is the navigation bar (**Figure 2.32**).

The arrows on the left of the bar allow you to navigate forward and backward through your editor pane history. You can also get at the same information by clicking the file-history menu (Control+1 on the keyboard).

The function menu (Control+2 on keyboard) shows a summary of all the class, function, method, and type declarations and definitions for the current file. Selecting one will jump to that point in your code.

There are also a number of special keywords you can put in your code to create marker labels in this menu. For example, putting the following before the `dealloc` method of a class

```
#pragma mark some comment here
```

would result in the function menu looking something like **Figure 2.33.**

Figure 2.31 Toggle the way completions are presented.

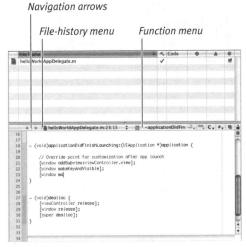

Figure 2.32 Arrows in the navigation bar and the file-history menu both let you navigate through the editor pane's history.

Figure 2.33 You can enhance the function menu to show developer comments.

Figure 2.34 Adding breaks to the function menu makes it easier to read.

Figure 2.35 The function menu showing multiple comment styles.

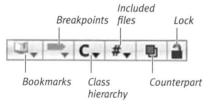

Figure 2.36 Pop-up menus in the navigation bar.

You can also break up the menu by adding separator labels, such as

```
#pragma mark -
```

which results in something like **Figure 2.34**.

There are also a number of special comment types:

```
//???: a question
//!!!: something important
//MARK: this is a mark
//TODO: a to-do item
//FIXME: something needs fixing
```

Figure 2.35 shows a code snippet containing all the special identifiers and the resulting menu.

The right side of the navigation bar (**Figure 2.36**) contains a number of useful pop-up menus and buttons:

◆ **Bookmarks**—Gives you access to *bookmarks* for the current file (you can also press Control+4 on the keyboard). Recall that bookmarks for your entire project are visible in the Groups & Files pane.

◆ **Breakpoints**—Allows you to jump between any breakpoints set in the current file.

◆ **Class hierarchy**—Lists all the superclasses and subclasses of your current file.

◆ **Included files**—Lists all the files that the current file includes or is included in.

◆ **Counterpart**—Allows you to jump between the implementation and header files (Option+Command+up arrow on keyboard).

◆ **Lock**—Lets you set the read-only state of the current file.

ABOUT THE XCODE IDE

You may have noticed the button at the top of the scroll bar on the right side of the editor pane. This is the handy split-view button, which lets you not only edit multiple parts of the same file at the same time but also open multiple files within an editor.

Figure 2.37 shows the application delegate with both the header and implementation file open for editing.

Creating new files

You create new files via the File > New File menu, which prompts Xcode to present a number of file templates for you to use during the application-creation process. In iPhone development you'll normally use templates from the iPhone OS section only. Within this section are four subsections:

◆ **Cocoa Touch Class**—Is the most common area you'll use; it provides templates for standard Objective-C iPhone classes.

◆ **Code Signing**—Allows you to create files related to signing your applications for ad hoc deployment.

◆ **Resource**—Provides templates for a number of resources, including Core Data models and application settings bundles.

◆ **User Interface**—Provides templates for creating the XIB files used in Interface Builder.

Now you'll add a custom UIView subclass to your application.

To add a class to your application:

1. Select Cocoa Touch Class from the left side of the template window, and select "Objective-C class" as the file template. Notice how UIView is selected in the "Subclass of" drop-down menu (**Figure 2.38**).

Figure 2.37 Splitting the editor allows you to see multiple parts of the same document at once.

Figure 2.38 Adding a new class file to the application.

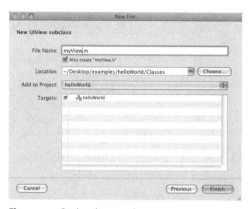

Figure 2.39 Saving the new class.

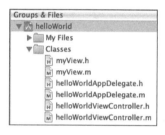

Figure 2.40
The Classes folder showing the newly added classes.

Figure 2.41 The Build Results window shows details of the project build.

2. Click Next, and save your file as myView.m. Make sure that "Also create 'myView.h'" is selected, and click Finish (**Figure 2.39**).

You should see your new myView.h and myView.m files in the Classes group of the Groups & Files pane (**Figure 2.40**). When you open the myView.m file, you can see that Xcode has created stub placeholders for the most common methods.

✔ Tip

■ When creating a new class, the "Created by" and Copyright comments at the top of the files come from the current user's Address Book card.

Building and running your application

To run your application, click Build and Go in the toolbar, or press Command+R. The Build Results window will open (**Figure 2.41**), displaying the status of your application target's build (you may have to enable this in the Building section of the Xcode preferences).

ABOUT THE XCODE IDE

The Build Results window lists any errors and warnings in your application. Clicking one will open an Xcode editor pane directly in the Build Results window (**Figure 2.42**), allowing you to fix the error without having to leave the current window. Double-clicking opens a new editor window.

Some build errors may not be immediately obvious, such as a misreferenced file in your project. By clicking the Build Transcript button (**Figure 2.43**), you can show or hide the build details. You can also set other build preferences with the buttons in this area of the Build Results window.

If there are no errors in your application, the iPhone Simulator will open, install, and launch your application.

Figure 2.42 The Build Results window showing an error in the code.

Build Transcript button

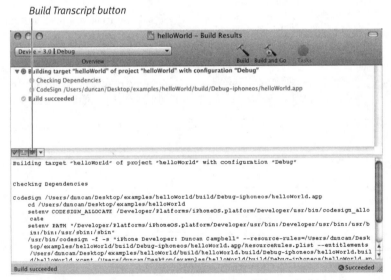

Figure 2.43 The Build Transcript button lets you show or hide your build details.

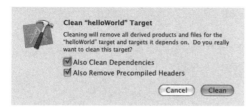

Figure 2.44 The Clean Target dialog box.

Building for iPhone vs. iPhone Simulator

If you look at the Overview toolbar item in both Xcode and the Build Results window, you'll notice it has a section called Active SDK (**Figure 2.45**).

This is how you determine whether you are deploying your application to an actual iPhone or to the iPhone Simulator.

Although the simulator will work out of the box, in order to install your application onto an iPhone (or iPod), you must have a provisioning profile and a development certificate installed on both your Mac and your iPhone.

You can find details of what these are and how to create and install them at the iPhone Dev Center Web site (*http://developer.apple.com/iphone*).

Figure 2.45
The Overview toolbar shows you whether you are building for the simulator or iPhone.

Cleaning

Each time you build your application target, Xcode performs only the actions required to update any files that were changed since the last build.

Xcode is not perfect, however, and sometimes it doesn't notice that a file has changed (such as when you replace an image in your project with another of the same name). In this situation, you need to perform what's known as a *clean*.

To clean a target, choose Build > Clean, or press Shift+Command+K on the keyboard.

Cleaning a target (**Figure 2.44**) removes any intermediate files created during the previous build process. The next time you build, every file will be processed.

For more details on the Xcode build system, see the "Building Products" section in the *Xcode Project Management Guide*.

Table 2.4 provides a summary of some of the common editor shortcuts.

Table 2.4

Common keyboard shortcuts	
SHORTCUT	DESCRIPTION
Shift+Command+E	Collapse/expand details pane
Option+Shift+Command+E	Collapse/expand details pane and Groups & Files pane
Option+Command+O	Open current document in new window
Option+left arrow	Go to previous word (+Shift to select)
Option+right arrow	Go to next word (+Shift to select)
Command+left arrow	Go to beginning of line (+Shift to select)
Command+right arrow	Go to end of line (+Shift to select)
Command+up arrow	Go to beginning of document (+Shift to select)
Command+down arrow	Go to end of document (+Shift to select)
Command+L	Go to line
Command+Z	Undo
Shift+Command+Z	Redo
Command+/	Comment/uncomment selected block
Command+D	Create bookmark
Command+\	Add/remove breakpoint
Control+Command+\	Deactivate/reactivate all breakpoints (projectwide)
Command+F	Find in current file
Command+G	Go to next match
Shift+Command+G	Go to previous match
Shift+Command+F	Find in project
Control+1	Open file-history menu
Control+2	Open function menu
Control+3	Open Included files menu
Control+4	Open Bookmarks menu
Option+Command+up arrow	Switch between header and implementation file
Command+double-click	Jump to definition of current symbol
Shift+Command+K	Clean current target
Command+B	Build application
Command+R	Build and run application
Command+Y	Build and debug application

About the iPhone Simulator

You will usually use the iPhone Simulator for the majority of your iPhone development. The simulator lets you build, run, and test iPhone applications on your computer rather than on an actual iPhone.

Although you can simulate most of the iPhone environment, the simulator can't do a number of tasks well, and it has several important differences from the iPhone environment.

The simulator has *significantly* better performance than an actual iPhone. Everything from application launch time and general UI speed to available memory are much improved on the simulator. How much better it performs will depend on the computer you are developing with, but if speed is important to your finished application, you should be testing your code on an actual iPhone as early as possible in your development cycle to get an accurate measure of its actual performance.

The simulator provides a number of functions that mimic an iPhone:

◆ **SDK version**—You can simulate your code running under multiple versions of the iPhone SDK.

◆ **Rotation and shakes**—The simulator can be rotated left and right as well as shaken, triggering the appropriate delegate methods in your view controllers.

◆ **Home and Lock buttons**—Both buttons work as they do on the iPhone.

continues on next page

ABOUT THE IPHONE SIMULATOR

◆ **Memory warnings**—You can trigger low-memory warnings, which can be very useful in making sure your applications handle low-memory situations gracefully.

◆ **Toggle in-call status bar**—This status bar allows you to see how your application would look with the in-call status bar active (**Figure 2.46**).

◆ **Touch**—Using the mouse, you can simulate either a single touch or, by holding the Option key, a two-finger touch. For more details on touch gestures in the simulator, see "Performing Gestures" in the iPhone Development Guide of the iPhone Reference Library.

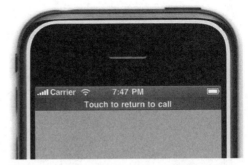

Figure 2.46 The simulator showing a call in progress.

The simulator can't do the following:

◆ No camera means you cannot simulate any of the image-capture functionality of the iPhone.

◆ Although there are options to rotate the simulator, you cannot fully simulate the accelerometer.

◆ Core Location and Map Kit will always report your location as Apple's headquarters in Cupertino.

◆ You cannot simulate more than two touches at once.

◆ The simulator has no iPod, iTunes, Calendar, Mail, SMS, Phone, or Maps applications.

◆ The Settings application has only limited functionality; for example, it doesn't have airplane mode or data settings.

◆ It doesn't have a proximity sensor.

Figure 2.47 Drag an image onto the simulator to have it open in Safari.

If your application needs access to any of these functions, you will need to test your code on an actual iPhone rather than on the simulator.

Since there is no camera on the simulator, to add photos to the Photos application, you must follow these steps.

To add photos:

1. Open the simulator, and make sure you are at the iPhone desktop screen.

2. Drag any image from your computer's desktop onto the iPhone Simulator. Safari will open on the simulator with your photo displayed (**Figure 2.47**).

3. Touch and hold the photo. A dialog box will pop up allowing you to save the image to the Photos application.

✔ Tips

- Once your applications are installed on the simulator, you can touch and hold to change their order or delete them—just as you can on a real iPhone.

- Choosing Reset Content and Settings in the iPhone Simulator menu will remove all applications and reset the simulator to its initial configuration. However, it also *deletes* the default address book and photo album data. You can back up this data before you reset the simulator by copying the contents of ~/Library/Application Support/iPhone Simulator/User.

ABOUT THE IPHONE SIMULATOR

About Interface Builder

Interface Builder (often abbreviated IB) is a visual tool used for creating your iPhone user interfaces.

IB lets you visually lay out the interface just as it would look on the iPhone, adding elements such as buttons, views, and labels and setting properties such as color and size.

You can also visually connect your interface to your application's code using a special system that encompasses outlets and actions.

An *outlet* is a connection from your code to your user interface. Imagine you have a label in your iPhone application that you want to display a message with. Using IB, you drag this label onto your interface. You then create an outlet between your code and your interface, which allows you to manipulate the properties of the label programmatically in your code.

An *action* goes the other way: from your interface to your application code. If you had a button on your interface that you wanted to have call a certain piece of code when clicked, you would create an action in your code and then hook up the button to this action in IB. When the button is clicked, the code is executed.

These concepts are common among many languages with visual design tools; however, the process of creating outlets and actions can be somewhat confusing at first. You'll examine this later in the chapter.

Your interface is saved as an XML-format XIB file. When you build your application, the XIB files are compiled into a deployable NIB file, which is then packaged up with your application bundle. At run time, your iPhone application will automatically unpackage and load these files to re-create your user interface.

Now you'll take a quick look at the various elements of the IB interface.

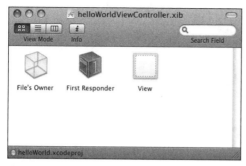

Figure 2.48 The contents of the XIB file.

In Xcode, double-click the helloWorldView Controller.xib file (in the XIB Files group of the Groups & Files pane) to open your XIB in IB.

There are three main parts to the IB interface: the document window, the Library window, and the inspector window.

✔ Tip

- NIB stands for "NeXT Interface Builder." The file format was originally created for the NeXT operating system in the 1980s. The newer XIB format was introduced in Xcode 3.0. In this chapter, XIB and NIB both mean an Interface Builder file.

About the document window

The document window shows the contents of the XIB file (**Figure 2.48**). In this example, you can see three objects.

- ◆ **File's Owner**—This is a proxy object representing an instance of a class (in this case the helloWorldViewController class). You will create your outlets and actions in objects like these.

- ◆ **First Responder**—Every XIB will have a First Responder object, providing an entry point for your interface into the responder chain, which consists of a list of objects connected together. Touch and motion events are sent to the first object in the chain (the firstResponder), which can choose to process it or pass it on up the chain to the next object via its nextResponder property.

  All UI objects (including UIViews and UIWindows) are responder objects, as is your UIApplication. You can create custom actions on this object and have your visual elements call these actions. Objects in the responder chain can then handle these custom actions.

continues on next page

ABOUT INTERFACE BUILDER

- **View**—This represents the interface of your iPhone application (in this example it is an instance of a `UIView` class).

  Note: Here you have only a single object placeholder and a single view. It is, however, quite possible (and common) to have more than one of each within a single XIB file.

Often an interface can have many nested UI controls on it: labels on buttons within views within yet more views. This can make it very difficult to determine which object is which in the document window. Although you can name your objects (by clicking the label underneath them), the View Mode options at the top left make it much easier to visualize these hierarchies. **Figure 2.49** shows the documents view of the interface with a button added to the view.

About the Library window

The Library window is divided into three main panes (**Figure 2.50**).

- **Organization**—Divides your objects into functional groups.

- **Item**—Lists the contents of the currently selected group (or groups), graphically depicting the functionality the object performs.

- **Detail**—Shows the name and a brief description of what the selected object is and what it does.

You can filter the items shown by entering search text in the filter control at the bottom of the Library window.

Notice the *mode* selector tabs at the top, which allow you to switch between user interface objects and media resources. Resources will include the images and sound files within your project.

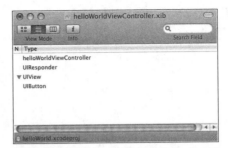

Figure 2.49 Changing the view mode of the XIB to visualize the object hierarchy.

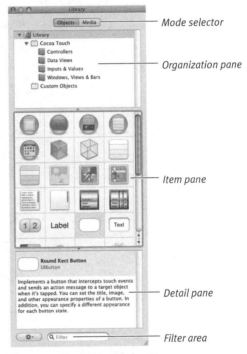

Figure 2.50 The Library window.

✔ Tips

- Just as with the Groups & Files pane of Xcode, you can create your own groups and smart groups in the Organization pane of the Library window.

- The *Action* menu at the bottom of the Library window allows you to modify the way items are presented.

Figure 2.51 The inspector window.

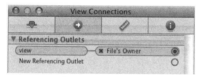

Figure 2.52 Outlets are visually represented in the Connections pane.

Figure 2.53 Control+click to view an object's outlets and connections.

About the inspector window

The inspector window (**Figure 2.51**) allows you to configure the properties and settings for each of the elements within the document window. It's divided into four panes.

◆ **Attributes**—This is the main area for setting the visual properties of your UI elements, such as colors, fonts, and text. You can also set drawing properties and choose whether an element can respond to touches from the iPhone screen.

  As you click each object in your document window, notice how the inspector window automatically updates to show the different properties and settings available for each object.

◆ **Connections**—This pane displays the outlets and actions for the currently selected object. If an outlet or action is connected, you will see the name of the object it is connected to (**Figure 2.52**). You'll take a look at how to go about connecting up outlets and actions later in this chapter. You can also see the connections for an object by Control+clicking it in the document window (**Figure 2.53**).

continues on next page

ABOUT INTERFACE BUILDER

◆ **Size**—This pane allows you to set the origin (the x and y coordinates) and size (width and height) of your visual elements. You can also adjust the autosizing behavior of your elements, which can be useful when your interface changes from portrait to landscape mode. Autosizing is intuitively shown by a small animation next to the control (**Figure 2.54**).

◆ **Identity**—The Identity pane shows you the class of your object, allowing you to override this with your own custom class should you choose to do so. You can visually add outlets and actions here and set the name used to display your objects in the document window (**Figure 2.55**).

The Identity pane is also the key to adding nonvisual instances of your own classes to your XIB files. After creating and saving your class in Xcode, simply drag an NSObject from the Library window and then rename its class to your own class name (**Figure 2.56**).

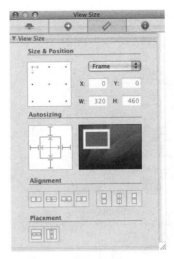

Figure 2.54
The Size pane of the inspector window.

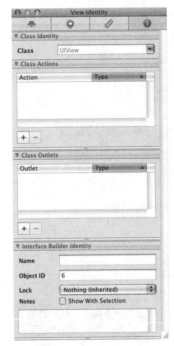

Figure 2.55
The Identity pane of the inspector window.

Figure 2.56
Changing a class in the Identity pane.

Figure 2.57 Visually lay out your application by dragging elements onto the iPhone canvas.

You'll now take a look at how to use all of this to create your own interface.

To create the interface:

1. Drag a UIButton from the Library window, drop it on your view, and set its text to Click Me.

2. Drag a UILabel from the Library window, and drop it on your view above the button (**Figure 2.57**).

3. Save your interface, go back to Xcode, and build and run your application.

You can click the button, but at the moment nothing happens.

Now you will update your application to have it display the current time when you click the button.

To update the application:

1. Back in IB, update the UIButton text to Show Current Time. You do this via the inspector window or just by double-clicking the button and typing. Notice how the button automatically resizes itself to fit the wider text. Resize your label to make it the same width as your button, and set the text alignment to center (the Alignment property is on the Attributes pane of the inspector window).

2. With File's Owner selected in the document window, select the Identity pane of the inspector. In the Class Actions area, click the Add (+) button, and set the action to buttonClick:.

3. In the Class Outlets section, add an outlet called labelTime. Also change the type to UILabel. The Identity pane should now look like **Figure 2.58**.

4. Making sure your File's Owner object is still selected in the document window, click the Connections pane of the inspector window.

5. Connect the outlet by clicking the small circle on the right side of the labelTime outlet. Keep your mouse button depressed, and drag to the label on your view to make the connection (**Figure 2.59**).

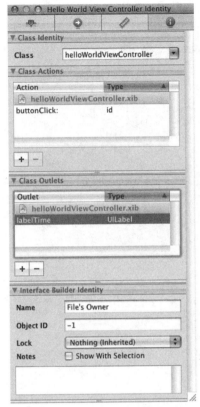

Figure 2.58 The Identity pane showing your object's connections and outlets.

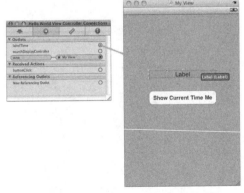

Figure 2.59 Hooking up the interface by dragging between elements.

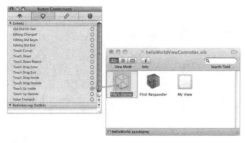

Figure 2.60 Connect actions by dragging between the actions window and the object you want to receive the action.

Figure 2.61 Updating your code with the outlets and actions you've just created.

6. To connect the action, you need to do the reverse. Click your button in the document window, select the Touch Up Inside event, and drag to your File's Owner object. Select the buttonClick: action when it pops up to make the connection (**Figure 2.60**).

7. Choose File > Write Class Files from the main menu. Then click Save (**Figure 2.61**).

8. Click Replace in the next dialog box (or, if you like, you can click Merge to see what is happening).

9. Back in Xcode, open the helloWorldView Controller.h file. Notice how IB has generated code for the outlet and the action:

```
@interface helloWorldViewController
 : UIViewController {
    IBOutlet UILabel *labelTime;
}
- (IBAction)buttonClick:(id)sender;
@end
```

continues on next page

ABOUT INTERFACE BUILDER

10. In helloWorldViewController.m, edit this stub code so that it looks like this:

```
- (IBAction)buttonClick:
→ (id)sender {

    NSDateFormatter *dateFormatter =
    → [[NSDateFormatter alloc] init];
    [dateFormatter setDateFormat:
    → @"hh:mm:ss"];

    labelTime.text = [dateFormatter
    → stringFromDate:[NSDate date]];

    [dateFormatter release];
}
```

11. Build and run your application. You should now be able to click the button, and the label will update to show the current time (**Figure 2.62**).

In the previous example, you got IB to automatically generate the stub code for your outlet and action. Although this is convenient, you wouldn't normally do it with anything other than an empty class. It's much more common to create your outlets and actions yourself in Xcode manually and then use IB to hook them up to your user interface. Now you'll take a look at how you do this.

To manually create outlets and actions:

1. In Xcode, open helloWorldView Controller.h, and edit it to look like **Code Listing 2.1**. You will have created two more outlets and replaced your buttonClick: action with one called controlChanged:.

Figure 2.62 The application running in the simulator.

Code Listing 2.1 The header file for the hello world application.

```
#import <UIKit/UIKit.h>
#import <Foundation/Foundation.h>

@interface helloWorldViewController : UIViewController
{
    IBOutlet UILabel *labelTime;
    IBOutlet UISwitch *dateSwitch;
    IBOutlet UISlider *fontSlider;
}

- (IBAction)controlChanged:(id)sender;

@end
```

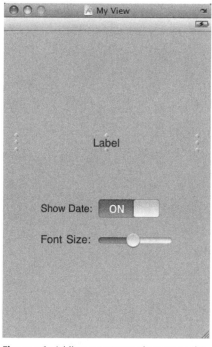

Figure 2.63 Adding some more elements to the interface.

2. Switch over to helloWorldViewController.m, and edit it to look like **Code Listing 2.2**. You have modified your code, moving the label update into its own method and adding the option to display the date or the time. You've also added the ability to modify the font size of the label. Notice also that you call this method in the viewDidLoad method. This is so the label shows correctly when the application first starts.

3. In the Groups & Files pane, double-click your helloWorldViewController.xib file to open IB. Delete the button from your interface, and drag two labels—a UISwitch and a UISlider—onto your view. Arrange them so they look like **Figure 2.63**. Notice how you've also increased the width of your time label to handle a larger font.

continues on next page

Code Listing 2.2 The updated code for the hello world application.

```
#import "helloWorldViewController.h"

@implementation helloWorldViewController

-(void)updateTimeLabel
{
    NSDateFormatter *dateFormatter = [[NSDateFormatter alloc] init];

    if (dateSwitch.on)
        [dateFormatter setDateFormat:@"dd-MMM-yyy, hh:mm:ss"];
    else
        [dateFormatter setDateFormat:@"hh:mm:ss"];

    labelTime.text = [dateFormatter stringFromDate:[NSDate date]];
    labelTime.font = [UIFont systemFontOfSize:fontSlider.value];
    [dateFormatter release];
}

- (IBAction)controlChanged:(id)sender {

    [self updateTimeLabel];
}

//update time when view first loads
-(void)viewDidLoad
{
    [self updateTimeLabel];
}

@end
```

4. Select your UISlider, and edit its Minimum Value setting to 10 and its Maximum Value setting to 25 (**Figure 2.64**).

5. Keeping your UISlider selected, press the Control key, and drag from the slider to the File's Owner object in the document window (**Figure 2.65**). Then select controlChanged: in the pop-up menu. This is a shortcut method of connecting outlets and actions: Instead of using the Connections menu, you can simply Control+drag between objects to have the default action connected. Also connect the outlet from the File's Owner to the UISlider.

6. Repeat step 5, but this time for the UISwitch control, again selecting the controlChanged: option. Notice how you can have multiple controls connected to the same action. Again, also connect the outlet from the File's Owner object to the UISwitch control.

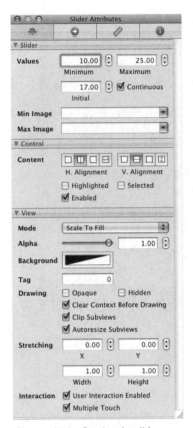

Figure 2.64 Configuring the slider.

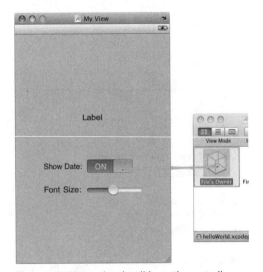

Figure 2.65 Connecting the slider to the controller.

Figure 2.66 The updated application.

Back in Xcode, build and run your application. You should be able to switch between the date and time, as well as change the font size by moving the slider (**Figure 2.66**).

✔ Tip

■ Although IB automatically scans your code for `IBAction` and `IBOutlet` definitions in your header files, it can occasionally miss them, and you'll find you can't see your outlets and actions in the inspector window. You can solve this by manually dragging the .h file of your class from the Xcode Groups & Files pane onto the IB documents window.

Why are there two XIB files in the project?

In the previous example, you may have noticed that you are working only with helloWorldViewController.xib, but your project actually contains two XIB files. So, what does MainWindow.xib do?

In the Xcode section, the <app>-Info.plist file has the property Main Nib File, which is the NIB that is loaded automatically when your iPhone application starts. MainWindow.xib is this file.

Opening MainWindow.xib, you can see several objects:

◆ **File's Owner**—An instance of `UIApplication` representing the entry point of your application, created by the `UIApplicationMain()` function call in main.m. You will only ever have a single `UIApplication` object in your iPhone applications.

continues on next page

Why are there two XIB files in the project? *(continued)*

◆ **helloWorld App Delegate**—An instance of your `helloWorldAppDelegate` class (the helloWorldAppDelegate.h and helloWorldAppDelegate.m files in your project). Since this object is the delegate of your `UIApplication`, it handles all of the startup behavior of your application. Notice it has `viewController` and `window` outlets.

◆ **helloWorld View Controller**—An instance of your `helloWorldViewController` class (the helloWorldViewController.h and helloWorldViewController.m files within your project). If you inspect this object in the inspector window you will notice that it has its NIB Name property set to helloWorldViewController (**Figure 2.67**). This tells the object to initialize itself from the helloWorldViewController.xib file. This is how the XIB file you have been working with so far gets loaded.

When an XIB is loaded, every object inside is created. By using this pattern of one XIB per view controller, you can lazily load your interface as you need it. This decreases your application's loading time and uses less memory. Having your views and view controller in individual XIB files also makes things easier to work with in IB—imagine how complex the outlets and actions would be if everything were in a single file!

◆ **Window**—Represents the top-level or root view in your application's interface. You will only ever have a single window in your application; views you create will be added as subviews to this object. Having this top-level view ensures that things like alert dialog boxes will always appear above your own views.

Figure 2.68 shows an overview of how the interface is created when your application is launched.

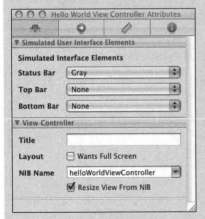

Figure 2.67 The NIB Name property.

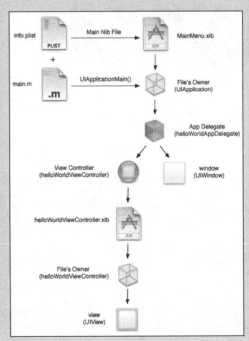

Figure 2.68 How the application is constructed.

Figure 2.69 The documentation browser.

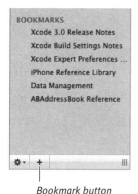

Figure 2.70
The Bookmarks pane.

Bookmark button

About the Documentation

As you saw earlier when looking at Xcode, the iPhone SDK includes a comprehensive and powerful documentation viewer. You can launch the documentation viewer by using the Help menu, by pressing Option+Command+?, or by selecting a symbol in your code and Option+double-clicking.

Documentation is presented in an HTML-based, multiframe layout that allows you to move around related information by clicking hyperlinks in the text, just as you would in a Web browser (**Figure 2.69**).

Above the main documentation pane, a history of your path through the pages is maintained, allowing you to navigate forward and backward or jump directly to a page via the pop-up menu.

In the left pane, you can subscribe to documentation feeds from Apple, which automatically update when new documentation becomes available. You can also bookmark the page you are currently viewing using the Bookmark button at the bottom (**Figure 2.70**). This adds a bookmark to the source list.

You can search the documentation by API (the fastest) or by document title; you can even search the full text of the documentation. The filter pane at the top allows you to limit searches to only the documentation sets and technologies in which you are interested.

ABOUT THE DOCUMENTATION

The Research Assistant is a mini–documentation browser designed to sit next to your Xcode editor window, which can be opened from the Help menu or by pressing Control+Command+? (**Figure 2.71**).

Documentation for the symbol at your pointer position will be automatically displayed, along with other useful information such as links to sample code and related APIs.

✔ Tips

- Pressing the Command key while clicking links in the documentation will make the page open in a new window.

- The latest documentation is also available online at *http://developer.apple.com/iphone*.

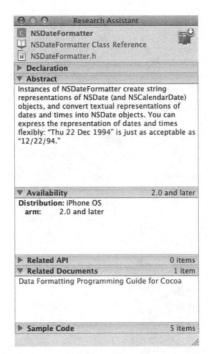

Figure 2.71 The Research Assistant.

COMMON TASKS

3

This chapter will show you some of the useful tips and tricks that are essential for building a great iPhone application. You'll start by looking at the application startup process, where to put your code, and how you set the various configuration options.

Next you'll see how easy it is to add user and application preferences to your applications. You'll also learn how to create an application preference page within the Settings application.

Then you'll learn about some of the techniques you can use to internationalize an iPhone application, making it available in different languages. Finally, you'll learn how to launch other applications from your own, as well as some techniques for sharing data between applications.

Application Startup and Configuration

In this section, you'll learn what happens when you tap the icon to launch your iPhone application. You'll see how you can respond to different stages in the application startup and shutdown processes. You'll also look at some of the configuration options available for your applications and how to work with user and application preferences.

Using the application delegate

The application delegate, represented by the UIApplicationDelegate class, is the starting point for all iPhone applications. Since there is only a single application delegate, it can be a useful place to put methods and variables you want to be available globally.

You add a reference to the application delegate from within your classes by writing this:

```
id appDelegate = [[UIApplication
→ sharedApplication] delegate];
```

(You also need to remember to import the header file of your application delegate).

However, since the application delegate needs to be loaded before your application can begin, it's probably good practice to avoid putting code there unless absolutely necessary. Instead, you can adopt a "lazy loading" style of programming where you create objects only when needed. This has the added benefit of keeping the memory footprint of your applications to a minimum.

The application delegate serves as both the first place (when your application loads) and the last place (before your application exits) that you can execute some code. It provides a number of important methods:

◆ applicationDidFinishLaunching:—This is the first method called when your application has loaded. This is a good place for you to perform application-wide initialization of data such as loading any previous state or settings.

◆ applicationDidFinishLaunchingWith Options:—If implemented, application DidFinishLaunching: will be ignored, and this method will be used instead. The launchOptions parameter is a dictionary containing information used in two scenarios:

▲ It will be used if your application was launched as the result of a "push" notification, in which case launch Options will contain a dictionary of information relating to the notification. See the *Apple Push Notification Service Programming Guide* for more information on working with push notifications.

▲ It will be used if your application was launched as a receiver of a URL resource. See the "Interapp Communication" section later in this chapter for more information.

◆ applicationWillTerminate:—This is the last chance to perform any action before your application exits. This is a good place for you to free memory and save application state or settings such as user preferences.

continues on next page

APPLICATION STARTUP AND CONFIGURATION

◆ `applicationDidReceiveMemoryWarning:`—
This is called whenever the device is
running low on memory due to improper
memory management or simply because
your application is trying to load too
much data into memory. Normally you
would attempt to free as much memory
as possible in this situation by releasing
any cached or unnecessary objects.

If this method is called, then the corresponding `didReceiveMemoryWarning`
delegate method will also be called on
every view controller class in your application. This gives you granular control over
your application, allowing you to clean up
memory on a per-view controller basis.
Although optional, it's recommended that
you try to implement this method, because
your application may become unstable or
crash if memory warnings are ignored.

◆ `applicationWillResignActive:`—This
is called just before your application
becomes inactive. This can happen if
another window pops up over your application (for example, an incoming phone
call) or if the device goes into a locked
state, either by going to sleep or by the
user pressing the power button.

◆ `applicationDidBecomeActive:`—This is
the reverse of the previous method and
will be called every time your application
becomes active. This obviously happens
when the application is first launched
but also when you dismiss any windows
that have appeared over your application
(for example, an incoming text message)
or when the device wakes from a locked
state. You can prevent your application
from going to sleep by writing this:

```
[[UIApplication sharedApplication]
→ setIdleTimerDisabled:YES];
```

✔ Tips

■ Some applications have splash screens
that display while the application is
loading. You can add a splash screen to
your own application by adding a file
called Default.png to the project. Rather
than displaying a graphical splash screen
(which can itself increase load time),
many developers opt to show an image
that replicates the initial screen of the
application.

■ After your application has launched, you
can use the `UIDevice` class to determine
information such as the make, model,
operating system name, and version of
the device on which it's running.

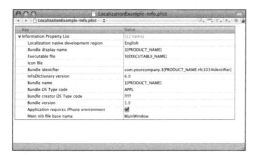

Figure 3.1 The Info.plist file contains the configuration settings for your application.

Understanding application settings

As mentioned in the "About the Xcode IDE" section in Chapter 2, "The iPhone Developers' Toolbox," the <app>-Info.plist file contains many of the preferences and settings used when launching your application (**Figure 3.1**). **Table 3.1** summarizes some of the more commonly used settings.

Table 3.1

Commonly used <app>-Info.plist settings	
KEY	DESCRIPTION
Application requires iPhone environment	If your application does not run on an iPod Touch, set this to True.
Application uses Wi-Fi	If your application requires Wi-Fi to function, you should set this property to True. Doing so will prompt the user to enable Wi-Fi if it is not already enabled. For power-saving, the iPhone automatically closes any Wi-Fi connections in your application after 30 minutes. Setting this property will prevent this from happening and keep the connection active.
Bundle display name	This sets the name of your application, displayed below the icon on the iPhone screen. You are limited to approximately 10 to 12 characters for an application name before the iPhone abbreviates the name.
Bundle identifier	This sets the unique identifier for your application setup in the iPhone Developer Program Portal website.
Bundle version	This sets the version number of your application. This is the used in the iTunes App Store and should be incremented each time you deploy a new version of your application.
Icon already includes gloss and bevel effects	By default, the iPhone applies a "gloss effect" to application icons. Setting this key to True will prevent this.
Icon file	This is the filename of your application's icon (added to your project).
Initial interface orientation	This determines whether your application starts in landscape or portrait mode.
Localizations	This is a comma-delimited list of localizations that your application supports. For example, if your application supports English and Japanese, you would use English,Japanese. You should then provide the appropriate localization strings for each language. See the "Localization" section later in this chapter for more details on how to localize an application.
Status bar is initially hidden	This allows you to launch your application without a status bar. Your application interface will automatically resize to fill the entire iPhone screen.
Status bar style	If you leave the status bar visible, this key allows you to select from one of three different display styles.
Main nib file base name	This is the XIB file loaded when your application first starts. You would not normally need to modify this value.
URL types	This is an array of URL identifiers supported by your application. See the "Interapp Communication" section later in this chapter for details on how to use this value.

Working with user preferences

User preferences are generally stored using the NSUserDefaults class, also known as the *defaults system*. You would normally read from the defaults system when your application first launches to restore any previous settings for the user or application.

The NSUserDefaults object is quite smart. When your application launches for the first time, there obviously won't be any user preferences (other than those you set programmatically). Once you set a value, the defaults system will automatically save it for you. The next time you launch the application and request the value, it will be returned to you. All the complexities of dealing with loading and saving files and values are hidden, and for performance everything is cached in memory. This cache is periodically refreshed automatically.

To begin using the defaults system, you first get a reference by writing this:

```
NSUserDefaults *prefs = [NSUserDefaults
→ standardUserDefaults];
```

You can then read values by using something like this:

```
NSInteger age = [prefs integerForKey:
→ @"age"];
```

You write values by using this:

```
NSInteger age = 30;
[prefs setInteger:age forKey:@"age"];
```

Code Listing 3.1 shows some examples of reading and writing to the defaults system.

The defaults system has methods for working with property list datatypes (NSNumber, NSString, NSData, NSArray, or NSDictionary). If you want to store more complex values, you need to *archive* the value and store it as an NSData instance. You can then *unarchive* when reading the value back to convert from an NSData instance to the original datatype.

For example, to archive and store a UIColor object in the defaults system, you would use this:

```
UIColor myColor = [UIColor blueColor];
NSData *colorData = [NSKeyedArchiver
→ archivedDataWithRootObject:myColor];
[prefs setObject:colorData forKey:
→ @"myColor"];
```

To then unarchive and restore the value, you write this:

```
NSData *colorData = [prefs objectForKey:
→ @"myColor"];
UIColor myColor = [NSKeyedUnarchiver
→ unarchiveObjectWithData:colorData];
```

✔ Tip

- While developing your applications, it is possible to force-quit them (by pressing Command+Q). Although this is not something that can happen when your application is in production, doing so may mean that the defaults system does not save correctly. You can get around this problem by calling the synchronize method, which will force the defaults system to be saved and written to disk.

Code Listing 3.1 Some examples of reading and writing to the defaults system.

```
NSUserDefaults *prefs = [NSUserDefaults standardUserDefaults];

//read values
BOOL homeOwner = [prefs boolForKey:@"homeOwner"];
NSInteger age = [prefs integerForKey:@"age"];
NSString *userName = [prefs stringForKey:@"userName"];
UIColor *favoriteColor;

//is value in user defaults?
NSData *colorData = [prefs objectForKey:@"favoriteColor"];

if (colorData != nil)
    favoriteColor = [NSKeyedUnarchiver unarchiveObjectWithData:colorData];
else
{
    UIColor *myColor = [UIColor blueColor];
    NSData *colorData = [NSKeyedArchiver archivedDataWithRootObject:myColor];
    [prefs setObject:colorData forKey:@"favoriteColor"];
}

//change some values
homeOwner = TRUE;
age = 30;
userName = @"Bob";

//save back to prefs
[prefs setBool:homeOwner forKey:@"homeOwner"];
[prefs setInteger:age forKey:@"age"];
[prefs setObject:userName forKey:@"userName"];
```

Application preferences

Just like user preferences, application preferences are stored and retrieved by using the NSUserDefaults class and are managed in the same way in your code.

The iPhone SDK provides a second mechanism for managing application preferences, allowing you to create a page in the global Settings application (**Figure 3.2**). The user can then edit the application preferences by using this page.

Figure 3.2 The Settings application can be used to edit your application settings.

To create a settings page for your application:

1. In Xcode, select File > New File.

2. Select the Resource section, and select Settings Bundle to create a new settings bundle (**Figure 3.3**).

3. Save the file as Settings.bundle.

4. Build and run your application.

Figure 3.3 Adding a settings bundle to your project.

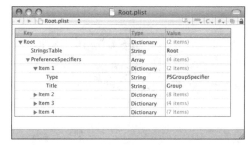

Figure 3.4 The settings page of your application.

Figure 3.5 The PreferenceSpecifiers key contains the various items in the settings page.

5. Switch to the Settings application. You will notice a new section with the same name as your application. Select this section to open the settings page showing four elements (**Figure 3.4**).

6. In Xcode, expand the Settings.bundle file in the Groups & Files pane, and select the Root.plist file.

7. In the editing window on the right, expand the PreferenceSpecifiers section (**Figure 3.5**).

   The four items (items 1–4) represent the four interface elements in the settings page from step 2. If you expand each element, you will notice they all have a Type key, which determines the control type to display.

Adding controls

You can add seven types of controls to your settings page:

◆ PSGroupSpecifier creates a new group of controls. **Figure 3.6** shows a settings page with three groups.

◆ PSTextFieldSpecifier creates a text field (**Figure 3.7**) where the user can enter a string of text. This control has several properties:

isSecure stops the text you are entering from being shown as it's typed. This is useful for passwords and other sensitive information.

DefaultValue lets you specify a default value if no value has been set.

KeyboardType allows you to specify which keyboard is shown when the user taps the control.

AutoCapitalizationType controls the type of capitalization that occurs as the user types.

◆ PSToggleSwitchSpecifier creates a toggle (on/off) switch. The DefaultValue property determines whether the switch is on or off by default.

◆ PSSliderSpecifier creates a slider. You use the MinimumValue and MaximumValue properties to determine the range of the slider, and you use the DefaultValue property to determine the starting value.

Figure 3.6 A settings page with three groups.

Figure 3.7 Entering text into a settings page.

APPLICATION STARTUP AND CONFIGURATION

Figure 3.8 Use the PSMultiValueSpecifier type to select from a set of multiple values.

Figure 3.9 Choosing from a set of values.

◆ `PSTitleValueSpecifier` creates a simple read-only label. Use the `DefaultValue` property to set the text of the label.

◆ `PSMultiValueSpecifier` creates a second view consisting of a table of values that the user can select from (**Figure 3.8**). The `Values` property contains an array of possible values. The corresponding `Titles` property contains the display labels for each value and accepts an array of values to display (**Figure 3.9**). The `DefaultValue` property determines which value is initially selected.

◆ `PSChildPaneSpecifier` allows you to create another settings view. By setting the `File` property to the name of another setting's plist, you can nest settings within settings.

For all the control types (except the slider that has no title), the `Title` property enables you to set the title text that appears to the left of the control.

The `Name` property of each control is the key you use to reference the setting with `NSUserDefaults`. For example, to get the value of the `PSToggleSwitchSpecifier` toggle switch defined in Item 3 of the `PreferenceSpecifiers` array you would write:

```
NSUserDefaults *prefs = [NSUserDefaults
→ standardUserDefaults];
BOOL enabled = [prefs boolForKey:
→ @"enabled_preference"];
```

Localization

Localization refers to the representation of currency, dates, times, and numbers for a regional variant of a language called a *locale*. For example, currency and dates are displayed differently for the United Kingdom than they are for the United States. *Internationalization*, on the other hand, refers to representing the text (and possibly other user interface elements) of your application in the end user's language. In this section, the term *localization* is used to mean both of these concepts.

You can localize numbers and dates by using the localization support of the `NSNumberFormatter` and `NSDateFormatter` classes. For example, to display a localized currency value, you can use this:

```
NSNumber *currencyValue = [NSNumber
↪ numberWithFloat:1000.23];

NSNumberFormatter *formatter =
↪ [[NSNumberFormatter alloc] init];

[formatter setNumberStyle:
↪ NSNumberFormatterCurrencyStyle];

NSLog(@"Formatted value for locale %@
↪ is: %@",

[[formatter locale] localeIdentifier],

[formatter stringFromNumber:
↪ currencyValue]);
```

The user's locale is automatically detected based on their phone settings.

Words and phrases, however, are unique to each language and must be treated differently. You must create a *strings file* for each language that you want your application to support. Strings files consist of a list of key-value pairs, where the "key" is the source representation of the word or phrase (which will be in the language used by the developer) and the "value" is the localized version of the word or phrase. **Figure 3.10** shows a sample strings file for a French strings file.

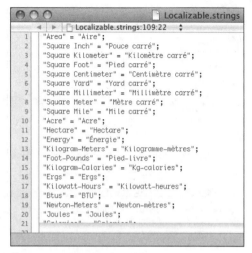

```
1   "Area" = "Aire";
2   "Square Inch" = "Pouce carré";
3   "Square Kilometer" = "Kilomètre carré";
4   "Square Foot" = "Pied carré";
5   "Square Centimeter" = "Centimètre carré";
6   "Square Yard" = "Yard carré";
7   "Square Millimeter" = "Millimètre carré";
8   "Square Meter" = "Mètre carré";
9   "Square Mile" = "Mile carré";
10  "Acre" = "Acre";
11  "Hectare" = "Hectare";
12  "Energy" = "Énergie";
13  "Kilogram-Meters" = "Kilogramme-mètres";
14  "Foot-Pounds" = "Pied-livre";
15  "Kilogram-Calories" = "Kg-calories";
16  "Ergs" = "Ergs";
17  "Kilowatt-Hours" = "Kilowatt-heures";
18  "Btus" = "BTU";
19  "Newton-Meters" = "Newton-mètres";
20  "Joules" = "Joules";
21
```

Figure 3.10 A French strings file.

Figure 3.11 Creating the en.lproj and fr.lproj directories in your project directory.

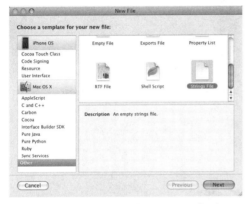

Figure 3.12 Adding a strings file to your application.

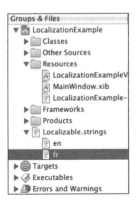

Figure 3.13 Xcode automatically groups together the strings files for a project.

To create a localized application:

1. Create a new view-based application, saving it as LocalizationExample.

2. Open the directory where you have just saved your project in Finder.

3. Create two directories: one representing English called en.lproj and one for French called fr.lproj (**Figure 3.11**).

   These directories are where you will be storing the localized resources for your project.

4. In Xcode, select File > New File.

5. In the Mac OS X section on the left of the New File dialog box, select the Other section, and choose Strings File from the file types (**Figure 3.12**).

6. Click Next, and save the file as Localizable.strings in the en.lproj directory created in step 3.

7. Repeat step 6, creating a second Localizable.strings file, but this time saving it in the fr.lproj directory.

   You should now see a new item in the Groups & Files pane in Xcode called Localizable.strings.

8. Expand this item, and you will see that Xcode has intelligently grouped both of your strings files together (**Figure 3.13**).

9. Select the English strings file ("en"), and enter the following:

   `"HelloKey" = "Hello World!";`

   This is a key-value pair, and the key (`HelloKey`) has a value of `"Hello World!"`. Notice you end the entry with a semicolon.

continues on next page

10. Repeat step 9, but this time add the entry to the French strings file ("fr"):

`"HelloKey" = "Bonjour Monde!";`

Again, you use the same key, only this time you have specified a different, localized value.

11. Switch to LocalizationExample.m, uncomment the `viewDidLoad` method, and write the following code:

```
CGRect lblFrame = CGRectMake
→ (110,10,200,40);

UILabel *lblLocalized = [[UILabel
→ alloc] initWithFrame:lblFrame];

lblLocalized.backgroundColor =
→ [UIColor clearColor];

lblLocalized.text = NSLocalized
→ String(@"HelloKey",nil);

[self.view addSubview:
→ lblLocalized];
```

Here you are just creating a label and adding it to your main view. Notice, however, that you set the text using the `NSLocalizedString` function. You pass this function a key for the localized text you want to display, and the function retrieves the localized text for you from the strings file.

12. Build and run your application.

You should see "Hello World!"

13. To see the French localization, switch to the Settings application, select General > International > Language, and choose French (**Figure 3.14**). Switch back to your application, and you should see the text now in French.

You can localize your application's settings and user interface in the same way by copying the <app>-Info.plist and XIB files to the localized en.lproj and fr.lproj directories.

Figure 3.14 Selecting a different language.

✔ Tips

- Notice that the second parameter of the `NSLocalizedString` function was not used. It's there to allow you to provide a comment for each of your localized strings. You can then use the *genstrings* tool to parse your source code and automatically generate strings files for you. For information on how to use the genstrings tool, see the "Strings Files" section of the *Apple Internationalization Programming Topics* documentation.

- In the example here, you created localized strings using the language codes for English ("en") and French ("fr") to name the directories. For a complete list of available language codes, refer to the Unicode Consortium homepage at *http://www.unicode.org*.

LOCALIZATION

Figure 3.15 Launching the Mail application.

Interapp Communication

Although the iPhone doesn't allow more than one application to run at a time, you can launch another application from your own, and you can share data between applications.

You can launch one application from another by using the `openURL:` method of the `UIApplication` class. For example, to open the Google homepage in the Safari application, you could write this:

```
NSURL *url = [NSURL URLWithString:
→ @"http://google.com"];
[[UIApplication sharedApplication]
→ openURL:url];
```

The `http://` part here is called a *URL scheme* and identifies the application you want to launch.

URL schemes exist for several of the other native iPhone applications and can be used to launch them in a similar manner.

For example, to launch the Mail application (**Figure 3.15**), you can use this:

```
NSURL *url = [NSURL URLWithString:
→ @"mailto:steve@apple.com?subject=
→ test"];
[[UIApplication sharedApplication]
→ openURL:url];
```

To launch the SMS application, you can write this:

```
NSURL *url = [NSURL URLWithString:
→ @"sms:555-1234"];
[[UIApplication sharedApplication]
→ openURL:url];
```

INTERAPP COMMUNICATION

To dial a phone number, you can use the following:

```
NSURL *url = [NSURL URLWithString:@"tel:
→ //555-1234"];

[[UIApplication sharedApplication]
→ openURL:url];
```

To launch the Maps application and search for *pizza* (**Figure 3.16**), you can use this:

```
NSURL *url = [NSURL URLWithString:
→ @"http://maps.google.com/maps?q=
→ pizza"];

[[UIApplication sharedApplication]
→ openURL:url];
```

You can also use a URL scheme to launch your own application.

To create an application with a custom URL scheme:

1. Create a new view-based application, saving it as URLSchemeExample.

2. In the Xcode Groups & Files pane, expand the Resource section, and select the <app>-Info.plist file.

3. Right-click the Information Property List key, and select Add Row. Select "URL types" from the list (**Figure 3.17**).

4. Expand Item 1, right-click URL identifier, and again select Add Row. Select URL Schemes from the list (**Figure 3.18**).

Figure 3.16 Launching the Maps application and finding some pizza.

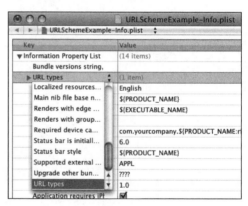

Figure 3.17 Adding a URL type.

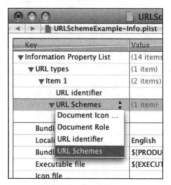

Figure 3.18 Adding a URL scheme.

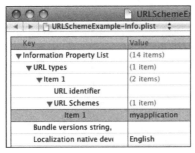

Figure 3.19 Setting the name of the URL scheme.

5. Select Item 1, and set the value to myapplication (**Figure 3.19**).

6. Open URLSchemeExampleViewController.m, uncomment the viewDidLoad method, and write the following:

```
[self.view setBackgroundColor:
 → [UIColor redColor]];
```

7. Build and run your application.

You should see a blank, red screen.

Your application doesn't do anything at the moment, but by running it (which installs the application on the iPhone or simulator), you have just registered the new URL scheme (myapplication) created in step 5.

8. You can now launch this application from a different application by using the following code:

```
NSURL *url = [NSURL URLWithString:
 → @"myapplication:"];
[[UIApplication sharedApplication]
 → openURL:url];
```

Sharing information between applications

When you launch an application using a URL scheme, the entire URL is passed to the application. This is how Safari knew to open the Google Web page in the earlier example.

To capture the URL, you need to implement the application:didFinishLaunchingWith Options: method within the application delegate. The launchOptions parameter of this method is a dictionary whose contents will contain both the URL and an identifier for the source application that launched your application.

To respond to being launched via a URL scheme:

1. Open the URLSchemeExampleApp Delegate.m file, and add the `application:didFinishLaunchingWithOptions:` delegate method.

```
if (launchOptions) {

    NSString *sourceApp = [launch
    → Options objectForKey:
    → UIApplicationLaunchOptionsSource
    → ApplicationKey];
    NSURL *url = [launchOptions
    → objectForKey:UIApplicationLaunch
    → OptionsURLKey];

    NSString *msg = [NSString
    → stringWithFormat:@"sourceApp:
    → %@, url: %@",sourceApp,url];

    UIAlertView *alert = [[UIAlertView
    → alloc] initWithTitle:@""
    → message:msg delegate:self
    → cancelButtonTitle:@"OK"
    → otherButtonTitles:nil];
    [alert show];
    [alert release];
}

[self applicationDidFinishLaunching:
→ application];
```

You first check to see whether the `launch Options` dictionary exists (it will be null if the application was launched normally), and then you extract two values from the dictionary:

`UIApplicationLaunchOptionsSource ApplicationKey` contains the bundle identifier for the source application that opened your application.

`UIApplicationLaunchOptionsURLKey` contains the complete URL (including the URL scheme itself).

For testing, you then create an alert view and display these values. In a real-world application, you could parse the URL to extract any information passed to your application.

2. Build and run the application to install it onto the iPhone or simulator.

Code Listing 3.2 shows the updated code.

continues on next page

Code Listing 3.2 The updated code to respond to being launched by a URL scheme.

```
#import "URLSchemeExampleAppDelegate.h"
#import "URLSchemeExampleViewController.h"

@implementation URLSchemeExampleAppDelegate

@synthesize window;
@synthesize viewController;

- (void)applicationDidFinishLaunching:(UIApplication *)application {

    // Override point for customization after app launch
    [window addSubview:viewController.view];
    [window makeKeyAndVisible];
}

- (BOOL)application:(UIApplication *)application didFinishLaunchingWithOptions:(NSDictionary *)launchOptions {

    if (launchOptions) {

        NSString *sourceApp = [launchOptions objectForKey:UIApplicationLaunchOptionsSourceApplicationKey];
        NSURL *url = [launchOptions objectForKey:UIApplicationLaunchOptionsURLKey];

        NSString *msg = [NSString stringWithFormat:@"sourceApp: %@, url: %@",sourceApp,url];

        UIAlertView *alert = [[UIAlertView alloc]
                                initWithTitle:@""
                                message:msg
                                delegate:self
                                cancelButtonTitle:@"OK"
                                otherButtonTitles:nil];
        [alert show];
        [alert release];
    }

    [self applicationDidFinishLaunching:application];

    return YES;
}

- (void)dealloc {

    [viewController release];
    [window release];
    [super dealloc];
}

@end
```

INTERAPP COMMUNICATION

3. Again, switch to the other application and change your code to this:

```
NSURL *url = [NSURL URLWithString:
→ @"myapplication:message=
→ helloworld"];

[[UIApplication sharedApplication]
→ openURL:url];
```

Your application will launch, and you should see an alert message similar to **Figure 3.20**.

Using the pasteboard

Another useful way of passing information between applications is by using the *pasteboard*. Items copied *to* the pasteboard from one application can be copied *from* the pasteboard by another application.

You can get a reference to the pasteboard by writing:

```
UIPasteboard *pasteboard = [UIPasteboard
→ generalPasteboard];
```

You can then place a string on the pasteboard by using this:

```
pasteboard.string = @"Hello World";
```

After launching your app via a call to openURL:, you can then retrieve the string from the pasteboard by writing this:

```
UIPasteboard *pasteboard = [UIPasteboard
→ generalPasteboard];

NSString *myString = pasteboard.string;
```

The UIPasteboard class contains convenience properties like this for NSString, UIImage, NSURL, and UIColor.

Figure 3.20 The application displaying the launchOptions values.

You can add multiple items to the pasteboard by using the setItems: method. For example, to add two strings to the pasteboard, you can use this:

```
UIPasteboard *pasteboard = [UIPasteboard
→ generalPasteboard];

NSDictionary *item1 = [NSDictionary
→ dictionaryWithObject:@"Hello World"
→ forKey:@"public.utf8-plain-text"];
NSDictionary *item2 = [NSDictionary
→ dictionaryWithObject:@"Goodbye World"
→ forKey:@"public.utf8-plain-text"];

NSArray *items = [NSArray arrayWith
→ Objects:item1,item2,nil];
[pasteboard setItems:items];
```

Each item is first added to an array as a dictionary and then added to the pasteboard using the setItems: method. You can later retrieve this array from the pasteboard using the items property.

The key for each dictionary is a uniform type identifier (UTI). For a list of available UTIs, refer to Uniform Type Identifiers Overview in the developer documentation.

INTERAPP COMMUNICATION

Code Listing 3.3 shows the code updated to retrieve a string from the pasteboard and display it in an alert view.

Code Listing 3.3 The code updated to use the pasteboard.

```
#import "URLSchemeExampleAppDelegate.h"
#import "URLSchemeExampleViewController.h"

@implementation URLSchemeExampleAppDelegate

@synthesize window;
@synthesize viewController;

- (void)applicationDidFinishLaunching:(UIApplication *)application {

    // Override point for customization after app launch
    [window addSubview:viewController.view];
    [window makeKeyAndVisible];
}

- (BOOL)application:(UIApplication *)application didFinishLaunchingWithOptions:(NSDictionary *)launchOptions {

    if (launchOptions) {

        UIPasteboard *pasteboard = [UIPasteboard generalPasteboard];
        NSString *msg = pasteboard.string;

        UIAlertView *alert = [[UIAlertView alloc]
                            initWithTitle:@""
                            message:msg
                            delegate:self
                            cancelButtonTitle:@"OK"
                            otherButtonTitles:nil];
        [alert show];
        [alert release];
    }

    [self applicationDidFinishLaunching:application];

    return YES;
}

- (void)dealloc {

    [viewController release];
    [window release];
    [super dealloc];
}

@end
```

iPhone User Interface Elements

The iPhone SDK offers a rich set of buttons, sliders, switches, and other user interface elements for you to use in creating your applications. These elements can be roughly divided into two main groups, views and controls.

Views provide the primary canvas and drawing functionality of your user interface. They also give your application the ability to handle touch events.

Controls extend upon this functionality and provide a way for users to interact with your application by defining what is known as the *target-action mechanism*: the ability for a control to send an *action* (method call) to a *target* (object) when an *event* (touch) occurs.

In this chapter, you'll look at the various views and controls available in the iPhone SDK and examine how to use them.

All the examples use the view-based Application template, with the code running in the view controller.

Views

A *view* is the common name given to instances of `UIView`. You can think of a view as your application's canvas; in other words, if you are adding UI elements to your iPhone's interface, you are adding them to a view. All the UI elements discussed in this chapter are themselves subclasses of `UIView` and so inherit its properties and behavior.

The root level of your iPhone application interface consists of a single `UIWindow` to which you would typically add one or more views to work with, instead of using `UIWindow` directly.

Since `UIView` is a subclass of `UIResponder`, it can receive touch events. For most views, you'll receive only a single-touch event unless you set the `multipleTouchEnabled` property to `TRUE`. You can determine whether a view can receive touch events by modifying its `userInteractionEnabled` property. You can also force a view to be the only view to receive touch events by setting the `exclusiveTouch` property to `YES`. (For more information on working with touch events, see Chapter 7, "Touches, Shakes, and Orientation.")

You can also nest views within each other in what's known as the *view hierarchy*. Child views are known as *subviews*, and a view's parent is its *superview*.

Frames

Views are represented by a rectangular region of the screen called a *frame*. The frame specifies the *origin* (x, y) and *size* (width, height) of the view, in relation to its parent superview. The origin of the coordinate system for all views is the upper-left corner of the screen (**Figure 4.1**).

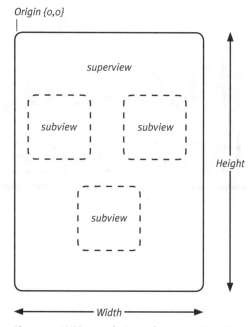

Figure 4.1 Child views (subviews) are nested inside their parent view (superview). A view's origin is at the top-left corner.

VIEWS

Figure 4.2 Adding a subview to the view controller's main view.

Code Listing 4.1 Creating a new view.

```
- (void)viewDidLoad {

    CGRect viewFrame = CGRectMake(10,10,100,100);
    UIView *myView = [[UIView alloc] initWithFrame:
                        viewFrame];

    myView.backgroundColor = [UIColor blueColor];

    [self.view addSubview:myView];
    [myView release];

}
```

To add a view to your application:

1. Create a `CGRect` to represent the frame of the view, and pass it as the first parameter of the view's `initWithFrame:` method:

   ```
   CGRect viewFrame = CGRectMake
   → (10,10,100,100);
   ```
   ```
   UIView *myView = [[UIView alloc]
   → initWithFrame:viewFrame];
   ```

   Here you are creating a view that is inset 10 pixels from the top left of its superview and that has a width and height of 100 pixels.

2. Since the view is transparent by default, set its background color before adding it to the view controller's existing view (**Figure 4.2**):

   ```
   myView.backgroundColor =
   → [UIColor blueColor];
   ```
   ```
   [[self view] addSubview:myView];
   ```

   Code Listing 4.1 shows the completed code.

✔ Tip

■ To improve performance, set your `UIView`'s `opaque` property to `YES` wherever possible.

VIEWS

Bounds

A view's *bounds* are similar to its frame, but the location and size are relative to the view's *own* coordinate system rather than those of its superview. In the previous example, the frame's origin is {10,10}, but the origin of its bounds is {0,0}. (The width and height for both the frame and the bounds are the same.)

The console output in **Figure 4.3** illustrates this: After moving the view 25 pixels in the x direction (using the view's center property), the frame origin is now {35,10}, whereas the bounds origin remains at {0,0}.

Let's say you want to create a view so that it completely fills its superview. A common mistake is to use the frame of the superview.

If you tried to run this code in your application, you'd see a gap at the top of the subview (**Figure 4.4**).

Recall that, in the project, the UIWindow is at the top level. The UIWindow has two subviews: the status bar and the main view 20 pixels below (**Figure 4.5**). The origin of the frame of the main view is actually {0,20}. (Remember, a view's frame is in relation to its superview's coordinate system.)

The solution to this problem is to use the *bounds* of the superview (**Code Listing 4.2**), which causes the view to correctly fill its superview.

✔ Tip

- You can use the NSStringFromCGRect() function to convert a CGRect into an NSString, making it useful for logging CGRects to the console via NSLog(). Other useful functions when dealing with CGRects are NSStringFromCGPoint() and NSStringFromCGSize().

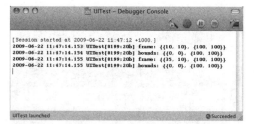

Figure 4.3 Console output after moving the view. Notice that although the frame changes, the bounds remain the same.

Figure 4.4 Setting the frame incorrectly by using the frame of the superview. Notice the gap at the top.

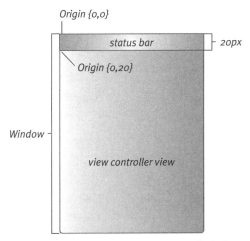

Origin {0,0}

status bar — 20px

Origin {0,20}

Window

view controller view

Figure 4.5 The enclosing `UIWindow` contains both the status bar and the view controller's view as subviews. Notice how the controller's view has an origin starting at `{0,20}` for its `frame`.

Code Listing 4.2 Initializing the view's frame with its superview's bounds.

```
Code
- (void)viewDidLoad {

    UIView *myView = [[UIView alloc] initWithFrame:
                            [self.view bounds]];

    myView.backgroundColor = [UIColor blueColor];

    [self.view addSubview:myView];
    [myView release];

}
```

Animation

Many properties of a view can be animated, including its `frame`, `bounds`, `backgroundColor`, `alpha` level, and more. You'll now look at some simple examples that illustrate additional view concepts.

To animate your view:

1. Retrieve the center of the view controller's main view:

   ```
   CGPoint frameCenter =
   → self.view.center;
   ```

2. Create a view, set its background color, and, just as you did earlier, add it to the main view:

   ```
   float width  = 50.0;

   float height = 50.0;

   CGRect viewFrame = CGRectMake
   → (frameCenter.x-width, frameCenter.
   → y-height,width*2, height*2);

   UIView *myView = [[UIView alloc]
   → initWithFrame:viewFrame];

   myView.backgroundColor =
   → [UIColor blueColor];

   [[self view] addSubview:myView];
   ```

   Here you are positioning your view in the center of its superview and giving it a width and height of 50 pixels.

3. Set up an *animation block*:

   ```
   [UIView beginAnimations:nil context:
   → NULL];

   [UIView setAnimationDuration:1.0];
   ```

   An animation block is a wrapper around a set of changes to animatable properties. In this example, the animation lasts for one second.

   continues on next page

4. Resize the view:

```
viewFrame = CGRectInset(viewFrame,
→ -width, -height);
[myView setFrame:viewFrame];
```

The CGRectInset() function takes a source rectangle and then creates a smaller or larger rectangle with the same center point. In this example, a negative value for the width and height creates a larger rectangle.

5. Close the animation block:

```
[UIView commitAnimations];
```

This will cause all of the settings within the animation block to be applied.

6. Build and run the application.

You should see the view grow in size over a period of one second. **Code Listing 4.3** shows the completed code.

✔ Tips

■ Try changing the setAnimationDuration: line to see how you can affect the speed of the animation.

■ Try setting some other properties on the view within the animation block (such as backgroundColor) to see what effect they have.

Code Listing 4.3 Animating a view.

```
- (void)viewDidLoad {

    [super viewDidLoad];

    CGPoint frameCenter = self.view.center;
    float width = 50.0;
    float height = 50.0;

    CGRect viewFrame = CGRectMake(frameCenter.x-width,frameCenter.y-height, width*2, height*2);

    UIView *myView = [[UIView alloc] initWithFrame:viewFrame];
    myView.backgroundColor = [UIColor blueColor];

    [[self view] addSubview:myView];

    [UIView beginAnimations:nil context:NULL];

    [UIView setAnimationDuration:1.0];
    viewFrame = CGRectInset(viewFrame, -width, -height);
    [myView setFrame:viewFrame];

    [UIView commitAnimations];

    [myView release];
}
```

Figure 4.6 Animating multiple views without using an autoresizing mask. Notice how the new subview ends up in the top-left corner of its superview.

Autosizing

When a view changes size or position, you often want any subviews contained within the view to change size or position in proportion to their containing superview. You can accomplish this by using a view's *autoresizing mask*. Now let's add a second subview inside the view you created in the previous exercise.

To add a subview:

1. Create a CGRect for the subview's frame, again using the shortcut CGRectInset() function:

   ```
   CGRect subViewFrame = CGRectInset
   → (myView.bounds,width/2.0,
   → height/2.0);
   ```
   ```
   UIView *mySubview = [[UIView alloc]
   → initWithFrame:subViewFrame];
   ```
   ```
   mySubview.backgroundColor =
   → [UIColor yellowColor];
   ```
   ```
   [myView addSubview:mySubview];
   ```

   This time, the positive width and height values for the CGRectInset function make the new view smaller. To make them stand out, give it a different background color.

2. Build and run the application (**Figure 4.6**). The new subview starts off in the center of its superview, but then it remains "pinned" to its initial location as the animation progresses and ends up in the top-left corner.

continues on next page

VIEWS

Code Listing 4.4 shows this code updated to use an autoresizing mask. Notice how you set all four margins of the subview using the bitwise OR operator (the | symbol) between the constant values (**Table 4.1**). Notice also that even though the animation is specified on the super-view, the subview still animates automatically. **Figure 4.7** shows the effect of using this mask.

3. You can visually set the `autoresizingMask` property in the size pane of the Inspector window in Interface Builder (**Figure 4.8**).

Figure 4.7 Using the autoresizing mask property, the subview remains in the center of its superview during an animation.

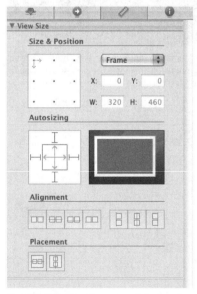

Figure 4.8 Setting the autoresizing mask in Interface Builder.

Code Listing 4.4 Using an autoresizing mask.

```objc
- (void)viewDidLoad {

    [super viewDidLoad];

    CGPoint frameCenter = self.view.center;
    float width = 50.0;
    float height = 50.0;

    CGRect viewFrame = CGRectMake(frameCenter.x-width,frameCenter.y-height, width*2, height*2);
    UIView *myView = [[UIView alloc] initWithFrame:viewFrame];
    myView.backgroundColor = [UIColor blueColor];

    //create subview
    CGRect subViewFrame = CGRectInset(myView.bounds, width/2.0, height/2.0);
    UIView *mySubview = [[UIView alloc] initWithFrame:subViewFrame];
    mySubview.backgroundColor = [UIColor yellowColor];

    //set autoresizing mask
    mySubview.autoresizingMask = UIViewAutoresizingFlexibleLeftMargin
                                 |
                                 UIViewAutoresizingFlexibleRightMargin
                                 |
                                 UIViewAutoresizingFlexibleTopMargin
                                 |
                                 UIViewAutoresizingFlexibleBottomMargin;

    [myView addSubview:mySubview];

    [[self view] addSubview:myView];

    //animate resize
    [UIView beginAnimations:nil context:NULL];

    [UIView setAnimationDuration:1.0];
    viewFrame = CGRectInset(viewFrame, -width, -height);
    [myView setFrame:viewFrame];

    [UIView commitAnimations];

    [mySubview release];
    [myView release];
}
```

Table 4.1

Available autoresizingMask values

VALUE	DESCRIPTION
UIViewAutoresizingNone	The view does not resize.
UIViewAutoresizingFlexibleLeftMargin	The view resizes by expanding or shrinking in the direction of the left margin.
UIViewAutoresizingFlexibleWidth	The view resizes by expanding or shrinking its width.
UIViewAutoresizingFlexibleRightMargin	The view resizes by expanding or shrinking in the direction of the right margin.
UIViewAutoresizingFlexibleTopMargin	The view resizes by expanding or shrinking in the direction of the top margin.
UIViewAutoresizingFlexibleHeight	The view resizes by expanding or shrinking its height.
UIViewAutoresizingFlexibleBottomMargin	The view resizes by expanding or shrinking in the direction of the bottom margin.

VIEWS

Custom drawing

By default, the visual representation of a UIView is fairly boring. You can manipulate the size, background color, and alpha levels of the view, but not much else.

Luckily, it's relatively simple to create your own UIView subclasses where you can implement custom drawing behavior. To see how this might be done, you'll now learn how to create a UIView subclass with rounded corners.

To create a custom rounded-corner view:

1. In Xcode, select File > New File. Create a new Objective-C class, making sure that "Subclass of" is set to UIView (**Figure 4.9**). Save the file as rounded-CornerView.

2. Open roundedCornerView.m, and modify your code to look like **Code Listing 4.5**.

3. Open UITestViewController.m, and replace all instances of UIView with roundedCornerView. Don't forget to also import the header file for roundedCornerView.h at the top of the file. **Code Listing 4.6** shows the updated code.

4. Build and run your application.

   Figure 4.10 shows the application with rounded corners for the views. As you can see, custom drawing happens in the drawRect: method of roundedCornerView. You set a couple of variables here—one to determine the width of the line you will be drawing and another to determine the color.

5. By setting the color to the superview's background color, you are essentially "erasing" any time you draw in the subview.

   ```
   float lineWidth = 10.0;
   UIColor *parentColor = [[self
   → superview] backgroundColor];
   ```

continues on page 110

Figure 4.9 Adding a custom class to draw the rounded corner view.

Figure 4.10 In the updated application, the views now have rounded corners.

VIEWS

Code Listing 4.5 The roundedCornerView class.

```
@implementation roundedCornerView


- (id)initWithFrame:(CGRect)frame {
    if (self = [super initWithFrame:frame])
    {
        self.opaque = TRUE;
    }
    return self;
}


void CGContextStrokeCorners(CGContextRef ctx, CGRect rect) {

    int radius = 12;

    CGFloat xOrigin = rect.origin.x;
    CGFloat yOrigin = rect.origin.y;

    CGFloat xMiddle = CGRectGetMidX(rect);
    CGFloat yMiddle = CGRectGetMidY(rect);

    CGFloat width  = rect.size.width;
    CGFloat height = rect.size.height;

    CGContextBeginPath(ctx);

    CGContextMoveToPoint(ctx, xOrigin, yMiddle);
    CGContextAddArcToPoint(ctx, xOrigin, yOrigin, xMiddle, yOrigin, radius);
    CGContextAddArcToPoint(ctx, width, yOrigin, width, yMiddle, radius);
    CGContextAddArcToPoint(ctx, width, height, xMiddle, height, radius);
    CGContextAddArcToPoint(ctx, xOrigin, height, xOrigin, yMiddle, radius);

    CGContextClosePath(ctx);
    CGContextStrokePath(ctx);
}

- (void)drawRect:(CGRect)rect {

    float lineWidth = 10.0;
    UIColor *parentColor = [[self superview] backgroundColor];

    CGContextRef ctx = UIGraphicsGetCurrentContext();
    CGContextSetStrokeColorWithColor(ctx, parentColor.CGColor);
    CGContextSetLineWidth(ctx, lineWidth);

    //draw corners
    CGContextStrokeCorners(ctx,rect);
}


- (void)dealloc {
    [super dealloc];
}


@end
```

6. Now you get a reference to the current graphics context and set the pen color and width.

A *graphics context* is a special type that represents the current drawing destination, in this case the custom view's contents.

```
CGContextRef ctx =
→ UIGraphicsGetCurrentContext();
CGContextSetStrokeColorWithColor
→ (ctx, parentColor.CGColor);
CGContextSetLineWidth(ctx,
→ lineWidth);
```

7. Finally, call a custom function that draws a line around the outside of the view, rounding at each corner:

```
CGContextStrokeCorners(ctx,rect);
```

Code Listing 4.6 Replacing regular views with the custom class.

```
Code

#import "UITestViewController.h"
#import "roundedCornerView.h"

@implementation UITestViewController

- (void)viewDidLoad {

    [super viewDidLoad];

    CGPoint frameCenter = self.view.center;
    float width  = 50;
    float height = 50;

    CGRect viewFrame = CGRectMake(frameCenter.x-width, frameCenter.y-height,width*2, height*2);
    roundedCornerView *myView = [[roundedCornerView alloc] initWithFrame:viewFrame];

    myView.backgroundColor = [UIColor blueColor];
    [[self view] addSubview:myView];

    CGRect subViewFrame = CGRectInset(myView.bounds,width/2,height/2);
    roundedCornerView *mySubview = [[roundedCornerView alloc] initWithFrame:subViewFrame];
    mySubview.autoresizingMask = UIViewAutoresizingFlexibleHeight | UIViewAutoresizingFlexibleWidth;
    mySubview.backgroundColor = [UIColor yellowColor];
    [myView addSubview:mySubview];

    [UIView beginAnimations:nil context:NULL];
    [UIView setAnimationDuration:1.0];

    viewFrame = CGRectInset(viewFrame, -width, -height);
    [myView setFrame:viewFrame];

    [UIView commitAnimations];

    [mySubview release];
    [myView release];
}
```

VIEWS

Transforms

You've already looked at resizing a view by increasing the width and height of its frame. Another way to perform the same task is by using a *transform*.

A transform maps the coordinates system of a view from one set of points to another. Transformations are applied to the *bounds* of a view. In addition to scaling, you can also rotate and move a view using transforms.

To resize your view using a scale transform:

◆ Add the following code to your application:
```
CGAffineTransform scale =
→ CGAffineTransformMakeScale
→ (2.0,2.0);
myView.transform = scale;
```
This creates a scale transform, doubling both the width and the height of your view.

or

Transforms can also be used to move views by using a *translate* transform:
```
CGAffineTransform translate =
→ CGAffineTransformMakeTranslation
→ (50,50);
myView.transform = translate;
```
This would cause a view to move by 50 pixels along both the x- and y-axes.

or

Finally, you can apply a *rotation* transform to rotate your views:
```
CGAffineTransform rotate =
→ CGAffineTransformMakeRotation
→ (radiansForDegrees(180));
myView.transform = rotate;
```
Because rotations are specified in radians, you use a function to convert from degrees.

VIEWS

To apply both a rotation transform and a scale transform to your view:

1. Update the code to look like the following:

```
CGAffineTransform scale =
→ CGAffineTransformMakeScale
→ (2.0,2.0);
CGAffineTransform rotate =
→ CGAffineTransformMakeRotation
→ (radiansForDegrees(180));
CGAffineTransform myTransform =
→ CGAffineTransformConcat
→ (scale,rotate);
myView.transform = myTransform;
```

Note how you can combine transformations using the `CGAffineTransform Concat()` function.

Code Listing 4.7 shows the completed code.

Code Listing 4.7 Rotating and scaling the view.

```
CGFloat radiansForDegrees(CGFloat degrees)
{
    return (M_PI * degrees / 180.0);
}

- (void)viewDidLoad {

    [super viewDidLoad];

    CGPoint frameCenter = self.view.center;
    float width  = 50;
    float height = 50;

    CGRect viewFrame = CGRectMake(frameCenter.x-width, frameCenter.y-height,width*2, height*2);
    roundedCornerView *myView = [[roundedCornerView alloc] initWithFrame:viewFrame];

    myView.backgroundColor = [UIColor blueColor];
    [[self view] addSubview:myView];

    CGRect subViewFrame = CGRectInset(myView.bounds,width/2,height/2);
    roundedCornerView *mySubview = [[roundedCornerView alloc] initWithFrame:subViewFrame];
    mySubview.backgroundColor = [UIColor yellowColor];
    [myView addSubview:mySubview];

    [UIView beginAnimations:nil context:NULL];

    [UIView setAnimationDuration:1.0];

    CGAffineTransform scale = CGAffineTransformMakeScale(2.0,2.0);
    CGAffineTransform rotate = CGAffineTransformMakeRotation(radiansForDegrees(180));
    CGAffineTransform myTransform = CGAffineTransformConcat(scale,rotate);
    myView.transform = myTransform;

    [UIView commitAnimations];

    [mySubview release];
    [myView release];
}
```

Figure 4.11 The view both rotating and scaling.

2. Build and run your application (**Figure 4.11**).

Your view should rotate and scale at the same time.

✔ Tips

■ You no longer need to set the `autoresizingMask` property of the subview because the transform is applied to the view and its subviews at the same time.

■ You can return a view to its original state by setting its `transform` property to `CGAffineTransformIdentity`.

Image Views

The `UIImageView` class extends `UIView` to provide support for displaying images. Its default initializer, `initWithImage:`, takes a `UIImage` as its only parameter (**Code Listing 4.8**):

```
UIImage *anImage = [UIImage
imageNamed:@"myImage.png"];
UIImageView *myImageView =
→ [[UIImageView alloc]
initWithImage:anImage];
```

Note that `initWithImage:` automatically adjusts the frame of the new image view to match the width and height of the image assigned (**Figure 4.12**).

If you resize the image view, you can see that the image automatically scales to fit (**Figure 4.13**):

```
CGSize viewSize =
→ myImageView.bounds.size;
//shrink width 50%
viewSize.width = viewSize.width * 0.5;
//keep height the same
viewSize.height = viewSize.height;

CGRect newFrame = CGRectMake
→ (0,0,viewSize.width, viewSize.height);
[myImageView setFrame:newFrame];
```

You can control scaling behavior by the `contentMode` property of `UIView`, which defaults to `UIViewContentModeScaleToFill`.

For example, to maintain the aspect ratio of the image, you would write this:

```
myImageView.contentMode =
→ UIViewContentModeScaleAspectFit;
```

Code Listing 4.8 Creating an image view.

```
- (void)viewDidLoad {

    UIImage *anImage = [UIImage imageNamed:
                        @"myImage.png"];
    UIImageView *myImageView = [[UIImageView alloc]
                        initWithImage:anImage];

    [self.view addSubview:myImageView];
    [myImageView release];
}
```

Figure 4.12 The image displaying a graphic.

Figure 4.13 Resizing the image view.

Figure 4.14 Resizing the image view while maintaining its aspect ratio.

Figure 4.14 shows the resulting image. Note that although the *image* itself is scaled, the *image view* still has the same bounds. Any part of the bounds not rendered in the image will be transparent.

Animating images

UIImageView lets you animate over an array of images, which is handy for creating progress animations. **Code Listing 4.9** shows the code updated to animate over three images.

To animate over an image:

1. Create the image view, and set its frame:

   ```
   CGRect viewFrame = CGRectMake
   → (0,0,200,200);

   UIImageView *myImageView =
   → [[UIImageView alloc]
   → initWithFrame:viewFrame];
   ```

continues on next page

Code Listing 4.9 Animating over an array of images.

```
- (void)viewDidLoad {

    [super viewDidLoad];

    NSArray *arrImages = [[NSArray alloc] initWithObjects:
                        [UIImage imageNamed:@"apple.png"],
                        [UIImage imageNamed:@"apple2.png"],
                        [UIImage imageNamed:@"apple3.png"],nil];

    CGRect viewFrame = CGRectMake(0,0,200,200);
    UIImageView *myImageView = [[UIImageView alloc] initWithFrame:viewFrame];

    [myImageView setAnimationImages:arrImages];

    [myImageView setAnimationRepeatCount:0];
    [myImageView setAnimationDuration:0.5];

    [self.view addSubview:myImageView];
    [myImageView startAnimating];

    [arrImages release];
    [myImageView release];
}
```

IMAGE VIEWS

2. Create and set the image array:

```
NSArray *arrImages =
→ [[NSArray alloc] initWithObjects:
   [UIImage imageNamed:@"apple.png"],
   [UIImage imageNamed:
   → @"apple2.png"],
   [UIImage imageNamed:
   → @"apple3.png"],nil];
[myImageView


setAnimationImages:arrImages];
[arrImages release];
```

3. You can control the speed of the animation (in seconds) and number of times the animation is repeated. The default is 0, making the animation loop indefinitely:

```
[myImageView setAnimationDuration:
→ 0.5];
[myImageView setAnimation
→ RepeatCount:0];
```

4. To begin the animation, add the following:

```
[myImageView startAnimating];
```

5. To stop the animation, you call `stopAnimating`.

✔ Tip

- For simplicity, the previous examples use `imageNamed:` to create the images. Although convenient, this method creates autoreleased objects that can't be manually released in a low-memory situation. So, it's usually wiser to use something like the `initWithContentsOfFile:` method and manually allocate/release your images.

Scrolling

Often your views will be larger than the visible area, and you need a way to scroll. For this, you use the UIScrollView class.

A scroll view acts as a container for a larger subview, allowing you to pan around the subview by touching the screen. Vertical and horizontal scroll bars indicate the position in the subview.

Code Listing 4.10 shows an example of using a scroll view.

To create a scroll view:

1. Set the frame as usual:

```
CGRect scrollFrame = CGRectMake
→ (20,90,280,280);
UIScrollView *scrollView =
→ [[UIScrollView alloc]
→ initWithFrame:scrollFrame];
```

2. Create an image view, assigning it an image that is larger than the scroll view:

```
UIImage *bigImage = [UIImage
→ imageNamed:@"appleLogo.jpg"];
UIImageView *largeImageView =
→ [[UIImageView alloc]
→ initWithImage:bigImage];
```

continues on next page

Code Listing 4.10 Using a scroll view.

```
- (void)viewDidLoad {

    [super viewDidLoad];

    CGRect scrollFrame = CGRectMake(20,90,280,280);
    UIScrollView *scrollView = [[UIScrollView alloc] initWithFrame:scrollFrame];

    UIImage *bigImage = [UIImage imageNamed:@"appleLogo.jpg"];
    largeImageView = [[UIImageView alloc] initWithImage:bigImage];

    [scrollView addSubview:largeImageView];
    scrollView.contentSize = largeImageView.frame.size; //important!

    [self.view addSubview:scrollView];

    [scrollView release];
}
```

117

3. Add the image view to the scroll view, and set the `contentSize` property of the scroll view:

```
[scrollView addSubview:
→ largeImageView];

scrollView.contentSize =
→ largeImageView.frame.size;
```

This is an important step: If you don't tell the scroll view how large its subview is, it won't know how to scroll at all.

4. Finally, add the scroll view to the main view:

```
[self.view addSubview:scrollView];
```

Figure 4.15 shows the scroll view with horizontal and vertical scroll bars indicating the current position in the image view. You can hide these scroll bars using the `showsHorizontalScrollIndicator` and `showsVerticalScrollIndicator` properties.

✔ Tip

■ If you play around with the previous code, you'll notice that if you scroll quickly to the edge of the subview, the scroll view actually moves a little too far before springing back. This behavior is controlled by the `bounce` property. You can restrict bouncing to the x- or y-axis using the `alwaysBounceHorizontal` and `alwaysBounceVertical` properties, or you can disable it entirely by setting `bounce` to NO.

Zoom

You can also zoom in and out of an image using a scroll view. The `minimumZoomScale` and `maximumZoomScale` properties control the scale by which you can zoom in and out. By default, both of these properties are set to the same value (`1.0`), which disables zooming. You must implement one of the `UIScrollViewDelegate` methods to return the view that is being zoomed.

Figure 4.15 Using a scroll view to pan around a large image.

To enable zooming:

1. Add the UIScrollViewDelegate protocol in the controller.h file:

   ```
   @interface UITestViewController :
   → UIViewController
   → <UIScrollViewDelegate>
   ```

2. Update the scroll view code to allow you to zoom out by 1/2 and in by 2x:

   ```
   scrollView.minimumZoomScale = 0.5;
   scrollView.maximumZoomScale = 2.0;
   scrollView.delegate = self;
   ```

   You've also set the delegate to be the controller (self).

3. Implement the -viewForZoomingInScroll View: delegate method, and return the image view. **Code Listing 4.11** shows the updated code.

Code Listing 4.11 Adding zoom to the scroll view.

```
                                        Code
- (void)viewDidLoad {

    [super viewDidLoad];

    CGRect scrollFrame = CGRectMake(20,90,280,280);
    UIScrollView *scrollView = [[UIScrollView alloc] initWithFrame:scrollFrame];
    scrollView.minimumZoomScale = 0.5;
    scrollView.maximumZoomScale = 2.0;
    scrollView.delegate = self;

    UIImage *bigImage = [UIImage imageNamed:@"appleLogo.jpg"];
    largeImageView = [[UIImageView alloc] initWithImage:bigImage];

    [scrollView addSubview:largeImageView];
    scrollView.contentSize = largeImageView.frame.size; //important!

    [self.view addSubview:scrollView];

    [scrollView release];
}
- (UIView *)viewForZoomingInScrollView:(UIScrollView *)scrollView
{
    return largeImageView;
}
```

Paging

Scroll views support the *paging* of their content—the ability to add multiple subviews as "pages" and then scroll between them as you might turn the pages of a book. Adding a `UIPageControl` will provide a visual depiction of your current page (**Figure 4.16**).

To create a page control:

1. Update the code to remove the image from the scroll view, and set some new properties:

```
float pageControlHeight = 18.0;
int pageCount = 3;

CGRect scrollViewRect =
→ [self.view bounds];
scrollViewRect.size.height -=
→ pageControlHeight;

myScrollView = [[UIScrollView alloc]
→ initWithFrame:scrollViewRect];
myScrollView.pagingEnabled = YES;
```

The `pagingEnabled` property turns paging on for the scroll view.

2. Since you have three pages, set the `contentView` of the scroll view to be three times wider than its frame. You'll also turn off the scroll view indicators:

```
myScrollView.contentSize =
→ CGSizeMake(scrollViewRect.size.
→ width * pageCount,1);
myScrollView.showsHorizontal
→ ScrollIndicator = NO;
myScrollView.showsVertical
→ ScrollIndicator = NO;
myScrollView.delegate = self;
```

3. Set up the page control by creating a frame below the scroll view, and add a target to the page control so that when it is tapped, it will call the `changePage:` method:

Figure 4.16 The page control indicating the total number of pages and the current page as a series of dots at the bottom of the iPhone's screen.

```
CGRect pageViewRect =
→ [self.view bounds];
pageViewRect.size.height =
→ pageControlHeight;
pageViewRect.origin.y =
→ scrollViewRect.size.height;

myPageControl = [[UIPageControl
→ alloc] initWithFrame:
→ pageViewRect];
myPageControl.backgroundColor =
→ [UIColor blackColor];
myPageControl.numberOfPages =
→ pageCount;
myPageControl.currentPage = 0;
[myPageControl addTarget:self
→ action:@selector(changePage:)
→ orControlEvents:UIControlEvent
→ ValueChanged];
```

4. Call the `createPages` method by adding three `UIViews` side by side to the scroll view to represent the three pages.

5. Set the `backgroundColor` property of the views.

   In a real-world application, these would be more interesting! At this stage, your scroll view will actually work, but you need some more work to get the page control to reflect the current page.

6. Implement the `scrollViewDidScroll:` delegate method:

```
CGFloat pageWidth = sender.frame.
→ size.width;
int page = floor((sender.content
→ Offset.x - pageWidth / 2) /
→ pageWidth) + 1;
myPageControl.currentPage = page;
```

   This simply does some math to calculate your current page during the scroll and then updates the page control accordingly.

continues on next page

SCROLLING

7. Finally, implement the changePage: method called when the page control is tapped:

```
int page = myPageControl.
→ currentPage;
CGRect frame = myScrollView.frame;
frame.origin.x = frame.size.width *
→ page;
frame.origin.y = 0;
[myScrollView scrollRectToVisible:
→ frame animated:YES];
```

This scrolls the scroll view horizontally based on the page you have selected in the page control. **Code Listing 4.12** shows the completed code.

Code Listing 4.12 Implementing a page control.

```
● ● ●                                    Code
UIScrollView *myScrollView;
UIPageControl *myPageControl;

@implementation UITestViewController

- (void)loadScrollViewWithPage:(UIView *)page
{
    int pageCount = [[myScrollView subviews] count];

    CGRect bounds = myScrollView.bounds;
    bounds.origin.x = bounds.size.width * pageCount;
    bounds.origin.y = 0;
    page.frame = bounds;
    [myScrollView addSubview:page];
}

- (void)createPages
{
    CGRect pageRect = myScrollView.frame;

    //create pages
    UIView *page1 = [[UIView alloc] initWithFrame:pageRect];
    page1.backgroundColor = [UIColor blueColor];
    UIView *page2 = [[UIView alloc] initWithFrame:pageRect];
    page2.backgroundColor = [UIColor redColor];
    UIView *page3 = [[UIView alloc] initWithFrame:pageRect];
    page3.backgroundColor = [UIColor greenColor];

    //add to scrollview
    [self loadScrollViewWithPage:page1];
    [self loadScrollViewWithPage:page2];
    [self loadScrollViewWithPage:page3];

    //cleanup
    [page1 release];
    [page2 release];
    [page3 release];
}
```

(code continues on next page)

Code Listing 4.12 *continued*

```
- (void)viewDidLoad {

    [super viewDidLoad];

    float pageControlHeight = 18.0;
    int pageCount = 3;

    CGRect scrollViewRect = [self.view bounds];
    scrollViewRect.size.height -= pageControlHeight;

    //create scrollview
    myScrollView = [[UIScrollView alloc] initWithFrame:scrollViewRect];
    myScrollView.pagingEnabled = YES;
    myScrollView.contentSize = CGSizeMake(scrollViewRect.size.width * pageCount,1);
    myScrollView.showsHorizontalScrollIndicator = NO;
    myScrollView.showsVerticalScrollIndicator = NO;
    myScrollView.delegate = self;

    //create pageview
    CGRect pageViewRect = [self.view bounds];
    pageViewRect.size.height = pageControlHeight;
    pageViewRect.origin.y = scrollViewRect.size.height;

    myPageControl = [[UIPageControl alloc] initWithFrame:pageViewRect];
    myPageControl.backgroundColor = [UIColor blackColor];
    myPageControl.numberOfPages = pageCount;
    myPageControl.currentPage = 0;
    [myPageControl addTarget:self action:@selector(changePage:) forControlEvents:UIControlEventValueChanged];

    //create pages
    [self createPages];

    //add to main view
    [self.view addSubview:myScrollView];
    [self.view addSubview:myPageControl];

    //cleanup
    [myPageControl release];
    [myScrollView release];
}

- (void)scrollViewDidScroll:(UIScrollView *)sender
{
    CGFloat pageWidth = sender.frame.size.width;
    int page = floor((sender.contentOffset.x - pageWidth / 2) / pageWidth) + 1;
    myPageControl.currentPage = page;
}

- (void)changePage:(id)sender
{
    int page = myPageControl.currentPage;

    // update the scroll view to the appropriate page
    CGRect frame = myScrollView.frame;
    frame.origin.x = frame.size.width * page;
    frame.origin.y = 0;
    [myScrollView scrollRectToVisible:frame animated:YES];
}
```

Labels

Instances of the UILabel class display a read-only view that can contain one or more lines of text. For example, to create a simple label and set its text, font, textColor, and backgroundColor properties (**Code Listing 4.13**):

```
myLabel.backgroundColor =
→ [UIColor clearColor];

myLabel.textColor = [UIColor redColor];

myLabel.font = [UIFont systemFontOfSize:
→ 18.0];

myLabel.text = @"Hello World!";
```

By default, a label is rendered as black text on a white background. You can also set a font by name:

```
myLabel.font = [UIFont fontWithName:
→ @"Verdana" size:18.0];
```

Table 4.2 shows the available fonts you can use.

If you don't specify a font size, the label will automatically reduce the font to fit the text within the label's frame. You can control how small the font gets with the minimumFontSize property, and you can disable this behavior entirely with the adjustsFontSizeToFitWidth property.

To add a shadow to a label's text, you could write the following:

```
myLabel.shadowColor =
→ [UIColor darkGrayColor];

myLabel.shadowOffset =
→ CGSizeMake(1.0,1.0);
```

The shadowOffset controls set how far on the x- and y-axes from the label's text the shadow is drawn. The default is {0,-1}.

The textAlignment property allows you to align the label text to the left (the default), center, or right.

Code Listing 4.13 Creating a label.

```
- (void)viewDidLoad {

    CGRect labelFrame = CGRectMake(10,10,200,44);

    UILabel *myLabel = [[UILabel alloc] initWithFrame:
                        labelFrame];

    myLabel.backgroundColor = [UIColor clearColor];
    myLabel.textColor = [UIColor redColor];
    myLabel.font = [UIFont systemFontOfSize:18.0];
    myLabel.text = @"Hello World!";

    [self.view addSubview:myLabel];
    [myLabel release];
}
```

Table 4.2

Fonts available on the iPhone	
FAMILY	NAME
American Typewriter	AmericanTypewriter, AmericanTypewriter-Bold
AppleGothic	AppleGothic
Arial	ArialMT, Arial-BoldMT, Arial-BoldItalicMT, Arial-ItalicMT
Arial Hebrew	ArialHebrew, ArialHebrew-Bold
Arial Rounded MT Bold	ArialRoundedMTBold
Arial Unicode MS	ArialUnicodeMS
Courier	Courier, Courier-BoldOblique, Courier-Oblique, Courier-Bold
Courier New	CourierNewPS-BoldMT, CourierNewPS-ItalicMT, CourierNewPS-BoldItalicMT, CourierNewPSMT
DB LCD Temp	DBLCDTempBlack
Geeza Pro	GeezaPro-Bold, GeezaPro
Georgia	Georgia-Bold, Georgia, Georgia-BoldItalic, Georgia-Italic
Hiragino Kaku Gothic ProN	HiraKakuProN-W6, HiraKakuProN-W3
Heiti J	STHeitiJ-Medium, STHeitiJ-Light
Heiti K	STHeitiK-Medium, STHeitiK-Light
Heiti SC	STHeitiSC-Medium, STHeitiSC-Light
Heiti TC	STHeitiTC-Light, STHeitiTC-Medium
Helvetica	Helvetica-Oblique, Helvetica-BoldOblique, Helvetica, Helvetica-Bold
Helvetica Neue	HelveticaNeue, HelveticaNeue-Bold
Marker Felt	MarkerFelt-Thin
Times New Roman	TimesNewRomanPSMT, TimesNewRomanPS-BoldMT, TimesNewRomanPS-BoldItalicMT, TimesNewRomanPS-ItalicMT
Thonburi	Thonburi-Bold, Thonburi
Trebuchet MS	TrebuchetMS-Italic, TrebuchetMS, TrebuchetMS-BoldItalic, TrebuchetMS-Bold
Verdana	Verdana-Bold, Verdana-BoldItalic, Verdana, Verdana-Italic
Zapfino	Zapfino

LABELS

125

The `lineBreakMode` property controls how a label wraps text that is too wide to fit within its frame. You can specify whether you want the text to be word or character wrapped, clipped, or truncated at the start, end, or middle of the text.

To display multiple lines of text in a label, use the `numberOfLines` property and the `\n` newline escape character:

```
myLabel.numberOfLines = 2;

myLabel.text = @"Hello World\nSecond
→ line";
```

The height of the label's `frame` property needs to be tall enough to accommodate the number of lines of text you specify, or the text will be wrapped using the value defined in the `lineBreakMode` property (**Code Listing 4.14**).

✔ Tip

■ Setting the `numberOfLines` property to `0` will make the label dynamically set the line count.

Code Listing 4.14 Setting various properties of a label.

```
- (void)viewDidLoad {

    CGRect labelFrame = CGRectMake(10,10,200,44);

    UILabel *myLabel = [[UILabel alloc] initWithFrame:
                        labelFrame];

    myLabel.backgroundColor = [UIColor clearColor];
    myLabel.textColor = [UIColor redColor];
    myLabel.font = [UIFont fontWithName:@"Verdana"
                        size:18.0];
    myLabel.numberOfLines = 2;
    myLabel.text = @"Hello World!\nSecond line";

    myLabel.shadowColor = [UIColor darkGrayColor];
    myLabel.shadowOffset = CGSizeMake(1.0,1.0);

    [self.view addSubview:myLabel];
    [myLabel release];
}
```

Figure 4.17 A progress view at 33 percent completion.

Progress and Activity Indicators

When performing tasks that may take some time, you often need to provide some kind of visual feedback to your users. If you know how long the task will take to complete, you can use a progress indicator to show the user how much of the task has been performed and how much still has to run. If you are unable to determine the duration of the task, use a "busy" indicator (such as the beach ball or hourglass on OS X).

The iPhone SDK provides classes for showing both progress and activity.

Indicating progress

When you want to show the progress of a task, use UIProgressView, a very simple class, consisting of only two properties.

You create a progress view and set its style using the initWithProgressViewStyle: method:

```
UIProgressView *myProgressView =
→ [[UIProgressView alloc]
→ initWithProgressViewStyle:
→ UIProgressViewStyleDefault];
```

The indicator appears as a horizontal bar that fills from left to right to show completion (**Figure 4.17**). This is controlled by the progress property, using a value between 0.0 (not started) and 1.0 (completed):

```
[myProgressView setProgress:0.33];
```

Although you set the frame of the progress view, the maximum height of a progress view is 9 pixels, so any larger value will be ignored.

Code Listing 4.15 shows an example of using UIProgressView with the progress updated in a timer to simulate a long-running task.

Figure 4.18 An activity indicator view.

✔ Tip

- The other progress bar style, UIProgress ViewStyleBar, also uses a horizontal bar indicator but is more suitable for using in a toolbar (explained in the following section).

Showing activity

For tasks of an indeterminate duration, you can use the UIActivityIndicatorView class, represented by an animated "spinner" graphic (**Figure 4.18**).

Code Listing 4.15 Updating the progress view.

```
⊖ ⊖ ⊖                              Code
NSTimer *timer;

@implementation UITestViewController

- (void)updateProgress:(NSTimer *)sender
{
    UIProgressView *progress = [sender userInfo];

    //have we completed?
    if (progress.progress == 1.0)
        [timer invalidate];
    else
        progress.progress += 0.05;
}

- (void)viewDidLoad {

    [super viewDidLoad];

    UIProgressView *myProgressView = [[UIProgressView alloc] initWithProgressViewStyle:UIProgressViewStyleDefault];

    CGRect progressFrame = CGRectMake(10,100,300,25);
    [myProgressView setFrame:progressFrame];

    [myProgressView setProgress:0.0];

    [self.view addSubview:myProgressView];

    [myProgressView release];

    //create timer
    timer = [[NSTimer scheduledTimerWithTimeInterval:0.1
                                    target:self
                                  selector:@selector(updateProgress:)
                                  userInfo:myProgressView
                                    repeats:YES] retain];
}
```

Similar to a progress view, you can create an activity indicator using the `initWithActivity IndicatorStyle:` method:

```
UIActivityIndicatorView *myActivityView
→ = [[UIActivityIndicatorView alloc]
→ initWithActivityIndicatorStyle:
→ UIActivityIndicatorViewStyleWhite];
```

The default size of an activity view is a 21-pixel square. If you use the `UIActivity IndicatorViewStyleWhiteLarge` style, this increases to a 36-pixel square.

Unlike the progress view, however, the frame property controls both the height and the width of the view. For activity views larger than 36 pixels, it's best to use the larger style so the image won't become pixelated.

The activity view will initially be invisible. Calling the `startAnimating` method shows the activity view and causes the spinner graphic to animate:

```
[myActivityView startAnimating];
```

Calling `stopAnimating` will stop the spinner animation, but you need to remember to set the `hidesWhenStopped` property if you want the activity view to hide (**Code Listing 4.16**).

Code Listing 4.16 Creating an activity indicator view.

```
- (void)viewDidLoad {

    [super viewDidLoad];

    [self.view setBackgroundColor:[UIColor blackColor]];

    UIActivityIndicatorView *myActivityView = [[UIActivityIndicatorView alloc]
                                    initWithActivityIndicatorStyle:UIActivityIndicatorViewStyleWhiteLarge];

    CGRect activityFrame = CGRectMake(130,100,50,50);
    [myActivityView setFrame:activityFrame];

    [myActivityView startAnimating];

    [self.view addSubview:myActivityView];

    [myActivityView release];
}
```

Alerts and Actions

Often in your applications you'll want to present a message to your users. Perhaps you want to alert them about an error or present them with options for a given action. As an iPhone developer, you handle these situations using *alert views* and *action sheets*.

Alerting users

To display an alert message, use the UIAlert View class. You define a title, message, and delegate, and then configure buttons to be shown in the view.

To display an alert view:

1. First, create a simple alert view (**Figure 4.19**):

```
UIAlertView *myAlert = [[UIAlertView
→ alloc] initWithTitle:@"title"
   message:@"message"
      delegate:nil
   cancelButtonTitle:@"OK",
   otherButtonTitles:nil];

[myAlert show];
```

2. Using the otherButtonTitles property, you can create the same alert view with up to four additional buttons (**Figure 4.20**):

```
UIAlertView *myAlert =
→ [[UIAlertView alloc] •
→ initWithTitle:@"title"
   message:@"message"
      delegate:nil
   cancelButtonTitle:@"OK"
   otherButtonTitles:@"button1",
   → @"button2", @"button3",
   → @"button4",nil];
```

If you have only two buttons in your alert view, they will be displayed side by side. Otherwise, buttons are added from top to bottom, with the cancel button always

Figure 4.19 A bare-bones alert view.

Figure 4.20 An alert view with several buttons added.

being at the very bottom. If you don't need the message or title text, there is room for five buttons in addition to the cancel button.

3. You can add buttons after creating your alert view by using the `addButtonWith` `Title:` method:

    ```
    [myAlert addButtonWithTitle:
    ⇢@"new button"];
    ```

4. To determine which button is tapped, set the delegate, and implement the `alertView:clickedButtonAtIndex:` delegate method (**Code Listing 4.17**). The `buttonIndex` parameter tells you which button was tapped, starting with the cancel button at index 0. Alert views close automatically when a button is tapped.

✔ Tips

■ Using the `dismissWithClickedButton` `Index:animated:` method, you can programmatically close an alert view without the user having to tap a button. This might be useful in a situation where you want to show an alert for a short time and then hide it automatically.

■ Another way to alert the user is by making the iPhone vibrate by calling the function `AudioServicesPlayAlertSound(kSystem SoundID_Vibrate)`. You'll need to add the `AudioToolbox` framework to your project for this to work.

Code Listing 4.17 Display an alert view.

```
- (void)viewDidLoad {

    [super viewDidLoad];

    UIAlertView *myAlert = [[UIAlertView alloc] initWithTitle:@"title"
                                               message:@"message"
                                              delegate:self
                                     cancelButtonTitle:@"OK"
                                     otherButtonTitles:nil];

    [myAlert addButtonWithTitle:@"new button"];
    [myAlert addButtonWithTitle:@"another button"];

    [myAlert show];

    [myAlert release];
}
- (void)alertView:(UIAlertView *)alertView clickedButtonAtIndex:(NSInteger)buttonIndex {

    NSLog(@"you clicked button: %i",buttonIndex);
}
```

Confirming an action

When presenting the user with a number of options, you can use a UIActionSheet.

To create an action sheet:

1. An action sheet is created in a similar way to an alert view (**Figure 4.21**):

```
UIActionSheet *mySheet =
→ [[UIActionSheet alloc]
→ initWithTitle:@"Do you really
→ want to delete?" delegate:nil
→ cancelButtonTitle:@"No"
→ destructiveButtonTitle:@"Yes"
→ otherButtonTitles:nil];

[mySheet showInView:self.view];
```

2. Define titles for three types of button.

   The *cancel* button is generally used to dismiss the action sheet.

   The *destructive* button acts as the confirmation of the action and is usually shown in red to indicate its importance.

   The *other* buttons are similar to the alert view and allow you to add more buttons.

   Setting any of these parameters to nil prevents the button type from showing.

3. Set the delegate, and implement the actionSheet:clickedButtonAtIndex: method, which is called when a button is tapped.

   You can compare the buttonIndex parameter to the action sheet's cancelButton Index and destructiveButtonIndex properties to determine which button was tapped.

   Code Listing 4.18 shows the code updated with some of these options.

Figure 4.21 An action sheet is "pinned" to the bottom of the screen, and it contains only a title.

Code Listing 4.18 Adding more options to the action sheet.

```
- (void)viewDidLoad {

    [super viewDidLoad];

    UIActionSheet *mySheet = [[UIActionSheet alloc] initWithTitle:@"Email Deletion Options"
                                          delegate:self
                                   cancelButtonTitle:@"Cancel"
                            destructiveButtonTitle:@"Delete Everything"
                                   otherButtonTitles:@"All Read Email", @"Spam Only",nil];


    mySheet.actionSheetStyle = UIActionSheetStyleBlackOpaque;
    [mySheet showInView:self.view];

    [mySheet release];
}

- (void)actionSheet:(UIActionSheet *)actionSheet clickedButtonAtIndex:(NSInteger)buttonIndex {

    BOOL cancelClicked = actionSheet.cancelButtonIndex == buttonIndex;
    BOOL destructiveButtonClicked = actionSheet.destructiveButtonIndex == buttonIndex;

    NSLog(@"button with index %i clicked (cancel:%i, destructive:%i)",buttonIndex,cancelClicked,destructiveButtonClicked);

}
```

Action sheets vs. alert views

Action sheets are functionally similar to alert views, with a number of important differences:

◆ Action sheets are attached to a view. The code used in the previous exercise attaches the action sheet to the controller's main view.

◆ You can optionally show the alert sheet from a tab bar or a toolbar using the showFromTab-Bar: and showFromToolbar: methods.

◆ Action sheets do not have a message property; they have a single title property.

◆ You can change how the action sheet looks by using the actionSheetStyle property. In addition to the default style, you can give your action sheet a black transparent or opaque style. Setting the style to UIActionSheetStyleAutomatic will give your action sheet the same appearance as the bottom bar if one exists.

Picker Views

The `UIPickerView` class allows users to "spin" a wheel-type control to select one or more values. Each picker view consists of one or more *components* consisting of one or more *rows*. Each component can be spun independently of the others. **Figure 4.22** shows the picker view being used to select a date value. There are three components in the control, representing the month, day, and year.

The number of components and rows in a picker view is determined by its *datasource*, an object that adopts the `UIPickerViewDataSource` protocol. The display and selection of the picker view content is handled by the *delegate*, which adopts the `UIPickerViewDelegate` protocol (the datasource and the delegate can be the same object).

Figure 4.22 A picker view being used to select a date.

To create a simple picker view:

1. Add the protocol declarations to your interface definition:

```
@interface UITestViewController :
→ UIViewController
→ <UIPickerViewDataSource,
→ UIPickerViewDelegate>
```

2. Create a picker view, and add it to the main view (**Code Listing 4.19**):

```
CGRect pickerFrame =
→ CGRectMake(0,120,0,0);

UIPickerView *myPicker =
→ [[UIPickerView alloc]
→ initWithFrame:pickerFrame];
myPicker.dataSource = self;
myPicker.delegate = self;

[self.view addSubview:myPicker];
```

Picker views are always 320 pixels by 216 pixels in size and cannot be resized.

3. The showsSelectionIndicator property creates a translucent bar across the control to indicate the selected row.

4. At a minimum, you need to implement two data source methods.

numberOfComponentsInPickerView: returns the number of segments or components in the picker view. In this example, you want a single component, so return the value 1.

pickerView:numberOfRowsInComponent: returns the number of rows for each component. Again, ignore the component parameter (since you have only a single component), and return the number of rows.

continues on next page

Code Listing 4.19 A bare-bones picker view implementation.

```
- (void)viewDidLoad {

    [super viewDidLoad];

    CGRect pickerFrame = CGRectMake(0,120,0,0);

    UIPickerView *myPicker = [[UIPickerView alloc] initWithFrame:pickerFrame];
    myPicker.dataSource = self;
    myPicker.delegate = self;
    myPicker.showsSelectionIndicator = YES;

    [self.view addSubview:myPicker];

    [myPicker release];
}
- (NSInteger)numberOfComponentsInPickerView:(UIPickerView *)pickerView {

    return 1;
}
- (NSInteger)pickerView:(UIPickerView *)pickerView numberOfRowsInComponent:(NSInteger)component {

    return 10;
}
- (NSString *)pickerView:(UIPickerView *)thePickerView titleForRow:(NSInteger)row forComponent:(NSInteger)component {

    return [NSString stringWithFormat:@"Row %i",row];
}
```

PICKER VIEWS

135

5. Implement the delegate `pickerView:`
`titleForRow:forComponent:` method,
returning an `NSString` representation of
the current row (**Figure 4.23**):

```
return [NSString stringWithFormat:
→ @"Row %i",row];
```

The picker view can display much more
interesting data than this simple example.
Components can be of different widths and,
rather than just simple text, can actually
have entire views embedded within them
(**Figure 4.24**).

To enhance the picker view:

1. After calling the `initComp1` and `initComp2`
methods to create some sample data,
update the `numberOfComponentsInPicker`
`View:` method to return two components
(one for each of the sample arrays). Also,
update the `pickerView:numberofRowsIn`
`Component:` method to return the size of
each array:

```
if (component == 0)
    return [comp1 count];
else
    return [comp2 count];
```

The arrays here contain different numbers
of elements; in other words, components
do not need the same number of rows.

2. Define a new delegate method, `picker`
`View:widthFormComponent:`, and set the
widths of the components to different
values:

```
if (component == 0)
    return 100.0;
else
    return 200.0;
```

Figure 4.23 The picker view shows the sample data.

Figure 4.24 The updated picker view. Not only do the
two components display different content, but they
also have different widths and numbers of items.

3. Implement the `pickerView:viewForRow:forComponent:reusingView:` delegate, returning either an image view or a label. This method allows you to embed almost any view subclass in a picker view component.

4. Finally, in the `pickerView:didSelectRow:inComponent:` delegate, log the selected row and component to the console.

   When you spin the picker view, this method isn't fired until the scrolling animation ends. **Code Listings 4.20** show the updated code.

Code Listing 4.20 The updated picker view.

```
⊖ ⊖ ⊖                              Code
NSMutableArray *comp1;
NSMutableArray *comp2;

@implementation UITestViewController

-(void)initComp1
{
    comp1 = [[NSMutableArray alloc] init];
    UIImageView *imgView;

    imgView = [[UIImageView alloc] initWithImage:[UIImage imageNamed:@"ca.png"]];
    [comp1 addObject:imgView];
    [imgView release];

    imgView = [[UIImageView alloc] initWithImage:[UIImage imageNamed:@"gb.png"]];
    [comp1 addObject:imgView];
    [imgView release];

    imgView = [[UIImageView alloc] initWithImage:[UIImage imageNamed:@"us.png"]];
    [comp1 addObject:imgView];
    [imgView release];
}

-(void)initComp2
{
    comp2 = [[NSMutableArray alloc] init];
    UILabel *lbl;

    lbl = [[UILabel alloc] initWithFrame:CGRectMake(0,0,100,44)];
    lbl.backgroundColor = [UIColor clearColor];
    lbl.text = @"Red";
    [comp2 addObject:lbl];
    [lbl release];

    lbl = [[UILabel alloc] initWithFrame:CGRectMake(0,0,100,44)];
    lbl.backgroundColor = [UIColor clearColor];
    lbl.text = @"Blue";
    [comp2 addObject:lbl];
    [lbl release];
}
```

(code continues on next page)

PICKER VIEWS

Code Listing 4.20 *continued*

```
○ ○ ○                                    Code
- (void)viewDidLoad {

    [super viewDidLoad];

    //create some sample data
    [self initComp1];
    [self initComp2];

    CGRect pickerFrame = CGRectMake(0,120,0,0);

    UIPickerView *myPicker = [[UIPickerView alloc] initWithFrame:pickerFrame];
    myPicker.dataSource = self;
    myPicker.delegate = self;
    myPicker.showsSelectionIndicator = YES;

    [self.view addSubview:myPicker];

    [myPicker release];
}
- (NSInteger)numberOfComponentsInPickerView:(UIPickerView *)pickerView {

    return 2;
}
- (NSInteger)pickerView:(UIPickerView *)pickerView numberOfRowsInComponent:(NSInteger)component {

    if (component == 0)
        return [comp1 count];
    else
        return [comp2 count];
}
- (CGFloat)pickerView:(UIPickerView *)pickerView widthForComponent:(NSInteger)component
{
    if (component == 0)
        return 100.0;
    else
        return 200.0;
}
- (UIView *)pickerView:(UIPickerView *)pickerView
          viewForRow:(NSInteger)row
        forComponent:(NSInteger)component
         reusingView:(UIView *)view {

    if (component == 0)
        return [comp1 objectAtIndex:row];
    else
        return [comp2 objectAtIndex:row];
}
- (void)pickerView:(UIPickerView *)pickerView didSelectRow:(NSInteger)row inComponent:(NSInteger)component {

    NSLog(@"row: %i, component:%i",row,component);
}
```

Picking dates and times

The iPhone SDK also has a special version of a picker, `UIDatePicker`, geared toward picking dates as well as times. The `datePickerMode` property determines the style of the picker. **Figure 4.25** shows a date picker with the default style of `UIDatePickerModeDateAndTime`.

Since the date picker is localized, it will automatically display dates and times in the format of the device locale. You can, however, override these settings to display dates and times for other locales.

You can set properties for start and end dates (for the date-style pickers) and for minute and countdown values (for the time-style pickers).

Figure 4.25 The default date picker lets you pick both the date and the time.

`UIDatePicker` is not actually a subclass of `UIPickerView`. It is a `UIControl` subclass that has a custom `UIPickerView` as a subview. This means that you use the target-action mechanism to manage the selection of values. As with other controls, you set the action:

```
[myPicker addTarget:self action:@selector(pickerChanged:) forControlEvents:
UIControlEventValueChanged];
```

The date picker creates a `UIControlEventValueChanged` event when a date or time is selected (**Code Listing 4.21**).

Code Listing 4.21 Implementing a date picker.

```
-(void)pickerChanged:(id)sender {

    NSLog(@"value: %@",[sender date]);
}

- (void)viewDidLoad {

    CGRect pickerFrame = CGRectMake(0,120,0,0);

    UIDatePicker *myPicker = [[UIDatePicker alloc]
                              initWithFrame:pickerFrame];

    [myPicker addTarget:self
            action:@selector(pickerChanged:)
        forControlEvents:UIControlEventValueChanged];

    [self.view addSubview:myPicker];
    [myPicker release];
}
```

Toolbars

You can create toolbars in iPhone applications using the UIToolbar class. A toolbar usually spans the entire width of the display and is aligned to either the top or the bottom of the screen (**Figure 4.26**).

To create a toolbar:

1. As with many other views, you can create a toolbar with the initWithFrame: method. Use the size of the main view to calculate the y position of the toolbar. This is important since you may not know the orientation of the iPhone and want the toolbar to sit at the bottom of the screen.

    ```
    CGSize viewSize =
    → self.view.frame.size;
    float toolbarHeight = 44.0;
    CGRect toolbarFrame = CGRectMake
    → (0,viewSize.height-toolbarHeight,
    → viewSize.width,toolbarHeight);
    UIToolbar *myToolbar =
    → [[UIToolbar alloc] initWithFrame:
    → toolbarFrame];
    ```

Figure 4.26 Most of the controls sit on the toolbar in Safari.

2. Set the autoresizingMask property of the toolbar to ensure that it stays in the same position (in this case, aligned to the bottom of the screen) even if the user rotates their iPhone.

    ```
    myToolbar.autoresizingMask =
    → UIViewAutoresizingFlexibleWidth |
    → UIViewAutoresizing
    → FlexibleLeftMargin |
    UIViewAutoresizingFlexibleRight
    → Margin | UIViewAutoresizing
    → FlexibleTopMargin;
    ```

3. You can change the color and translucency of the toolbar using the tintColor and translucent properties:

    ```
    myToolbar.tintColor =
    → [UIColor redColor];
    myToolbar.translucent = YES;
    ```

Figure 4.27 A toolbar showing the three toolbar item styles available for the initWithTitle:style:target :action: method.

Figure 4.28 Some of the available system item styles.

Toolbar items

Buttons you add to a toolbar are known as *toolbar items* and are created using the UIBarButtonItem class. Several types of buttons are available, and you can create them in several ways:

◆ The simplest way to create a button with some title text is by using the initWith Title:style:target:action: method (**Figure 4.27**). Use the target and action parameters to indicate which method to call when the button is pressed.

◆ Similarly, the initWithImage:style: target:action: method lets you create a button with an image instead of text. The button will automatically resize its width to that of the image.

◆ You can create a button from your own custom UIView subclass using the initWithCustomView: method. However, you must set the target and action properties manually.

◆ The final way is to use the initWithBar ButtonSystemItem:target:action: method.

The iPhone SDK offers a set of predefined buttons, known as *system items*, to ensure your application adheres to the iPhone interface guidelines. Use them whenever possible.

There are system items for play, pause, and stop buttons, as well as for search, trash, and camera (**Figure 4.28**). For a complete list of system items available, refer to the UIBarButtonSystemItem type in the developer documentation.

TOOLBARS

You will often use two particular system item types: UIBarButtonSystemItemFlexibleSpace and UIBarButtonSystemItemFixedSpace. Both are not visible and represent spaces on a toolbar. The flexible-space item lets you force a button to the other side of the toolbar, while the fixed-space item simply lets you add a space between buttons. You can set the width property of a fixed-space item to determine how wide you want the space to be.

Once you've created these buttons, add them to an NSArray and then use the setItems: method of the UIToolbar to add them to the toolbar itself. The optional animated: parameter allows you to have buttons fade in as they are added to the toolbar.

Code Listing 4.22 shows the updated code, with buttons of various types and a flexible-space item being used to push a button to the right side of the toolbar. If you try rotating the phone, you will notice that the toolbar and buttons correctly align themselves regardless of orientation (**Figure 4.29**).

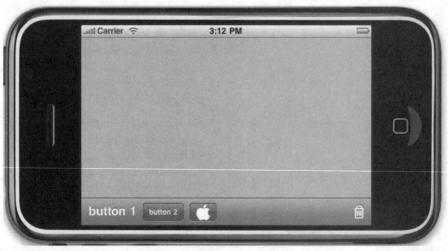

Figure 4.29 The toolbar has correctly sized itself with the iPhone in landscape mode. The trash toolbar item is aligned to the right.

Code Listing 4.22 Creating several different types of toolbar items.

```
● ● ●                                    Code
- (void)buttonClick:(id)sender {

    NSLog(@"you clicked button: %@",[sender title]);
}

- (void)viewDidLoad {

    [super viewDidLoad];

    CGSize viewSize = self.view.frame.size;
    float toolbarHeight = 44.0;
    CGRect toolbarFrame = CGRectMake(0,viewSize.height-toolbarHeight,viewSize.width,toolbarHeight);

    UIToolbar *myToolbar = [[UIToolbar alloc] initWithFrame:toolbarFrame];

    myToolbar.autoresizingMask = UIViewAutoresizingFlexibleWidth
                                 |
                                 UIViewAutoresizingFlexibleLeftMargin
                                 |
                                 UIViewAutoresizingFlexibleRightMargin
                                 |
                                 UIViewAutoresizingFlexibleTopMargin;

    UIBarButtonItem *button1 = [[UIBarButtonItem alloc] initWithTitle:@"button 1"
                                                    style:UIBarButtonItemStylePlain target:self
                                                    action:@selector(buttonClick:)];

    UIBarButtonItem *button2 = [[UIBarButtonItem alloc] initWithTitle:@"button 2"
                                                    style:UIBarButtonItemStyleBordered
                                                    target:self
                                                    action:@selector(buttonClick:)];

    UIBarButtonItem *button3 = [[UIBarButtonItem alloc] initWithImage:[UIImage imageNamed:@"apple_icon.png"]
                                                    style:UIBarButtonItemStyleBordered
                                                    target:self
                                                    action:@selector(buttonClick:)];

    UIBarButtonItem *flexButton = [[UIBarButtonItem alloc] initWithBarButtonSystemItem:UIBarButtonSystemItemFlexibleSpace
                                                    target:nil
                                                    action:nil];

    UIBarButtonItem *trashButton = [[UIBarButtonItem alloc] initWithBarButtonSystemItem:UIBarButtonSystemItemTrash
                                                    target:self
                                                    action:@selector(buttonClick:)];

    NSArray *buttons = [[NSArray alloc] initWithObjects:button1,button2,button3, flexButton,trashButton,nil];

    //cleanup
    [button1 release];
    [button2 release];
    [button3 release];
    [flexButton release];
    [trashButton release];

    [myToolbar setItems:buttons animated:NO];

    [buttons release];

    [self.view addSubview:myToolbar];

    [myToolbar release];
}
```

Text

For entering text into your applications, the iPhone SDK provides two classes, UIText Field and UITextView. Both allow the user to enter and edit text using an onscreen keyboard and support features such as cut/copy and paste, spell check, and more, but the two classes function differently.

To create a text field:

1. You can use the UITextField class to enter small amounts of text, such as user names, passwords, or search terms. This field is limited to a single line of text.

2. As with most other views, you use the initWithFrame: method to create them:

```
CGRect textRect = CGRectMake
→ (10,10,300,20);
UITextField *myTextField =
→ [[UITextField alloc]
→ initWithFrame:textRect];
myTextField.backgroundColor =
→ [UIColor whiteColor];
```

This also sets the background color of the text field; otherwise, it's transparent by default. Text fields also don't have a border by default.

3. Use the borderStyle property to choose from four different styles (**Figure 4.30**).

The UITextBorderStyleRoundedRect style has a white background and will ignore the backgroundColor property. If you set a custom UIImage as the background, the borderStyle property will be ignored.

4. You can set the text font, color, and alignment to apply to the entire text field.

Text fields do not support the styling of individual text elements.

Figure 4.30 Border styles available for text fields.

Clicking the clear button removes any text in the text field.

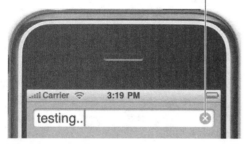

Figure 4.31 Press the clear button to remove any text in the text field.

Figure 4.32 Two of the keyboards available by setting the keyboardType property of a text field.

5. You can set your text field to automatically resize the font to accommodate larger text:

```
myTextField.font =
→ [UIFont systemFontOfSize:22.0];
myTextField.adjustsFontSizeTo
→ FitWidth = YES;
myTextField.minimumFontSize = 2.0;
```

This example sets the initial font size as 22 and then tells the text field to automatically shrink the font to a minimum size of 2 if the text is wider than the text field's bounds.

6. Setting the clearsOnBeginEditing property to YES will clear any existing text when you first touch the control:

```
myTextField.clearsOnBeginEditing =
→ YES;
myTextField.clearButtonMode =
→ UITextFieldViewModeWhileEditing;
```

The clearButtonMode property adds a small button to the end of the text field, letting you clear the text at any time (**Figure 4.31**). You can determine when this button is shown, such as only when editing the text.

To use keyboards:

1. Tap in the text field to open a keyboard from the bottom of the screen.

2. You can choose from a number of keyboard styles (**Figure 4.32**), each designed for particular situations such as entering numbers or using a web browser.

3. Set the style with the keyboardType property.

By default, the keyboard will automatically suggest words as you type.

continues on next page

TEXT

4. To disable this function, set the
autocorrectionType property to
UITextAutocorrectTypeNo.

5. Set the autocaptializationType property to determine whether the keyboard
capitalizes your typing by word, sentence,
or even all characters.

6. You can change the text on the Return key
via the returnKeyType property.

7. Use the enablesReturnKeyAutomatically
property to determine whether the
Return key is enabled even if you haven't
entered any text into the text field.

   In **Code Listing 4.23**, the secureTextEntry
property is set to YES, which is useful
for text fields that contain passwords or
other sensitive information. As you enter
text, you will see only the last letter typed.

8. You may have noticed that the keyboard
doesn't disappear when you press the
Return key. To hide the text field, you
must implement the textFieldShould
Return: delegate and tell the text field to
resign its first responder status:

```
[textField resignFirstResponder];
return YES;
```

Code Listing 4.23 Creating a secure text field.

```
- (void)viewDidLoad {

    CGRect textRect = CGRectMake(10,10,300,31);
    UITextField *myField = [[UITextField alloc]
                            initWithFrame:textRect];
    myField.borderStyle = UITextBorderStyleRoundedRect;

    myField.font = [UIFont systemFontOfSize:22.0];
    myField.adjustsFontSizeToFitWidth = YES;
    myField.minimumFontSize = 2.0;

    myField.clearButtonMode = UITextFieldViewModeWhileEditing;
    myField.keyboardType = UIKeyboardTypeDefault;
    myField.autocorrectionType = UITextAutocorrectionTypeNo;
    myField.autocapitalizationType = UITextAutocapitalizationTypeNone;
    myField.returnKeyType = UIReturnKeyDone;

    myField.secureTextEntry = YES;

    [self.view addSubview:myField];
    [myField release];
}
```

TEXT

9. Similarly, you can make the keyboard appear automatically when the view is loaded by setting the first responder status in the `viewDidLoad:` method:

`[myTextField becomeFirstResponder];`

10. To prevent the keyboard from showing at all, which is useful if you are implementing your own custom keyboard, return `NO` from the `textFieldShould BeginEditing:` delegate method.

✔ Tip

■ For a complete list of keyboard options, refer to the "UITextInputTraits Protocol" section of the developer documentation.

Restricting content

You can also use the delegate methods to control the text being entered into the text field. The `textField:shouldChangeCharacters InRange:replacementString:` delegate is called whenever the text is changed. You could, for example, use this method to restrict the number of characters entered. **Code Listing 4.24** shows a text field that allows a maximum of ten characters.

Code Listing 4.24 Limiting the contents of a text field to ten characters.

```
- (BOOL)textField:(UITextField *)textField
shouldChangeCharactersInRange:(NSRange)range
replacementString:(NSString *)string
{
    //limit text field to 10 chars
    int MAX_CHARS = 10;
    NSMutableString *newText = [NSMutableString
                        stringWithString:textField.text];
    [newText replaceCharactersInRange:range
                        withString:string];
    return ([newText length] <= MAX_CHARS);
}
```

TEXT

You should check the length of the replacement rather than just looking at the length of the text in the text field, since the text field's contents can be altered via copy and paste as well as by using the keyboard.

For the same reason, simply changing the keyboard type to numeric does not guarantee that a user will enter only numeric values (since a user could paste non-numeric values into the field). **Code Listing 4.25** shows the same delegate method, this time restricting the text field to allow numeric values only.

Text views

The UITextView class allows for multiline editable text. Although similar to text fields, text views feature a number of important differences.

Text views don't have any support for automatically reducing the font size like text fields have. Also, they don't have any support for clearing the text other than through programmatically setting the text property. There is also no support for secure text entry.

As with text fields, text views also apply the same text style to the entire text. Apple recommends using a UIWebView (see the "Web Views" section) if you require multiple styles in your text.

Data detectors

Text views can analyze their contents and convert any links or phone numbers into tappable links by using a capability known as *data detectors*. Tapping the link will either launch the browser or call the phone number.

Code Listing 4.25 Restricting the contents of a text field to numeric values.

```
- (BOOL)textField:(UITextField *)textField
shouldChangeCharactersInRange:(NSRange)range
replacementString:(NSString *)string
{
    //limit text field to numeric values only
    NSCharacterSet *numberSet = [NSCharacterSet
                            decimalDigitCharacterSet];
    for (NSUInteger i=0; i<[string length]; i++)
    {
        unichar ch = [string characterAtIndex:i];
        if (![numberSet characterIsMember:ch])
            return NO;
    }
    return YES;
}
```

Figure 4.33 A text view with an active data detector.

Two data detector types are available: `UIData DetectorTypePhoneNumber` for phone numbers and `UIDataDetectorTypeLink` for Web `http:` links. To enable both, set the `data DetectorTypes` property:

```
myTextView.dataDetectorTypes =
→ UIDataDetectorTypeAll;
```

There's one caveat with data detectors: The default behavior of text views is to show the keyboard when tapped, so you can't tap the link of a data detector. For data detectors to work, you must set the `editable` property of the text view to `NO`. In **Figure 4.33**, the URL is underlined just as it would be in a web browser. Tapping it will launch the Safari application.

Hiding the keyboard

A text view's keyboard behaves the same as a text field, with one important difference: Since a text view supports multiline editing, pressing the Return button on the keyboard will insert a carriage return instead of calling a delegate method. Just as with the text field, resign the text view's first responder status to hide the keyboard when you have finished editing the text. This is often done as an action within another control.

Scrolling the interface

You may have noticed that since the iPhone's keyboards are very large, they take up a lot of the screen and can overlap other controls when shown. It would be handy if your interface moved up when the keyboard appeared and then moved back down once it disappeared.

TEXT

You can make that happen by placing the controls inside a UIScrollView. When the keyboard appears, you simply scroll everything up, scrolling back down when the keyboard hides.

To scroll the interface in response to the keyboard:

1. Create and add a scroll view, making it the full size of the main view:

```
CGRect viewRect =
→ [self.view bounds];
myScrollView = [[UIScrollView alloc]
→ initWithFrame:viewRect];
myScrollView.contentSize =
→ viewRect.size;
[self.view addSubview:myScrollView];
```

2. Add the controls to the scroll view instead of the main view (since you want them to scroll).

3. Implement the textViewDidBeginEditing: delegate method, which is called when the keyboard is shown.

Here you need to calculate both the bottom of the text view and the top of the keyboard and then tell the scroll view to scroll the difference. You must also look at the orientation property of the iPhone because the keyboard will have a different height in portrait mode than in landscape mode.

4. Implement the textViewDidEndEditing: delegate so that when the keyboard is hidden, you scroll the text view to its original position. **Code Listing 4.26** shows the completed code.

Code Listing 4.26 Scrolling an interface in response to a keyboard.

```
UIScrollView *myScrollView;
UITextView *myTextView;

@implementation UITestViewController

-(void)buttonClick:(id)sender
{
    [myTextView resignFirstResponder];
}

- (void)viewDidLoad {

    CGRect viewRect = [self.view bounds];
    myScrollView = [[UIScrollView alloc] initWithFrame:viewRect];
    myScrollView.contentSize = viewRect.size;
    [self.view addSubview:myScrollView];

    CGRect buttonFrame = CGRectMake(10,10,60,32);
    UIButton *keyboardToggle = [UIButton buttonWithType:UIButtonTypeRoundedRect];
    [keyboardToggle setTitle:@"hide" forState:UIControlStateNormal];
    [keyboardToggle addTarget:self action:@selector(buttonClick:) forControlEvents:UIControlEventTouchUpInside];
    keyboardToggle.frame = buttonFrame;
    [myScrollView addSubview:keyboardToggle];

    CGRect textRect = CGRectMake(10,60,300,200);
    myTextView = [[UITextView alloc] initWithFrame:textRect];

    myTextView.font = [UIFont systemFontOfSize:22.0];
    myTextView.keyboardType = UIKeyboardTypeDefault;
    myTextView.returnKeyType = UIReturnKeyGo;
    myTextView.delegate = self;

    [myScrollView addSubview:myTextView];

    [myTextView release];
    [myScrollView release];
}

- (void)textViewDidBeginEditing:(UITextView *)textView {

    float keyboardHeight;
    if ([UIDevice currentDevice].orientation == UIDeviceOrientationPortrait | UIDeviceOrientationPortraitUpsideDown)
        keyboardHeight = 216.0;
    else
        keyboardHeight = 162.0;

    CGRect textViewRect = textView.frame;
    float textViewBottom = textViewRect.origin.y + textViewRect.size.height;
    CGRect viewRect = [myScrollView bounds];
    float keyboardTop = viewRect.size.height-keyboardHeight;
    float scrollOffset = fabs(textViewBottom - keyboardTop);
    [myScrollView setContentOffset:CGPointMake(0, scrollOffset) animated:YES];
}

- (void)textViewDidEndEditing:(UITextView *)textView {

    [myScrollView setContentOffset:CGPointMake(0, 0) animated:YES];
}
```

Web Views

Just as with iPhone's native Safari application, you can display web-based content in your own applications by using the UIWebView class. (In fact, Safari on the iPhone uses a UIWebView for display.)

Web views provide touch-based control for zooming in and out of pages, panning, and scrolling. Tapping links can load pages, and tapping in text controls will open a keyboard for data entry.

To display a web page in your application:

1. Just as with other views, you can add web views to your interface in the usual way:

```
CGRect webRect = CGRectMake
→ (10,10,300,400);
UIWebView *myWebView =
→ [[UIWebView alloc]
→ initWithFrame:webRect];
myWebView.scalesPageToFit = YES;
```

The scalesPageToFit property ensures that larger pages are zoomed out or in enough to fit correctly in the current frame as well as letting you zoom in and out in response to pinch gestures.

What's the status?

Web views provide four optional delegate methods that will notify you about changes in the status of loading a web page:

webView:shouldStartLoadWithRequest: navigationType: is sent before the web view begins to load the content and is a handy place to handle navigation within your web views (see the "Loading local content and handling hyperlinks" section).

webViewDidStartLoad: is sent when your web page starts loading and is a good place to show a progress indicator.

webViewDidFinishLoad: is sent when the web view finishes loading a page and is a good place for you to stop a progress indicator. This will not be sent if the page fails to load for any reason.

webView:didFailLoadWithError: is sent if an error occurs in loading the web page.

Figure 4.34 A web view displaying the Google homepage.

2. Use the loadRequest: method to load content into the web view, which takes an NSURLRequest object as its only parameter:

NSURL *url = [NSURL URLWithString:
→ @"http://www.google.com"];

NSURLRequest *request =
→ [NSURLRequest requestWithURL:url];

[myWebView loadRequest:request];

[self.view addSubview:myWebView];

This would load the Google homepage (**Figure 4.34**).

3. If your page is taking a long time or you want to cancel loading, use the stopLoading method. You can also check the loading property to make sure the page is actually in the process of loading.

If you are building a web browser–type interface with Forward and Backward buttons, you can use the `canGoForward` and `canGoBackward` properties to determine whether your buttons should be enabled, and you can use the `goForward` and `goBackward` methods to navigate through the web view's page history.

Although there is no direct access to the page history, you can easily maintain history via the delegate methods mentioned in the "What's the status?" sidebar. **Code Listing 4.27** shows the code updated to include an activity indicator when the page is loading.

Code Listing 4.27 Implementing a web view.

```
UIActivityIndicatorView *activity;

@implementation UITestViewController

- (void)viewDidLoad {

    [super viewDidLoad];

    [self.view setBackgroundColor:[UIColor blackColor]];

    CGRect webRect = CGRectMake(10,10,300,380);
    UIWebView *myWebView = [[UIWebView alloc] initWithFrame:webRect];
    myWebView.scalesPageToFit = YES;

    myWebView.delegate = self;

    NSURL *url = [NSURL URLWithString:@"http://www.google.com"];
    NSURLRequest *request = [NSURLRequest requestWithURL:url];
    [myWebView loadRequest:request];

    [self.view addSubview:myWebView];

    activity = [[UIActivityIndicatorView alloc] initWithActivityIndicatorStyle:UIActivityIndicatorViewStyleWhiteLarge];
    [activity setCenter:CGPointMake(160,420)];
    [self.view addSubview:activity];

    [myWebView release];
}
- (void)webViewDidStartLoad:(UIWebView *)webView
{
    [activity startAnimating];
}

- (void)webViewDidFinishLoad:(UIWebView *)webView
{
    [activity stopAnimating];
    [webView stringByEvaluatingJavaScriptFromString:@"alert('Finished Loading!');"];
}

- (void)webView:(UIWebView *)webView didFailLoadWithError:(NSError *)error
{
    [activity stopAnimating];
    NSLog(@"Error: %@",error);
}
```

Running JavaScript

You can execute JavaScript in a web view by using the `stringByEvaluatingJavaScript FromString:` method. For example, if you wanted to open an alert dialog box in your web view, write the following:

```
[webView stringByEvaluatingJavaScript
→ FromString:@"alert('Hello World!');"];
```

This lets you manipulate your web page's style sheet or DOM or even call existing JavaScript functions defined within the page itself. For example, to change the background color of your web page, you could write the following:

```
[webView stringByEvaluatingJavaScript
→ FromString:@"document.bgColor=
→ \"#000000\";"];
```

To call the JavaScript function `myFunction` defined in the web page, you could use this:

```
[webView stringByEvaluatingJavaScript
→ FromString:@"myFunction();"];
```

For performance reasons, any JavaScript you call must execute fully within ten seconds and must be less than 10MB in size.

WEB VIEWS

Loading local content and handling hyperlinks

You can also use web views to display *local* content, such as an .html file that ships in your application bundle. This makes web views handy for displaying content that mixes graphics with text or requires multiple text styles. (Remember that UILabels and UITextViews are restricted to only a single style per control.)

To load content from a local file:

1. Use the loadHTMLString:baseURL: method to load content contained in the resources folder of the application bundle:

   myWebView.scalesPageToFit = NO;

   NSString *htmlPath = [[[NSBundle
   → mainBundle] resourcePath]
   → stringByAppendingPathComponent:
   → @"myPage.html"];

   NSString *htmlContent = [NSString st
   → ringWithContentsOfFile:htmlPath];

   [myWebView loadHTMLString:
   → htmlContent baseURL:nil];

   This time, scalePageToFit has been set to NO because you don't want the user to be able to zoom in and out of the web view as if it were a web page.

   Figure 4.35 shows the application with a hyperlink in the page.

2. To prevent a user from tapping any hyperlinks in the document, you can set userInteractionEnabled to NO for the web view. This also disables the ability to scroll content that may be longer than the control can fit on the screen at once.

   or

   To disable links entirely, return NO from the webView:shouldStartLoadWith Request:navigationType: delegate method.

Figure 4.35 A web view displaying some local content.

3. To open a link in the native Safari application, you could write the following in the `webView:shouldStartLoadWithRequest:navigationType:` delegate method (**Code Listing 4.28**):

```
NSURL *pageURL = [request URL];

if ( ([[pageURL scheme]
→ isEqualToString: @"http"]) &&
→ (navigationType == UIWebView
→ NavigationTypeLinkClicked ))

[[UIApplication sharedApplication]
→ openURL:pageURL];

return NO;
```

Here you are trapping only `http:` links. Other link types, such as `https:`, would have no effect.

✔ Tip

- When implementing this type of functionality, it's common to warn the user they are navigating away from your application and have them confirm the action. You can do this with the `UIAlertView` described in the exercise, "To display an alert view," earlier in this chapter.

Code Listing 4.28 Capturing clicks on a web view.

```
- (void)viewDidLoad {

    [super viewDidLoad];

    CGRect webRect = CGRectMake(10,10,300,400);
    UIWebView *myWebView = [[UIWebView alloc] initWithFrame:webRect];

    myWebView.delegate = self;

    myWebView.scalesPageToFit = NO;
    NSString *htmlPath = [[[NSBundle mainBundle] resourcePath] stringByAppendingPathComponent:@"myPage.html"];
    NSString *htmlContent = [NSString stringWithContentsOfFile:htmlPath];

    [myWebView loadHTMLString:htmlContent baseURL:nil];

    [self.view addSubview:myWebView];

    [myWebView release];
}

- (BOOL)webView:(UIWebView *)webView
        shouldStartLoadWithRequest:(NSURLRequest *)request
        navigationType:(UIWebViewNavigationType)navigationType {
    NSURL *pageURL = [request URL];

    if ( ([[pageURL scheme] isEqualToString: @"http"]) && (navigationType == UIWebViewNavigationTypeLinkClicked ))
    {
        [[UIApplication sharedApplication] openURL:pageURL];
        return NO;
    }

    return YES;
}
```

Controls

Almost all the drawing functionality you've learned about so far also applies to controls. Most controls inherit their class from UIControl, and as you can see in **Figure 4.36**, UIControl is a subclass of UIView; this is how controls know how to draw themselves.

You'll never actually create instances of UIControl directly the way you do with UIView. UIControl is simply used to define a common set of functionality and behavior for its subclasses.

As mentioned at the beginning of this chapter, controls use the target-action mechanism to respond to touch events. Since the iPhone is a Multi-Touch device, many different events can occur, such as tapping, multitapping, dragging, and releasing. Luckily, each control has been designed to respond to only those events appropriate for its usage, and each does so in an intuitive and consistent manner.

You'll now take a closer look at the controls available to iPhone developers.

Buttons

When adding buttons to your application, you'll use the UIButton class. The default initializer for buttons is the buttonWithType: method:

```
UIButton *myButton =
→ [[UIButton buttonWithType:
→ UIButtonTypeRoundedRect];
```

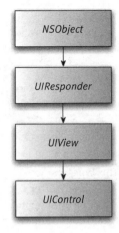

Figure 4.36 The UIControl class hierarchy.

Figure 4.37 The default button types for UIButton.

Figure 4.37 shows the default buttons types available.

To be notified when a button changes state, add a target and action:

```
[myButton addTarget:self action:
→ @selector(buttonClick:)
→ forControlEvents:UIControlEvent
→ TouchUpInside];
```

The UIControlEventTouchUpInside event is most commonly used for handling regular button presses.

The UIButtonTypeCustom type lets you create buttons with images or even draw them yourself using your own custom drawing code (as discussed earlier in the "Views" section).

To create a button with an image:

1. Specify an image for the button's default state using NSControlStateNormal:

   ```
   UIImage *buttonImage =
   → [UIImage imageNamed:
   → @"myButtonImage.png"];
   ```

   ```
   [myButton setImage:buttonImage
   → forState:UIControlStateNormal];
   ```

   UIButton will automatically apply highlight effects to indicate that the button is pressed or disabled.

2. You can also set multiple appearance properties for each of these states, including the title text, font, and color.

   You can use different images for the four different states: the default (as shown in step 1), highlighted, selected, and disabled. This enables you to create buttons to represent other controls.

CONTROLS

To create a checkbox button:

1. Assign images for both of the buttons' states:

```
[checkbox setImage:[UIImage
→ imageNamed:@"checkbox_off.png"]
→ forState:UIControlStateNormal];
[checkbox setImage:[UIImage
→ imageNamed:@"checkbox_on.png"]
→ forState:UIControlStateSelected];
```

2. Set the target method to call when the button is tapped:

```
[checkbox addTarget:self action:
→ @selector(checkboxClick:)
→ forControlEvents:UIControlEvent
→ TouchUpInside];
```

3. In the checkboxClick: method, simply flip the button's selected property:

```
btn.selected = !btn.selected;
```

Since you've previously defined images for the two different states, the button automatically updates to display the correct image. **Code Listing 4.29** shows the updated code.

✔ Tip

■ If you specify an image or title for any button type other than UIButtonTypeRoundedRect, the button effectively becomes a button of UIButtonTypeCustom.

Code Listing 4.29 Creating a check box.

```
- (void)checkboxClick:(UIButton *)sender {

    sender.selected = ! sender.selected;
}

- (void)viewDidLoad {

    UIButton *checkbox = [UIButton buttonWithType:
                            UIButtonTypeCustom];

    CGRect checkboxRect = CGRectMake(135,150,36,36);
    [checkbox setFrame:checkboxRect];

    [checkbox setImage:[UIImage
                    imageNamed:@"checkbox_off.png"]
            forState:UIControlStateNormal];
    [checkbox setImage:[UIImage
                    imageNamed:@"checkbox_on.png"]
            forState:UIControlStateSelected];

    [checkbox addTarget:self
            action:@selector(checkboxClick:)
        forControlEvents:UIControlEventTouchUpInside];

    [self.view addSubview:checkbox];

}
```

Figure 4.38 Switches are used extensively in the Settings application of the iPhone.

Switches

Switches, represented by the UISwitch class, let you create an on/off control (**Figure 4.38**).

To create a switch:

1. Use the initWithFrame: method:

   CGRect switchRect = CGRectMake
   → (120,50,0,0);
   UISwitch *mySwitch = [[UISwitch
   → alloc] initWithFrame:switchRect];

   Since switches are always the same size, the width and height properties are ignored.

2. When you change a switch's value, it generates a UIControlEventValueChanged event:

   [mySwitch addTarget:self action:
   → @selector(switchAction:)
   → forControlEvents:UIControlEvent
   → ValueChanged];

3. To turn a switch on/off, call the setOn:Animated: method:

   [mySwitch setOn:YES animated:YES];

Switches don't have any properties for modifying the default visual appearance, but with a little digging, you can control a couple of elements.

Figure 4.39 shows the control hierarchy of a UISwitch. The "on" and "off" elements are both UILabels. You can manipulate the text, font, color, and more.

To alter the appearance of a switch:

1. To retrieve the two UILabels within the switch that hold the switch's text , you can use this:

```
UIView *mainView = [[[[mySwitch
→ subviews] objectAtIndex:0]
→ subviews] objectAtIndex:2];

UILabel *onLabel = [[mainView
→ subviews] objectAtIndex:0];

UILabel *offLabel = [[mainView
→ subviews] objectAtIndex:1];
```

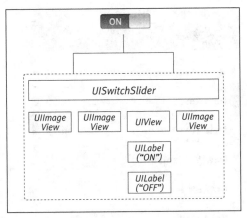

Figure 4.39 The control hierarchy that makes up a UISwitch.

2. Now you can change the text and color of these labels. The choice of text values is quite limited since the labels are small in size and are clipped by their containing view:

```
onLabel.text      = @"YES";
offLabel.text     = @"NO";
```

```
onLabel.textColor = [UIColor yellow
↪Color];
offLabel.textColor = [UIColor green
↪Color];
```

3. When setting the text values you should localize your replacement text wherever possible. **Code Listing 4.30** shows the updated code.

Code Listing 4.30 Customizing the switch control.

```
-(void)switchAction:(id)sender
{
    NSLog(@"switch changed");
}

- (void)viewDidLoad {

    [super viewDidLoad];

    CGRect switchRect = CGRectMake(120,50,0,0);
    UISwitch *mySwitch = [[UISwitch alloc] initWithFrame:switchRect];
    [mySwitch addTarget:self action:@selector(switchAction:) forControlEvents:UIControlEventValueChanged];

    //customize the appearance
    UIView *mainView = [[[[mySwitch subviews] objectAtIndex:0] subviews] objectAtIndex:2];
    UILabel *onLabel = [[mainView subviews] objectAtIndex:0];
    UILabel *offLabel = [[mainView subviews] objectAtIndex:1];

    //change the text
    onLabel.text      = @"YES";
    offLabel.text     = @"NO";

    //change the text color
    onLabel.textColor = [UIColor yellowColor];
    offLabel.textColor = [UIColor greenColor];

    [self.view addSubview:mySwitch];

    [mySwitch release];
}
```

CONTROLS

Sliders

Although switches have only two possible states, sliders let you select from a range of values on a horizontal bar, or *track*, with a *thumb* indicator that can be moved from side to side to select values (**Figure 4.40**).

Unlike the UISwitch, there's quite a lot you can do to customize the visual appearance of sliders, such as putting images to represent the values at either end of the track. You can also customize the thumb image and the graphics that appear on the track on both sides of the thumb as the values change (**Figure 4.41**).

Just as with the UISwitch, sliders create a UIControlEventValueChanged event when their value is changed. By setting the continuous property, you can choose to have these events fired either as the slider is changed or at the end of a change. **Code Listing 4.31** demonstrates this with a custom UISlider, with minimum, maximum, and thumb images. In the sliderAction: method, you are forcing a "step" behavior, making the slider jump to the next value in increments of ten. A label added to the view displays the current slider value.

✔ Tips

- Although not specified in the developer documentation, setting the thumb image of a UISlider also hides the tracking image. You must also set the minimum and maximum track images.

- The stretchableImageWithLeftCapWidth: topCapHeight: method lets you create an image that can stretch in the center but does not stretch on either side, as shown in the rounded edges of the track images.

Figure 4.40 The brightness slider control indicates the change in value with graphics at both ends of the control.

Figure 4.41 A custom slider control.

CONTROLS

Code Listing 4.31 Implementing a custom slider.

```
○ ○ ○                                    Code
UILabel *lblSliderValue;

@implementation UITestViewController

-(void)sliderAction:(id)sender
{
    int stepAmount  = 10;
    float stepValue = (abs([(UISlider *)sender value]) / stepAmount) * stepAmount;
    [sender setValue:stepValue];

    lblSliderValue.text = [NSString stringWithFormat:@"%d",(int)stepValue];
}


- (void)viewDidLoad {

    [super viewDidLoad];

    CGRect sliderRect = CGRectMake(20,50,280,40);
    UISlider *mySlider = [[UISlider alloc] initWithFrame:sliderRect];

    mySlider.minimumValue = 0;
    mySlider.maximumValue = 100;
    mySlider.continuous   = YES;

    //images
    UIImage *leftTrackImage  = [[UIImage imageNamed:@"left_slider.png"] stretchableImageWithLeftCapWidth:5.0 topCapHeight:0.0];
    UIImage *rightTrackImage = [[UIImage imageNamed:@"right_slider.png"] stretchableImageWithLeftCapWidth:5.0 topCapHeight:0.0];
    UIImage *thumbImage      = [UIImage imageNamed:@"apple_thumb.png"];
    UIImage *minSliderImage  = [UIImage imageNamed:@"apple_min.png"];
    UIImage *maxSliderImage  = [UIImage imageNamed:@"apple_max.png"];

    [mySlider setThumbImage:thumbImage forState:UIControlStateNormal];
    [mySlider setMinimumTrackImage:leftTrackImage forState:UIControlStateNormal];
    [mySlider setMaximumTrackImage:rightTrackImage forState:UIControlStateNormal];
    [mySlider setMinimumValueImage:minSliderImage];
    [mySlider setMaximumValueImage:maxSliderImage];
    [mySlider setValue:50.0f];

    //handle value change events
    [mySlider addTarget:self action:@selector(sliderAction:) forControlEvents:UIControlEventValueChanged];

    //label to show current value
    CGRect lblRect = CGRectMake(145,100,100,20);
    lblSliderValue = [[UILabel alloc] initWithFrame:lblRect];
    lblSliderValue.backgroundColor = [UIColor clearColor];

    lblSliderValue.text = [NSString stringWithFormat:@"%d",(int)mySlider.value];

    //add slider to main view
    [self.view addSubview:mySlider];
    [self.view addSubview:lblSliderValue];

    [lblSliderValue release];
    [mySlider release];
}
```

CONTROLS

Segmented controls

The UISegmentedControl consists of a horizontal control divided into segments (**Figure 4.42**). Segmented controls are useful for allowing users to pick from a group or set of values.

Each segment functions as its own button. By default, selecting a segment will deselect the others in the control (much as a radio button does in HTML). You can alter this behavior by setting the momentary property.

Figure 4.42 A segment control.

To create a segmented control:

1. Create an array of UIImages or NSStrings, and then call the default initializer init WithItems: (**Code Listing 4.32**).

2. Set the frame, and the control will automatically resize to accommodate its segments.
   Each segment will initially be the same size.

3. Set the width of individual segments using the setWidth:forSegmentIndex: method.
   This will automatically resize any other segments that have not had their widths explicitly set to fit within the control.

4. Select segments using the setSelected SegmentIndex: method.

5. Disable individual segments using the setEnabled:forSegementAtIndex: method.

6. Add more segments using insertSegments WithImage:atIndex:animated:

   or

   insertSegmentsWithTitle:atIndex: animated:.

7. Set the animated property to YES so your segments will "slide in" as they are added.

8. To remove segments, use the remove SegmentsAtIndex:animated: method.

9. Use removeAllSegments to clear the entire control.

Code Listing 4.32 Creating a segment control.

```
- (void)viewDidLoad {

    NSArray *arrSegments = [[NSArray alloc] initWithObjects:
                              [NSString stringWithString:@"0"],
                              [NSString stringWithString:@"1"],
                              [NSString stringWithString:@"2"],
                              nil];

    UISegmentedControl *mySegment = [[UISegmentedControl alloc]
                                        initWithItems:arrSegments];

    CGRect segmentRect = CGRectMake(10,50,300,40);
    [mySegment setFrame:segmentRect];

    [self.view addSubview:mySegment];
    [arrSegments release];
    [mySegment release];
}
```

CONTROLS

Segment control styles

Segment controls have three different styles (**Figure 4.43**), which can be set using the `segmentedControlStyle` property. Set the style to `UISegmentedControlStyleBar` to change the color of the control via the `tintColor` property, but depending on the color you use, you may not be able to see the difference between selected and unselected. **Code Listing 4.33** shows an example of how to use some of the properties of a segmented control.

Use the `UISegmentControl` to create a "glass" alternative to a `UIButton`. Use the `tintColor` property to change the color of the button.

Figure 4.43 The three styles available for segmented controls.

Code Listing 4.33 Setting some of the segment control properties.

```
- (void)segmentClick:(id)sender {

    NSLog(@"clicked: %d",[sender selectedSegmentIndex]);

}

- (void)viewDidLoad {

    NSArray *arrSegments = [[NSArray alloc] initWithObjects:
                            [NSString stringWithString:@"0"],
                            [NSString stringWithString:@"1"],
                            [NSString stringWithString:@"2"],
                            nil];

    UISegmentedControl *mySegment = [[UISegmentedControl alloc]
                                initWithItems:arrSegments];

    CGRect segmentRect = CGRectMake(10,50,300,40);
    [mySegment setFrame:segmentRect];

    [mySegment addTarget:self
                action:@selector(segmentClick:)
        forControlEvents:UIControlEventValueChanged];

    [mySegment setSegmentedControlStyle:UISegmentedControlStyleBar];
    [mySegment setTintColor:[UIColor darkGrayColor]];

    //select first item
    [mySegment setSelectedSegmentIndex:0];

    //change a segment size
    [mySegment setWidth:120.0 forSegmentAtIndex:1];

    //add a new segment
    [mySegment insertSegmentWithTitle:@"new" atIndex:2 animated:YES];

    [self.view addSubview:mySegment];
    [arrSegments release];
    [mySegment release];
}
```

5

TABS AND TABLES

At the core of most iPhone applications, the view controller classes allow you to manage the visual elements that make up your application's interface in a consistent fashion while eliminating redundant code. View controllers are the *C* in the MVC design pattern, providing the layer between your data model and your user interface.

In this chapter, you'll see how to work with these classes. You'll start by looking at the base `UIViewController` class from which the other view controller classes inherit and see how it provides a lot of the core functionality required by any iPhone application. Then you'll see how you can add a tab-based interface using the `UITabBarController` class.

Finally, you'll investigate how to use the `UITableViewController` and `UINavigation Controller` classes to present tabular, hierarchical data.

View Controllers

The UIViewController class is the main class used to control most views (a view being a single screen within your application) and provides the base class for the UITabBarController and UINavigation Controller classes discussed later in this chapter.

Each view controller has a single *main* view—represented by the view property—which it alone owns. Main views cannot be shared between view controllers. The main view will generally have one or more *subviews* containing the actual content of your application (other views, controls, and user-interface elements). For more information on views, see Chapter 4, "iPhone User Interface Elements."

These are a view controller's main responsibilities:

◆ To manage the presentation of its views, responding to events such as changes in the iPhone's orientation or low-memory situations

◆ To act as the coordinator between the user interface and the application's data model (See the "Model View Controller" section in Chapter 1, "Objective-C and Cocoa," for more information.)

Presenting views

As mentioned, each view controller contains a main view that you would normally use as the canvas for your application's user interface. You can put your code in a number of places when working with view controllers:

◆ loadView—Although you should not call this method directly, if you create your own views manually, then you should override this method and assign them to the view controller's view property.

- `viewDidLoad`—This method is called just after the view controller loads its views into memory and is a good place for you to perform any additional initialization. Many of the code examples in this book use this method as the point at which to create the user interface.

- `viewDidUnload`—Conversely, this is called when the view controller releases its views from memory and is a good place for you to clean up any objects you may have created within the view controller.

- `viewWillAppear:`—This is called when the view is about to be added to a window and is not yet visible. It's a good place to perform any customization such as changing the view's orientation. If you implement any code in this method, make sure you also call `[super viewWillAppear:]`.

- `viewDidAppear:`—This is called when the view has been added to a window and is a good place to place code that needs to run after the view has been presented. If you implement any code in this method, make sure you also call `[super viewDidAppear:]`.

- `viewWillDisappear:`—This is called when the view is about to be removed from a window and is a good place for you revert to any changes that may have been made when `viewWillAppear:` was called. If you implement any code in this method, make sure you also call `[super viewWillDisappear:]`.

- `viewDidDisappear:`—This is called when the view is dismissed, covered, or hidden from view. If you implement any code in this method, make sure you also call `[super viewDidDisappear:]`.

Code Listing 5.1 shows an example of changing the background color and adding a button to the main view within the `viewDidLoad` method.

Responding to changes in orientation

Another responsibility of a view controller is to respond to changes in the iPhone's orientation and automatically rotate the interface where appropriate. The `shouldAutorotateToInterface Orientation:` method is called immediately after the iPhone is rotated. If you want to autorotate to all four orientations (up, down, left, and right), you can simply return YES from this method. Otherwise, you can examine the `interfaceOrientation` property and return YES or NO based on the device's current orientation.

To create an application that responds to changes in orientation:

1. Create a new view-based application, saving it as OrientationExample.

2. Open the OrientationExampleView Controller.h file, and create an instance variable to display the orientation (**Code Listing 5.2**).

Code Listing 5.1 Adding a button to the main view within the `viewDidLoad` method.

```
- (void)viewDidLoad {

    CGRect labelFrame = CGRectMake(10,10,300,38);
    orientationLabel = [[UILabel alloc] initWithFrame:labelFrame];
    orientationLabel.textAlignment = UITextAlignmentCenter;
    orientationLabel.autoresizingMask = UIViewAutoresizingFlexibleWidth;
    orientationLabel.text = [self getOrientationName];

    [self.view addSubview:orientationLabel];
}
```

Code Listing 5.2 The header file of the orientation example.

```
#import <UIKit/UIKit.h>

@interface OrientationExampleViewController : UIViewController {

    UILabel *orientationLabel;
}

@end
```

3. Switch to the OrientationExampleView
Controller.m file, uncomment the `viewDid`
`Load` method, and add the following:

```
CGRect labelFrame = CGRectMake
→ (10,10,300,38);

orientationLabel = [[UILabel alloc]
→ initWithFrame:labelFrame];

orientationLabel.textAlignment =
→ UITextAlignmentCenter;

orientationLabel.autoresizingMask =
→ UIViewAutoresizingFlexibleWidth;

orientationLabel.text =
→ [self getOrientationName];


[self.view addSubview:
→ orientationLabel];
```

You first create a label that spans the
width of the screen. Notice how you set
the text alignment of the label to be cen-
tered so that when the iPhone is rotated,
your text will remain in the center of the
label. Likewise, you set the `autoresizing`
`Mask` property so that the label stretches
its width automatically when the iPhone
is rotated from portrait to landscape
mode. Finally, you call a method to set the
text of the label.

continues on next page

VIEW CONTROLLERS

4. Implement the `getOrientationName` method:

```
switch (self.interfaceOrientation)
{
    case UIInterfaceOrientation
    →Portrait:
        return @"Portrait";
        break;

    case UIInterfaceOrientation
    →PortraitUpsideDown:
        return @"Portrait (upside
        →down)";
        break;

    case UIInterfaceOrientation
    →LandscapeLeft:
        return @"Landscape (left)";
        break;

    case UIInterfaceOrientation
    →LandscapeRight:
        return @"Landscape (right)";
        break;
}
```

This method looks at the current orientation of the iPhone (via the view controller's `interfaceOrientation` property) and returns a descriptive string.

5. Next, implement the `didRotateFrom InterfaceOrientation:` method:

```
orientationLabel.text =
→[self getOrientationName];
```

This method is called just after the orientation of the iPhone changes. Here you simply update the label text.

6. Uncomment the `shouldAutorotateTo`
   `InterfaceOrientation:` method, and add
   the following code:

   `return YES;`

   This will allow your interface to be
   autorotated in any direction.

7. Build and run the application.

   If you rotate your iPhone, the label should
   automatically rotate and continue to fill
   the width of the screen. The text should
   also change to indicate the iPhone's
   current orientation. Try changing the
   allowed orientations by modifying the
   `shouldAutorotateToInterfaceOrientation:`
   method. **Code Listing 5.3** shows the
   completed code.

✔ Tip

- Several methods are available for you to
  track changes in orientation:

  `willRotateToInterfaceOrientation:`
  `duration:`—This is called just before rotation takes place. It's a good place for you
  to pause any activity that may be happening in the user interface and to disable
  the ability for the user to interact with
  the application until the interface has
  completed rotating.

  `willAnimateRotationToInterface`
  `Orientation:duration:`—This is called
  with the rotation animation block itself
  and is a good place for you to write
  custom code to override the default rotation animation. For example, you could
  change the rotation to a cross-dissolve
  animation.

  `didRotateFromInterfaceOrientation:`—
  This is called once the rotation has
  completed and is a good place for you to
  reenable your user interface and reallow
  user interactions with your application if
  you disabled them earlier.

Code Listing 5.3 The completed orientation example.

```
#import "OrientationExampleViewController.h"

@implementation OrientationExampleViewController

- (NSString *)getOrientationName {

    switch (self.interfaceOrientation)
    {
        case UIInterfaceOrientationPortrait:
            return @"Portrait";
            break;

        case UIInterfaceOrientationPortraitUpsideDown:
            return @"Portrait (upside down)";
            break;

        case UIInterfaceOrientationLandscapeLeft:
            return @"Landscape (left)";
            break;

        case UIInterfaceOrientationLandscapeRight:
            return @"Landscape (right)";
            break;
    }

    return @"Unknown";
}

- (void)viewDidLoad {

    CGRect labelFrame = CGRectMake(10,10,300,38);
    orientationLabel = [[UILabel alloc] initWithFrame:labelFrame];
    orientationLabel.textAlignment = UITextAlignmentCenter;
    orientationLabel.autoresizingMask = UIViewAutoresizingFlexibleWidth;
    orientationLabel.text = [self getOrientationName];

    [self.view addSubview:orientationLabel];
}

- (void)didRotateFromInterfaceOrientation:(UIInterfaceOrientation)fromInterfaceOrientation {

    orientationLabel.text = [self getOrientationName];
}

- (BOOL)shouldAutorotateToInterfaceOrientation:(UIInterfaceOrientation)interfaceOrientation {

    return YES;
}

- (void)didReceiveMemoryWarning {

    [super didReceiveMemoryWarning];
}

- (void)dealloc {

    [orientationLabel release];

    [super dealloc];
}
@end
```

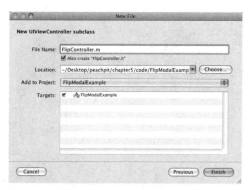

Figure 5.1 Adding a second view controller class.

Code Listing 5.4 The header file of the flip modal example.

```
●○○                    Code
#import <UIKit/UIKit.h>
#import "FlipController.h"

@interface FlipModalExampleViewController:UIViewController
{
    FlipController *flip;
}

@end
```

Displaying modal views

You display a view modally by presenting one view controller from another view controller. Modal views are animated onto the screen, and you can determine an animation type to use. This can be helpful in providing meaning to the action you are performing. For example, it's common to provide settings for an application by "flipping" the settings view over the main view.

To display a view modally using a "flip" animation:

1. Create a new view-based application, saving it as FlipModalExample.

2. Select File > New, and add a new UIViewController subclass.

   Save the file as FlipViewController.m. Make sure that "Also create 'FlipController.h'" is selected (**Figure 5.1**).

3. Open the FlipModalExampleView Controller.h file, import the header file, and create an instance variable to hold the flip view controller (**Code Listing 5.4**).

continues on next page

4. Switch to the FlipModalExampleView
    Controller.m file, uncomment the `view
    DidLoad` method, and add the following:

    ```
    flip = [[FlipController alloc]
    → init];

    UIButton *viewButton = [UIButton
    → buttonWithType:UIButtonTypeRounded
    → Rect];
    CGRect buttonFrame = CGRectMake
    → (110,10,100,38);
    [viewButton setFrame:buttonFrame];
    [viewButton setTitle:@"Show"
    → forState:UIControlStateNormal];
    [viewButton addTarget:self action:
    → @selector(buttonClick:)
    → forControlEvents:UIControlEvent
    → TouchUpInside];
    [self.view addSubview:viewButton];
    ```

    Here you create the flip controller and then
    add a button to your main controller view.

5. Implement the `buttonClick:` method:

    ```
    flip.modalTransitionStyle = UIModal
    → TransitionStyleFlipHorizontal;

    [self presentModalViewController:
    → flip animated:YES];
    ```

    Setting the `modalTransitionStyle` prop-
    erty of your flip controller to `UIModal
    TransitionStyleFlipHorizontal` uses
    a "flip" animation when the new view con-
    troller is shown modally.

6. Switch to FlipController.m, uncomment
    the `viewDidLoad` method, and add the
    following:

    ```
    [self.view setBackgroundColor:
    → [UIColor redColor]];

    UIButton *viewButton =
    → [UIButton buttonWithType:
    → UIButtonTypeRoundedRect];
    CGRect buttonFrame = CGRectMake
    → (110,10,100,38);
    ```

```
[viewButton setFrame:buttonFrame];
[viewButton setTitle:@"Hide"
→ forState:UIControlStateNormal];
[viewButton addTarget:self action:@
selector(buttonClick:) forControlEve
nts:UIControlEventTouchUpInside];
[self.view addSubview:viewButton];
```

This is almost the same code as with your main view controller, but you set the background of the view to make it obvious which view is showing.

7. Implement the second buttonClick: method:

```
[self dismissModalViewController
→ Animated:YES];
```

This tells the main view controller to hide the flip controller. The message is automatically forwarded to the main view controller (since it is the one dismissing the modal view). This is handy since it means you don't have to declare any public methods or create a reference to the parent view controller.

8. Build and run the application.

Pressing Show will cause the view to flip and show the other view controller's view modally. Pressing Hide will flip the view back. **Code Listing 5.5** shows the completed code.

✔ Tip

■ When presenting a view modally, you can pick from three animation styles:

UIModalTransitionStyleCoverVertical is the default style and slides the view from the bottom to over the current view.

UIModalTransitionStyleFlipHorizontal is the style used in the example here and flips the view from right to left.

UIModalTransitionStyleCrossDissolve fades the current view out and the new view in using a cross-dissolve.

All three of these styles perform the reverse animation when the view is dismissed.

Code Listing 5.5 The completed flip modal application.

```
//
// FlipModalExampleViewController.m
// FlipModalExample
//

#import "FlipModalExampleViewController.h"

@implementation FlipModalExampleViewController

- (void)buttonClick:(id)sender {

    flip.modalTransitionStyle = UIModalTransitionStyleFlipHorizontal;
    [self presentModalViewController:flip animated:YES];
}
```

(code continues on next page)

VIEW CONTROLLERS

Code Listing 5.5 *continued*

```
●○○                                    Code
- (void)viewDidLoad {

    flip = [[FlipController alloc] init];

    UIButton *viewButton = [UIButton buttonWithType:UIButtonTypeRoundedRect];
    CGRect buttonFrame = CGRectMake(110,10,100,38);
    [viewButton setFrame:buttonFrame];
    [viewButton setTitle:@"Show" forState:UIControlStateNormal];
    [viewButton addTarget:self
                action:@selector(buttonClick:)
          forControlEvents:UIControlEventTouchUpInside];
    [self.view addSubview:viewButton];
}


- (void)didReceiveMemoryWarning {

    [super didReceiveMemoryWarning];
}

- (void)dealloc {

    [flip release];
    [super dealloc];
}

@end

//
// FlipController.m
// FlipModalExample
//

#import "FlipController.h"

@implementation FlipController

- (void)buttonClick:(id)sender {

    [self dismissModalViewControllerAnimated:YES];
}

- (void)viewDidLoad {

    [self.view setBackgroundColor:[UIColor redColor]];

    UIButton *viewButton = [UIButton buttonWithType:UIButtonTypeRoundedRect];
    CGRect buttonFrame = CGRectMake(110,10,100,38);
    [viewButton setFrame:buttonFrame];
    [viewButton setTitle:@"Hide" forState:UIControlStateNormal];
    [viewButton addTarget:self
                action:@selector(buttonClick:)
          forControlEvents:UIControlEventTouchUpInside];
    [self.view addSubview:viewButton];
}

- (void)didReceiveMemoryWarning {

    [super didReceiveMemoryWarning];
}

- (void)dealloc {

    [super dealloc];
}

@end
```

Handling low-memory conditions

View controllers can automatically handle low-memory scenarios by releasing and cleaning up any views that aren't needed, such as when a view doesn't have a super-view. When a memory warning is issued (via the `UIApplication` delegate), each view controller also receives a notification via the `didReceiveMemoryWarning` method. You can override this method to perform any memory cleanup within your own code. However, if you do so, make sure you also call `[super didReceiveMemoryWarning]`. You can also put your cleanup code in the `viewDidUnload` method, which will be called if the view controller decides it can release its views.

Since you would normally have multiple view controllers in your application, each with their own views and subviews, this provides a very granular memory management model where you can determine what you should release and when.

VIEW CONTROLLERS

Tab Views

You can use the UITabBarController class to create a multipage interface. Pages are displayed by selecting a tab from a tab bar at the bottom of the screen (**Figure 5.2**).

Each page of the tab bar controller is a view controller. When a tab is selected, the view of the corresponding view controller is displayed above the tab bar.

To create an application with tabs:

1. Create a new view-based application, saving it as TabExample.

2. Select File > New, and add a new UIView Controller subclass.

   Save the file as Tab1Controller.m. Make sure that "Also create 'Tab1Controller.h'" is selected (**Figure 5.3**).

3. Repeat step 2, adding two more UIView Controller subclasses named Tab2 Controller and Tab3Controller.

4. Open TabExampleViewController.h, import the three tab controllers, create instance variables to represent the three tabs, and change the class name to UITabBarController (**Code Listing 5.6**).

Figure 5.2 The World Clock application uses tabs to switch between clock types.

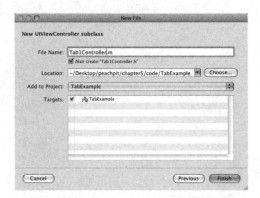

Figure 5.3 Adding a new UIViewController subclass.

Code Listing 5.6 The header file for the tab example.

```
#import <UIKit/UIKit.h>
#import "Tab1Controller.h"
#import "Tab2Controller.h"
#import "Tab3Controller.h"

@interface TabExampleViewController : UITabBarController {

    Tab1Controller *tab1;
    Tab2Controller *tab2;
    Tab3Controller *tab3;
}

@end
```

5. Switch to TabExampleViewController.m, uncomment the `viewDidLoad` method, and add the following code:

```
tab1 = [[Tab1Controller alloc]
→ init];

tab2 = [[Tab2Controller alloc]
→ init];

tab3 = [[Tab3Controller alloc]
→ init];

NSArray *arrTabs = [NSArray array
→ WithObjects:tab1,tab2,tab3,nil];

[self setViewControllers:arrTabs
→ animated:YES];
```

Here you create three tabs, add them to an array, and then assign them to the `viewControllers` property, which will create a tab for each element.

6. Switch to Tab1Controller.m, uncomment the `viewDidLoad` method, and add the following code to set the background color:

```
[self.view
setBackgroundColor:[UIColor
→ redColor]];
```

7. Repeat step 6 for Tab2Controller.m and Tab3Controller.m. Make sure you use a different color each time.

8. Build and run your application.

You should see a tab bar with three tabs. As you select a tab, the area above the tab bar will change color.

✔ Tip

■ You can select a tab in your code by using the `selectedIndex` property of the `UITabBarController`. This can be useful when you are developing your application, allowing you to launch your application on the page on which you are currently working.

What happens if I have too many tabs?

In the exercises in this section, you added only a limited number of tabs to the tab bar. If you were to add so many that the tab bar ran out of room, a new special More tab would appear on the right edge of the tab bar (**Figure 5.4**). Selecting this allows the user to customize the tab bar by choosing which tabs they want to display. You can restrict which tabs the user can edit by removing the corresponding view controller from the array in the `customizableViewControllers` property.

Figure 5.4 The More tab.

Adding graphics and titles to tabs

Although this example showed you how easy it is to create an application with tabs, the tabs themselves are not particularly helpful. It would be much better if each one had a title or graphic on it so that you knew what it actually did. Luckily, `UIViewController` has a property called `tabBarItem` that is designed for exactly this purpose.

To update the application to use tab bar items:

1. Open Tab1Controller.m, and create an `init:` method:

   ```
   UITabBarItem *tab = [[UITabBarItem
   → alloc] initWithTitle:@"Tab 1"
   → image:nil tag:0];
   [self setTabBarItem:tab];
   [tab release];
   ```

   Here you create a new tab item and set its title only.

2. Open Tab2Controller.m, and again create an `init:` method:

   ```
   UITabBarItem *tab = [[UITabBarItem
   → alloc] initWithTabBarSystemItem:
   → UITabBarSystemItemFavorites
   → tag:1];
   [self setTabBarItem:tab];
   [tab release];
   ```

   This time you are using the `initWithTab BarSystemItem:` method to create the tab item. The iPhone has a number of system tabs that can be used for common functionality and are used in many of the built-in applications. Using a system item adds both a graphic and a label to the tab. For more information on the available system items, refer to the *UITabBarItem Class Reference* in the developer documentation.

Figure 5.5 The completed tab example application.

3. Open Tab3Controller.m, and create a third init: method:

```
UITabBarItem *tab = [[UITabBarItem
→ alloc] initWithTitle:@"Tab 3"
→ image:nil tag:2];

[tab setBadgeValue:@"New!"];

[self setTabBarItem:tab];

[tab release];
```

Just as in step 1, you set a title, but no graphic, for the tab. However, this time, you also set the badgeValue property. This will add a red oval to the upper-right corner of your tab. This technique is commonly used to alert a user to a change in the contents of the tab.

4. Build and run the application (**Figure 5.5**). **Code Listing 5.7** and **Code Listing 5.8** show the completed code.

✔ Tips

■ In this example, you created the tab bar item in the init: method instead of in the viewDidLoad method. You did this because viewDidLoad is not actually called until the view controller displays its view, which would mean that the tab would not draw its contents until it had been selected.

■ You can use the delegate of a UITabBar Controller (which must implement the UITabBarControllerDelegate protocol) to disable tabs.

TAB VIEWS

Code Listing 5.7 The implementation files for the three tab view controllers.

```
@implementation Tab1Controller

- (id)init
{
    if (self = [super init])
    {
        UITabBarItem *tab = [[UITabBarItem alloc]
                              initWithTitle:@"Tab 1l"
                              image:nil
                              tag:0];
        [self setTabBarItem:tab];
        [tab release];
    }
    return self;
}

- (void)viewDidLoad {

    [self.view
      setBackgroundColor:[UIColor redColor]];
}

- (void)dealloc {
    [super dealloc];
}

@end

@implementation Tab2Controller

- (id)init
{
    if (self = [super init])
    {
        UITabBarItem *tab = [[UITabBarItem alloc]
                              initWithTabBarSystemItem:UITabBarSystemItemFavorites
                              tag:1];
        [self setTabBarItem:tab];
        [tab release];
    }
    return self;
}

- (void)viewDidLoad {

    [self.view
      setBackgroundColor:[UIColor blueColor]];
}

- (void)dealloc {
    [super dealloc];
}

@end

@implementation Tab3Controller

- (id)init
{
    if (self = [super init])
    {
        UITabBarItem *tab = [[UITabBarItem alloc]
                              initWithTitle:@"Tab 3"
                              image:nil
                              tag:2];
        [tab setBadgeValue:@"New!"];
        [self setTabBarItem:tab];
        [tab release];
    }
    return self;
}
```

(code continues on next page)

Code Listing 5.7 *continued*

```
- (void)viewDidLoad {

    [self.view
     setBackgroundColor:[UIColor greenColor]];
}

- (void)dealloc {
    [super dealloc];
}

@end
```

Code Listing 5.8 The tab bar controller implementation file.

```
#import "TabExampleViewController.h"

@implementation TabExampleViewController

- (void)viewDidLoad {

    tab1 = [[Tab1Controller alloc] init];
    tab2 = [[Tab2Controller alloc] init];
    tab3 = [[Tab3Controller alloc] init];

    NSArray *arrTabs = [NSArray arrayWithObjects:tab1,tab2,tab3,nil];
    [self setViewControllers:arrTabs animated:YES];
}

- (void)dealloc {

    [tab1 release];
    [tab2 release];
    [tab3 release];

    [super dealloc];
}

@end
```

Table Views

Table views—represented by the UITableView class—are the main interface element used to display lists and hierarchical data on the iPhone. Table views are used everywhere; the Settings, Clock, Notes, Mail, and Contact applications all use table views as the main interface element.

Tables views represent their data in *rows* and *sections*. A row is an individual item in the table view. Rows can be grouped into zero or more sections. Sections can have both a header and a footer (**Figure 5.6**).

The content of a row is called a *cell* and is represented by the UITableViewCell class. You can use a cell's textLabel and detail TextLabel properties for displaying text, and you can use its imageView property for displaying images. Several different styles of cell exist, and you can also create your own custom cells.

To use a table view, you must implement a *data source* and, optionally, a *delegate*. The data source provides the table view with its contents and determines what (if anything) can be edited. The delegate manages the selection and editing of rows and the display of section information.

Several of the delegate and data source methods have an NSIndexPath as a parameter. Using the section and row properties of this object is how you determine exactly to what in your table view you are referring.

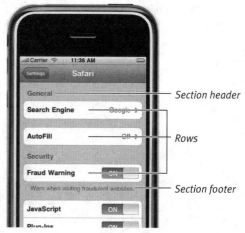

Figure 5.6 The various elements of a table view.

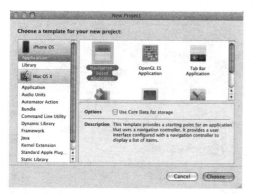

Figure 5.7 Creating a navigation-based application.

Although you could create and add a table view much as you do with any other view, all the examples in this section use the `UITableViewController` class, which is designed specifically to manage a table view. Table view controllers are already configured as both the data source and the delegate of their own table view, and they have some additional functionality for updating a navigation bar when editing a table view.

To create an application with a table view:

1. Create a new navigation-based application, saving it as TableViewExample (**Figure 5.7**).

2. Open RootViewController.h, and create the instance variable you will use to hold your table contents:

   `NSArray *arrCountries;`

3. Switch to RootViewController.m, uncomment the `viewDidLoad` method, and add the following code:

   ```
   self.title = @"Countries";
   arrCountries = [[NSArray alloc]
   → initWithObjects: @"Australia",
   → @"Canada",@"Germany",@"France",
   → @"Great Britain",@"Italy",
   → @"Japan",@"New Zealand",
   → @"United States",nil];
   ```

   Here you are setting the title of the toolbar and creating an array of country names.

4. Edit the `tableView:numberOfRowsIn Section:` method to look like this:

   `return [arrCountries count];`

   This method is how the table view knows how many rows it should display. In this example, you return the size of your array.

continues on next page

TABLE VIEWS

5. Update the `tableView:cellForRowAt`
`IndexPath:` method to look like the
following:

```
static NSString *CellIdentifier =
→ @"Cell";
    UITableViewCell *cell =
    → [tableView dequeueReusable
    → CellWithIdentifier:
    → CellIdentifier];
if (cell == nil) {
    cell = [[[UITableViewCell
    → alloc] initWithStyle:
    → UITableViewCellStyleDefault
    → reuseIdentifier:Cell
    → Identifier] autorelease];
}

// Configure the cell.
cell.textLabel.text = [arrCountries
→ objectAtIndex:indexPath.row];
NSString *imageName =
→ [NSString stringWithFormat:
→ @"%@.png",[arrCountries
→ objectAtIndex:indexPath.row]];
cell.imageView.image = [UIImage
→ imageNamed:imageName];
return cell;
```

Most of this code is unchanged from the
template—you need to implement only
the cell contents. Here you set the text by
looking at the current row of the table and
retrieving that value from your countries
array. You also set an image for the cell;
the image is a PNG file with the same
name as the country. You will need to add
a PNG graphic for each country's flag to
your project. You can easily find these by
visiting *http://images.google.com*.

6. Build and run the application.

You should see a list of countries with
flags next to them (**Figure 5.8**). **Code
Listing 5.9** shows the completed code.

Figure 5.8 The table view application.

✔ Tip

- You may have noticed in `tableView:cell`
`ForRowAtIndexPath:` you gave your cell
an identifier and used the `dequeue`
`ReusableCellWithIdentifier:` method
when you created the cell. For performance reasons, each unique type of cell
is stored in a *reuse queue*. You can then
check this queue to see whether a cell is
available for reuse, rather than creating a
new one.

Code Listing 5.9 The code for the table view application.

```
#import "RootViewController.h"

@implementation RootViewController

- (void)viewDidLoad {

    self.title = @"Countries";
    arrCountries = [[NSArray alloc] initWithObjects:
                    @"Australia",
                    @"Canada",
                    @"Germany",
                    @"France",
                    @"Great Britain",
                    @"Italy",
                    @"Japan",
                    @"New Zealand",
                    @"United States",nil];
}

- (NSInteger)numberOfSectionsInTableView:(UITableView *)tableView {

    return 1;
}

- (NSInteger)tableView:(UITableView *)tableView numberOfRowsInSection:(NSInteger)section {

    return [arrCountries count];
}

- (UITableViewCell *)tableView:(UITableView *)tableView cellForRowAtIndexPath:(NSIndexPath *)indexPath {

    static NSString *CellIdentifier = @"Cell";

    UITableViewCell *cell = [tableView dequeueReusableCellWithIdentifier:CellIdentifier];
    if (cell == nil) {
        cell = [[[UITableViewCell alloc]
                initWithStyle:UITableViewCellStyleDefault
                reuseIdentifier:CellIdentifier] autorelease];
    }

    // Configure the cell.
    cell.textLabel.text = [arrCountries objectAtIndex:indexPath.row];
    NSString *imageName = [NSString stringWithFormat:@"%@.png",[arrCountries objectAtIndex:indexPath.row]];
    cell.imageView.image = [UIImage imageNamed:imageName];

    return cell;
}

- (void)dealloc {

    [arrCountries release];

    [super dealloc];
}

@end
```

TABLE VIEWS

Grouping rows into sections and styles

As mentioned earlier, you can group your table view's rows into *sections*, which can be useful for displaying sets of related information. When using sections, it's also common to use the grouped style for your table view, which is the style used in the Settings application (**Figure 5.9**). This style represents cells as rounded rectangles with a shaded background.

To update the application to use sections and a grouped table view:

1. Open the RootViewController.h file, and modify the code to create three instance variables (**Code Listing 5.10**):

   ```
   NSArray *arrAsiaPacific;
   NSArray *arrEurope;
   NSArray *arrNorthAmerica;
   ```

   This time you are going to split the countries into three sections.

2. Switch to RootViewController.m, and update the viewDidLoad method:

   ```
   arrAsiaPacific = [[NSArray alloc] in
   → itWithObjects:@"Australia",
   → @"Japan",@"New Zealand",nil];
   arrEurope = [[NSArray alloc]
   → initWithObjects:@"Germany",
   → @"France",@"Great Britain",
   → @"Italy",nil];
   arrNorthAmerica = [[NSArray alloc]
   → initWithObjects:@"Canada",
   → @"United States",nil];
   ```

   Here you are creating an array for each section of your table view.

Figure 5.9 The Settings application uses the grouped table style.

Code Listing 5.10 The header file for the grouped table view application.

```
@interface RootViewController : UITableViewController
{
    NSArray *arrAsiaPacific;
    NSArray *arrEurope;
    NSArray *arrNorthAmerica;
}
@end
```

3. Update the `tableView:numberOfRowsIn Section:` method to look like this:

```
switch(section)
{
    case 0:
    return [arrAsiaPacific count];
    break;
    case 1:
    return [arrEurope count];
    break;
    case 2:
    return [arrNorthAmerica count];
    break;
    default:
    return 0;
    break;
}
```

This checks which section is being requested and then returns the size of the corresponding array.

continues on next page

4. Similarly, you need to update the `table View:cellForRowAtIndexPath:` method to check the correct array when you are creating the table view cell:

```
NSString *country;
switch(indexPath.section)
{
   case 0:
   country = [arrAsiaPacific
   ⇥ objectAtIndex:indexPath.row];
   break;
   case 1:
   country = [arrEurope
   ⇥ objectAtIndex:indexPath.row];
   break;
   case 2:
   country = [arrNorthAmerica
   ⇥ objectAtIndex:indexPath.row];
   break;
}
NSString *imageName = [NSString
⇥ stringWithFormat:@"%@.png",
⇥ country];
cell.imageView.image = [UIImage
⇥ imageNamed:imageName];
cell.textLabel.text = country;

return cell;
```

5. Update the `numberOfSectionsInTable View:` method to return the correct number of sections:

```
return 3;
```

6. Implement the `tableView:titleFor HeaderInSection:` method to create the title text above each section:

```
switch(section)
{
   case 0:
   return @"Asia Pacific";
   break;
```

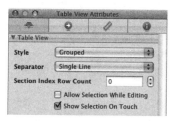

Figure 5.10 Setting the table view style in Interface Builder.

Figure 5.11 The grouped table view application.

```
        case 1:
            return @"Europe";
            break;
        case 2:
            return @"North America";
            break;
        default:
            return nil;
            break;
    }
```

7. Update the style of your table view using Interface Builder (**Figure 5.10**).

   Since the property is read-only, you can't edit it through code.

8. Build and run your application.

   You should now see your data grouped into three sections (**Figure 5.11**). **Code Listing 5.11** shows the updated code.

Code Listing 5.11 The code for the grouped table view application.

```
#import "RootViewController.h"

@implementation RootViewController

- (void)viewDidLoad {

    //create test data
    arrAsiaPacific = [[NSArray alloc] initWithObjects:@"Australia",@"Japan",@"New Zealand",nil];
    arrEurope = [[NSArray alloc] initWithObjects:@"Germany",@"France",@"Great Britain",@"Italy",nil];
    arrNorthAmerica = [[NSArray alloc] initWithObjects:@"Canada",@"United States",nil];
}


- (NSString *)tableView:(UITableView *)tableView titleForHeaderInSection:(NSInteger)section
{
    switch(section) {
        case 0:
            return @"Asia Pacific";
            break;
        case 1:
            return @"Europe";
            break;
```

(code continues on next page)

Code Listing 5.11 *continued*

```
          case 2:
              return @"North America";
              break;
          default:
              return nil;
              break;
    }
}

- (NSInteger)numberOfSectionsInTableView:(UITableView *)tableView {

    return 3;
}

- (NSInteger)tableView:(UITableView *)tableView numberOfRowsInSection:(NSInteger)section {

    switch(section) {
        case 0:
            return [arrAsiaPacific count];
            break;
        case 1:
            return [arrEurope count];
            break;
        case 2:
            return [arrNorthAmerica count];
            break;
        default:
            return 0;
            break;
    }
}

- (UITableViewCell *)tableView:(UITableView *)tableView cellForRowAtIndexPath:(NSIndexPath *)indexPath {

    static NSString *CellIdentifier = @"Cell";

    UITableViewCell *cell = [tableView dequeueReusableCellWithIdentifier:CellIdentifier];
    if (cell == nil) {
        cell = [[[UITableViewCell alloc]
                initWithStyle:UITableViewCellStyleDefault
                reuseIdentifier:CellIdentifier] autorelease];
    }

    // Configure the cell.
    NSString *country;
    switch(indexPath.section) {
        case 0:
            country = [arrAsiaPacific objectAtIndex:indexPath.row];
            break;
        case 1:
            country = [arrEurope objectAtIndex:indexPath.row];
            break;
        case 2:
            country = [arrNorthAmerica objectAtIndex:indexPath.row];
            break;
    }

    NSString *imageName = [NSString stringWithFormat:@"%@.png",country];
    cell.imageView.image = [UIImage imageNamed:imageName];
    cell.textLabel.text = country;

    return cell;
}

- (void)dealloc {

    [arrAsiaPacific release];
    [arrEurope release];
    [arrNorthAmerica release];

    [super dealloc];
}

@end
```

Editing and searching table views

Now you'll take a closer look at some of the data source methods you can use to edit your table view. You'll see how you can drag the table view rows to reorder them, as well as how to delete rows. You'll also add a UISearchBar control to the table view and write some code to allow you to filter the table view contents.

To create an editable table view that can be searched:

1. Create a new navigation-based application, saving it as EditTableViewExample.

2. Repeat steps 1–6 from the earlier exercise, "To create an application with a table view."

3. Open RootViewController.h, and create some new instance variables (**Code Listing 5.12**).

   Notice that you have changed the countries array to a *mutable* array. This is necessary since you will be changing the contents of the array when you search, edit, and delete items.

   continues on next page

Code Listing 5.12 The header file for the editable table view application.

```
@interface RootViewController : UITableViewController  <UISearchBarDelegate>
{
    NSMutableArray *arrCountries;
    NSMutableArray *arrTemp;
    UISearchBar *search;
    UIBarButtonItem *searchDoneButton;
}

@end
```

4. Switch to RootViewController.m, and modify the `viewDidLoad` method:

```
arrTemp = [arrCountries mutable
→ Copy];
```

You first create a new array, copying the countries array. This is going to be used as temporary storage when you filter the table view by searching.

```
CGRect tableFrame = [self.tableView
→ frame];
```

```
CGRect searchRect = tableFrame;
```

```
searchRect.size.height = 40;
```

```
search = [[UISearchBar alloc]
→ initWithFrame:searchRect];
```

```
search.delegate = self;
```

```
self.tableView.tableHeaderView =
→ search;
```

Next you create a search bar and attach it to the top of the table view by assigning it to the `tableHeaderView` property.

```
self.navigationItem.rightBarButton
→ Item = self.editButtonItem;
```

Then you set the navigation bar's right button to be the control that edits the table view. The `editButtonItem` automatically switches your table view between edit modes.

```
searchDoneButton = [[UIBarButtonItem
→ alloc] initWithBarButtonSystem
→ Item:UIBarButtonSystemItemDone
→ target:self action:@selector
→ (searchDone:)];
```

Finally, you create a bar button that you will use for searching.

5. Implement the `tableView:canMoveRowAt IndexPath:` method. By returning YES, you are allowing any row to be moved. You can see which the user is attempting to move by looking at the `indexPath.row` property.

6. Implement the `tableView:moveRowAt` `IndexPath:toIndexPath:` method that is called when the user rearranges a row:

```
NSString *name = [arrCountries
→ objectAtIndex:fromIndexPath.row];
[arrCountries removeObjectAtIndex:
→ fromIndexPath.row];
[arrCountries insertObject:name
→ atIndex:toIndexPath.row];
```

Although the table view will reorder itself, you also need to manually update the order of your countries array.

7. Implement the `tableView:commitEditing` `Style:forRowAtIndexPath:` method.

You check the editing style to see whether the user has deleted a row and, if so, remove it from the two arrays. You then call the `deleteRowsAtIndexPaths:with` `RowAnimation:` method to remove the row from the table view using a fade animation.

8. Implement the `searchBarTextDidBegin` `Editing:` delegate method:

```
self.navigationItem.rightBarButton
→ Item = searchDoneButton;
```

This method is called when the search keyboard appears. You swap the table view edit button with the search button you created earlier, allowing the user to exit from the search.

9. Implement the `searchBarSearchButton` `Clicked:` method, which is called when the user clicks "search" on the search keyboard.

This method calls a function that swaps the edit button in and hides the search bar keyboard.

continues on next page

TABLE VIEWS

10. Implement the `searchBar:textDid` `Change:` method, which is called when the user starts typing in the search bar. This in turn calls the `searchDone:` method:

```
NSString *searchFor = search.text;

[arrCountries release];
arrCountries = [arrTemp
→ mutableCopy];

if ([searchFor length] > 0) {

    NSPredicate *pred = [NSPredicate
    → predicateWithFormat:@"SELF
    → contains[c] %@",searchFor];
    [arrCountries filterUsing
    → Predicate:pred];
}

[self.tableView reloadData];
```

Here you reset the countries array so that you are dealing with the complete set of countries. You next create a predicate with the search text. A *predicate* is a special object that allows you to perform filtering of data. By calling the `filter` `UsingPredicate:` method of your countries array, you can filter the array to contain only the text entered in the search bar. Finally, calling `reloadData` tells your data to redraw itself, re-requesting all of its data using its data source methods. Since you have filtered the countries array, you will see only those countries that match the search text.

Figure 5.12 The editable table view application.

11. Build and run the application.

If you click the edit button, the table view will go into edit mode. You can reorder the rows by dragging using the handle on the right side of each row (**Figure 5.12**). Clicking the delete graphic on the left side of a row allows you to remove the row from the table view. If you tap in the search bar area, a keyboard will appear. The data in the table view will be filtered as you type. **Code Listing 5.13** shows the completed code.

✔ Tip

■ To prevent the delete button from appearing while still allowing the rows to be reordered, you can return `UITableView CellEditingStyleNone` from the `table View:editingStyleForRowAtIndexPath:` delegate method.

Code Listing 5.13 The completed code for the editable table view application.

```
#import "RootViewController.h"

@implementation RootViewController

- (void)viewDidLoad {

    self.title = @"Countries";
    arrCountries = [[NSMutableArray alloc] initWithObjects:
                    @"Australia",
                    @"Canada",
                    @"Germany",
                    @"France",
                    @"Great Britain",
                    @"Italy",
                    @"Japan",
                    @"New Zealand",
                    @"United States",nil];
    arrTemp = [arrCountries mutableCopy];

    CGRect tableFrame = [self.tableView frame];
    CGRect searchRect = tableFrame;
    searchRect.size.height = 40;
    search = [[UISearchBar alloc] initWithFrame:searchRect];
    search.delegate = self;
    self.tableView.tableHeaderView = search;

    self.navigationItem.rightBarButtonItem = self.editButtonItem;
    searchDoneButton = [[UIBarButtonItem alloc]
                        initWithBarButtonSystemItem:UIBarButtonSystemItemDone
                        target:self
                        action:@selector(searchDone:)];
}

- (NSInteger)tableView:(UITableView *)tableView numberOfRowsInSection:(NSInteger)section {

    return [arrCountries count];
}

- (UITableViewCell *)tableView:(UITableView *)tableView cellForRowAtIndexPath:(NSIndexPath *)indexPath {

    static NSString *CellIdentifier = @"Cell";

    UITableViewCell *cell = [tableView dequeueReusableCellWithIdentifier:CellIdentifier];
    if (cell == nil) {
        cell = [[[UITableViewCell alloc]
                initWithStyle:UITableViewCellStyleDefault
                reuseIdentifier:CellIdentifier] autorelease];
    }

    // Configure the cell.
    cell.textLabel.text = [arrCountries objectAtIndex:indexPath.row];
    NSString *imageName = [NSString stringWithFormat:@"%@.png",[arrCountries objectAtIndex:indexPath.row]];
    cell.imageView.image = [UIImage imageNamed:imageName];

    return cell;
}

- (NSInteger)numberOfSectionsInTableView:(UITableView *)tableView {

    return 1;
}

- (BOOL)tableView:(UITableView *)tableView canMoveRowAtIndexPath:(NSIndexPath *)indexPath
{
    return YES;
}
```

(code continues on next page)

Code Listing 5.13 *continued*

```
000                                    Code
- (void)tableView:(UITableView *)tableView
moveRowAtIndexPath:(NSIndexPath *)fromIndexPath
     toIndexPath:(NSIndexPath *)toIndexPath
{
    //re-order array
    NSString *name = [arrCountries objectAtIndex:fromIndexPath.row];
    [arrCountries removeObjectAtIndex:fromIndexPath.row];
    [arrCountries insertObject:name atIndex:toIndexPath.row];
}

- (void)tableView:(UITableView *)tableView
commitEditingStyle:(UITableViewCellEditingStyle)editingStyle
forRowAtIndexPath:(NSIndexPath *)indexPath
{
    if (editingStyle == UITableViewCellEditingStyleDelete)
    {
        [arrTemp removeObject:[arrCountries objectAtIndex:indexPath.row]];
        [arrCountries removeObjectAtIndex:indexPath.row];
        [tableView
         deleteRowsAtIndexPaths:[NSArray arrayWithObject:indexPath]
         withRowAnimation:UITableViewRowAnimationFade];
    }
}

- (void)searchDone:(id)sender {

    self.navigationItem.rightBarButtonItem = self.editButtonItem;
    [search resignFirstResponder];
}

- (void)doSearch {

    NSString *searchFor = search.text;

    [arrCountries release];
    arrCountries = [arrTemp mutableCopy];

    if ([searchFor length] > 0) {
        NSPredicate *pred = [NSPredicate predicateWithFormat:@"SELF contains[c] %@",searchFor];
        [arrCountries filterUsingPredicate:pred];
    }

    [self.tableView reloadData];
}

- (void)searchBarTextDidBeginEditing:(UISearchBar *)searchBar {

    self.navigationItem.rightBarButtonItem = searchDoneButton;
}

- (void)searchBar:(UISearchBar *)searchBar textDidChange:(NSString *)searchText {

    [self doSearch];
}

- (void)searchBarSearchButtonClicked:(UISearchBar *)searchBar {
    [self searchDone:nil];
}

- (void)dealloc {

    [arrCountries release];
    [arrTemp release];
    [search release];
    [searchDoneButton release];

    [super dealloc];
}

@end
```

Drilling down in table views

So far, the examples have presented a table
view with only a single level of data. It's common, however, for data to be hierarchical,
and you will often want to provide an interface where the user can select an item and
then be presented with a subset of related
items. This "drill-down" concept is used frequently and is surprisingly easy to implement
using table views.

Before you see how to do this, it's worth
learning about another important class you
will be using to add this functionality: the
navigation controller.

A navigation controller, represented by the
`UINavigationController` class, is a special
type of view controller designed to help you
navigate through hierarchical content known
as the *navigation stack*. View controllers are
pushed onto the navigation stack to display
them and then *popped* off the navigation
stack when you are finished with them.

Navigation controllers typically display a
navigation bar at the top of the screen that
indicates the current (topmost) controller
on the stack. (You have actually been using
a navigation controller in all the table view
examples so far.) This bar will update as view
controllers are pushed onto and popped off
the navigation stack. This bar is also usually
where any edit controls related to the view
would sit. The view of the current view controller is displayed below this navigation bar
(**Figure 5.13**).

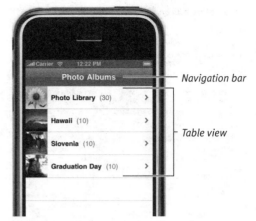

Figure 5.13 A navigation controller
with a navigation bar and a table view.

Figure 5.14 Adding a second view controller class to hold your table view details.

Code Listing 5.14 The header file for the drill-down details of the table view controller.

```
● ● ●                    Code
#import <UIKit/UIKit.h>

@interface DetailViewController : UITableViewController
{
    NSArray *content;
}

@property (nonatomic, retain) NSArray *content;

@end
```

To create a table view with drill-down behavior:

1. Create a new navigation-based application, saving it as DrillDownExample.

2. Select File > New, and add a new UIViewController (**Figure 5.14**) subclass.
   Save the file as DetailViewController.m. Make sure that "Also create 'DetailView Controller.h'" is selected.

3. Open the DetailViewController.h file, change the class type to UITableView Controller, and create a new property that you'll use to hold the table view details (**Code Listing 5.14**).

4. Switch to DetailsViewController.m, uncomment the viewWillAppear method, and add the following code:
   ```
   self.title = @"Details";
   [self.tableView reloadData];
   ```
   Here you are setting the title and telling the table view to reload. Note that this time you are using the viewDidAppear method (instead of viewDidLoad as in the other exercises in this chapter). This method will be run every time your details view is shown. By using the reloadData method call, you know your table view will always contain the correct data.

5. Implement the rest of this class as shown in **Code Listing 5.15**, which is the same code you used for previous exercises in this chapter.

6. Switch to RootViewController.h, import the DetailsViewController.h file, and create some instance variables that you will use to hold your table data and the details view (**Code Listing 5.16**).

continues on page 207

Code Listing 5.15 The completed code for the drill-down details of the table view controller.

```
#import "DetailViewController.h"

@implementation DetailViewController

@synthesize content;

- (void)viewWillAppear:(BOOL)animated {

    self.title = @"Details";
    [self.tableView reloadData];
}

- (NSInteger)tableView:(UITableView *)tableView numberOfRowsInSection:(NSInteger)section {

    return [content count];
}

- (UITableViewCell *)tableView:(UITableView *)tableView cellForRowAtIndexPath:(NSIndexPath *)indexPath {

    static NSString *CellIdentifier = @"Details";

    UITableViewCell *cell = [tableView dequeueReusableCellWithIdentifier:CellIdentifier];
    if (cell == nil) {
        cell = [[[UITableViewCell alloc]
                initWithStyle:UITableViewCellStyleDefault
                reuseIdentifier:CellIdentifier] autorelease];
    }

    cell.textLabel.text = [content objectAtIndex:indexPath.row];

    return cell;
}

- (void)dealloc {

    [content release];
    [super dealloc];
}

@end
```

Code Listing 5.16 The main header file for the
drill-down details application.

```
#import "DetailViewController.h"

@interface RootViewController : UITableViewController
{
    NSArray *arrCountries;
    NSArray *arrUSACities;
    NSArray *arrAustraliaCities;
    DetailViewController *details;
}

@end
```

7. Switch to RootViewController.m, uncomment the viewDidLoad method, and add the following code:

```
arrCountries = [[NSArray alloc]
→ initWithObjects: @"Australia",
→ @"United States",nil];
arrUSACities = [[NSArray alloc]
→ initWithObjects: @"Boston",
→ @"San Francisco",@"New York",nil];
arrAustraliaCities = [[NSArray
→ alloc] initWithObjects:
→ @"Brisbane",@"Perth",@"Sydney",
→ nil];

details = [[DetailViewController
→ alloc] initWithStyle:UITableView
→ StyleGrouped];
```

Here you create three arrays: the first is your main array, and the other two are used for the details view. Notice that you can create the details view with a grouped style using the initWithStyle: method.

8. Implement the tableView:didSelectRow AtIndexPath: delegate method that is called when you select a row:

```
if (indexPath.row == 0)
    [details
setContent:arrAustraliaCities];
else
    [details setContent:arrUSACities];

[[self navigationController]
→ pushViewController:details
→ animated:YES];
```

Here you check which row the user has selected, assigning the appropriate array to the details view controller. You then push the view controller onto the stack of the navigation controller, causing it to be animated onto the screen.

continues on next page

TABLE VIEWS

9. The rest of the code is almost exactly as in previous exercises, except you set the `accessoryType` property when creating the cells:

```
cell.accessoryType = UITableView
→ CellAccessoryDisclosureIndicator;
```

This adds a disclosure triangle to the right side of the cell, providing a visual cue to the user that they will see detailed data by selecting the row.

10. Build and run your application (**Figure 5.15**).

Selecting either row will cause the details view to be shown. Pressing the back button in the navigation bar will take you to the main screen. **Code Listing 5.17** shows the completed code.

Figure 5.15 The details screen of the drill-down table view application.

Code Listing 5.17 The completed drill-down table view application.

```
#import "RootViewController.h"

@implementation RootViewController

- (void)viewDidLoad {

    self.title = @"Countries";
    arrCountries = [[NSArray alloc] initWithObjects: @"Australia",@"United States",nil];
    arrUSACities = [[NSArray alloc] initWithObjects: @"Boston",@"San Francisco",@"New York",nil];
    arrAustraliaCities = [[NSArray alloc] initWithObjects: @"Brisbane",@"Perth",@"Sydney",nil];

    details = [[DetailViewController alloc] initWithStyle:UITableViewStyleGrouped];
}

- (void)tableView:(UITableView *)tableView didSelectRowAtIndexPath:(NSIndexPath *)indexPath {

    if (indexPath.row == 0)
        [details setContent:arrAustraliaCities];
    else
        [details setContent:arrUSACities];

    [[self navigationController] pushViewController:details animated:YES];
}

- (NSInteger)tableView:(UITableView *)tableView numberOfRowsInSection:(NSInteger)section {

    return [arrCountries count];
}

- (UITableViewCell *)tableView:(UITableView *)tableView cellForRowAtIndexPath:(NSIndexPath *)indexPath {

    static NSString *CellIdentifier = @"Cell";

    UITableViewCell *cell = [tableView dequeueReusableCellWithIdentifier:CellIdentifier];
    if (cell == nil) {
        cell = [[[UITableViewCell alloc]
                initWithStyle:UITableViewCellStyleDefault
                reuseIdentifier:CellIdentifier] autorelease];
    }

    cell.textLabel.text = [arrCountries objectAtIndex:indexPath.row];
    cell.accessoryType = UITableViewCellAccessoryDisclosureIndicator;

    return cell;
}

- (void)dealloc {

    [arrCountries release];
    [arrUSACities release];
    [arrAustraliaCities release];
    [details release];

    [super dealloc];
}

@end
```

TABLE VIEWS

Creating custom cells

So far, you've been using the default cell style in your table views (represented by the `UITableViewCellStyleDefault` type). **Figure 5.16** shows the four styles available.

However, you are not restricted to displaying text and images. You can create your own custom cell types to fully control the appearance and contents of the cell (**Figure 5.17**).

Next you'll learn how you can create a custom cell type that will allow you to add an on/off switch and a button to your table view.

Figure 5.16 The four styles for table cells.

Figure 5.17 The Settings application makes extensive use of custom cells.

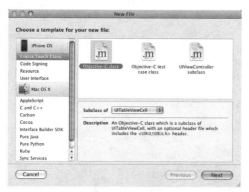

Figure 5.18 Adding a custom cell class to hold your table view details.

Code Listing 5.18 The header file for the custom cell class.

```
#import <UIKit/UIKit.h>

@interface MyCustomCell : UITableViewCell {

    UIView  *view;
}

@property (nonatomic, retain) UIView *view;


@end
```

To create a table view with custom cells:

1. Create a new navigation-based application, saving it as CustomCellExample.

2. Select File > New, and add a new Objective-C class.

   Make sure that the Subclass drop-down is set to `UITableViewCell` (**Figure 5.18**), and save it as MyCustomCell.m. Make sure that "Also create 'MyCustomCell.h'" is selected.

3. Open MyCustomCell.h, and create a property (**Code Listing 5.18**). This will be the view that holds your custom control.

4. Switch to MyCustomCell.m, and add the following to the `initWithStyle:reuse Identifier:` method:

   `self.selectionStyle = UITableView` `→ CellSelectionStyleNone;`

   This disables selection of the entire cell; you don't want the cell to be selected because you will be manipulating your control instead.

5. Implement the `setView:` method:

   `if (view)`

   `    [view removeFromSuperview];`

   `view = aView;`

   `[self.view retain];`

   `[self.contentView addSubview:aView];`

   `[self layoutSubviews];`

   This adds a view (from the view property) to the cell's `contentView` and then tells the cell to draw its subviews.

continues on next page

TABLE VIEWS

6. Implement the layoutSubviews method:

```
float xOffset = 10.0;

[super layoutSubviews];
CGRect contentRect =
→ [self.contentView bounds];

CGRect viewFrame = CGRectMake
→ (contentRect.size.width -
→ self.view.bounds.size.width -
→ xOffset,round((contentRect.size.
→ height - self.view.bounds.size.
→ height) / 2.0),self.view.bounds.
→ size.width,self.view.bounds.size.
→ height);
view.frame = viewFrame;
```

Here you add the view (defined in the view property) to the right side of the cell's contentView. **Code Listing 5.19** shows the complete code for your custom cell class.

7. Open RootViewController.h, and import the header file for your custom cell.

8. Create instance variables to hold two controls for your custom cells and an array to hold the table view content (**Code Listing 5.20**).

continues on page 214

Code Listing 5.19 The completed custom cell class.

```
                                    Code

#import "MyCustomCell.h"

@implementation MyCustomCell

@synthesize view;

- (id)initWithStyle:(UITableViewCellStyle)style reuseIdentifier:(NSString *)reuseIdentifier {

    if (self = [super initWithStyle:style reuseIdentifier:reuseIdentifier]) {

        self.selectionStyle = UITableViewCellSelectionStyleNone;
    }
    return self;
}

- (void)setSelected:(BOOL)selected animated:(BOOL)animated {

    [super setSelected:selected animated:animated];
}

- (void)setView:(UIView *)aView {

    if (view)
        [view removeFromSuperview];
    view = aView;
    [self.view retain];
    [self.contentView addSubview:aView];

    [self layoutSubviews];
}

- (void)layoutSubviews {

    float xOffset = 10.0;

    [super layoutSubviews];
    CGRect contentRect = [self.contentView bounds];

    CGRect viewFrame = CGRectMake(contentRect.size.width - self.view.bounds.size.width - xOffset,
                                  round((contentRect.size.height - self.view.bounds.size.height) / 2.0),
                                  self.view.bounds.size.width,
                                  self.view.bounds.size.height);
    view.frame = viewFrame;
}

- (void)dealloc {

    [view release];

    [super dealloc];
}
@end
```

Code Listing 5.20 The header file for the main table
view controller class of the custom cell example.

```
                        Code
#import "MyCustomCell.h"

@interface RootViewController : UITableViewController
{
    UISwitch *mySwitch;
    UIButton *myButton;
    NSArray *arrCells;
}
@end
```

9. Switch to RootViewController.m, uncomment the viewDidLoad method, and add the following code:

```
mySwitch = [[UISwitch alloc]
 initWithFrame:CGRectZero];
[mySwitch addTarget:self action:
 @selector(switchAction:)
 forControlEvents:UIControlEvent
 ValueChanged];
[mySwitch setOn:YES];


myButton = [UIButton buttonWithType:
 UIButtonTypeRoundedRect];
[myButton setFrame:CGRectMake
 (0,0,80,30)];
[myButton addTarget:self action:
 @selector(buttonAction:)
 forControlEvents:UIControlEvent
 TouchUpInside];
[myButton setTitle:@"Tap Me!"
 forState:UIControlStateNormal];


arrCells = [[NSArray alloc]
 initWithObjects:@"Item 1",
 @"Item 2",@"Item 3",nil];
```

Here you create a switch and a button that you are going to be adding to your custom cells. Notice how you define the target-action methods for both of them within this class also. In this example, you just log the actions to the console. You also create an array to hold the text for the table view just as you did in previous exercises.

10. Implement the `tableView:numberOfRows InSection:` method to return the size of your array, and implement the `table View:cellForRowAtIndexPath:` method:

```
UITableViewCell *cell = nil;
    static NSString *CellIdentifier =
→ @"Cell";
    static NSString *ViewCell
→ Identifier = @"ViewCell";


switch (indexPath.row) {

    case 0:
        cell = [tableView dequeue
        → ReusableCellWithIdentifier:
        → ViewCellIdentifier];
        if (cell == nil)
            cell = [[[MyCustomCell
            → alloc] initWithStyle:
            → UITableViewCellStyle
            → Default reuseIdentifier:
            → ViewCellIdentifier]
            → autorelease];

        cell.textLabel.text =
        → [arrCells objectAtIndex:
        → indexPath.row];
        ((MyCustomCell *)cell).view =
        → mySwitch;
        break;

    case 1:
        cell = [tableView dequeue
        → ReusableCellWithIdentifier:
        → ViewCellIdentifier];
        if (cell == nil)
```

continues on next page

```
        cell = [[[MyCustomCell
        → alloc] initWithStyle:
        → UITableViewCellStyle
        → Default reuseIdentifier:
        → ViewCellIdentifier]
        → autorelease];

    cell.textLabel.text =
    [arrCells objectAtIndex:
    → indexPath.row];
    ((MyCustomCell *)cell).view =
    → myButton;
    break;

default:
    cell = [tableView dequeue
    → ReusableCellWithIdentifier:
    → CellIdentifier];
    if (cell == nil)
        cell = [[[UITableViewCell
        → alloc] initWithStyle:
        → UITableViewCellStyle
        → Default reuseIdentifier:
        → CellIdentifier]
        → autorelease];

    cell.textLabel.text =
    → [arrCells objectAtIndex:
    → indexPath.row];
    break;
}

return cell;
```

Since you are using custom cells, you need to determine which row is being requested via indexPath.row. For the first two rows, you create a custom cell. Notice how you set the view of the custom cell to the switch or the button. For other rows (the default case), the code is the same as in the previous exercise, "To create an appliction with a table view."

Figure 5.19 The completed custom cell application.

11. Build and run the application.

Figure 5.19 shows the completed application with two custom cells displayed. Selecting the switch or tapping the button will log a message to the console. **Code Listing 5.21** shows the completed code.

✔ Tip

■ This is obviously a simple example, adding only a single view to the cell, but you should be able to see how you could extend it to add multiple controls to your own custom cells. For more information on working with table views, see the *Table View Programming Guide for iPhone OS* in the developer documentation.

Code Listing 5.21 The completed code for the custom cell example.

```
#import "RootViewController.h"

@implementation RootViewController

- (void)switchAction:(id)sender
{
    NSLog(@"switch changed");
}

- (void)buttonAction:(id)sender
{
    NSLog(@"button tapped");
}

- (void)viewDidLoad {

    mySwitch = [[UISwitch alloc] initWithFrame:CGRectZero];
    [mySwitch addTarget:self action:@selector(switchAction:) forControlEvents:UIControlEventValueChanged];
    [mySwitch setOn:YES];

    myButton = [UIButton buttonWithType:UIButtonTypeRoundedRect];
    [myButton setFrame:CGRectMake(0,0,80,30)];
    [myButton addTarget:self action:@selector(buttonAction:) forControlEvents:UIControlEventTouchUpInside];
    [myButton setTitle:@"Tap Me!" forState:UIControlStateNormal];

    arrCells = [[NSArray alloc] initWithObjects:@"Item 1",@"Item 2",@"Item 3",nil];
}
```

(code continues on next page)

TABLE VIEWS

Code Listing 5.21 *continued*

```
○○○                                    Code
- (NSInteger)tableView:(UITableView *)tableView numberOfRowsInSection:(NSInteger)section {

    return [arrCells count];
}

- (UITableViewCell *)tableView:(UITableView *)tableView cellForRowAtIndexPath:(NSIndexPath *)indexPath {

    UITableViewCell *cell = nil;
    static NSString *CellIdentifier = @"Cell";
    static NSString *ViewCellIdentifier = @"ViewCell";

    switch (indexPath.row) {

        case 0:
            cell = [tableView dequeueReusableCellWithIdentifier:ViewCellIdentifier];
            if (cell == nil)
                cell = [[[MyCustomCell alloc]
                            initWithStyle:UITableViewCellStyleDefault
                            reuseIdentifier:ViewCellIdentifier] autorelease];

            cell.textLabel.text = [arrCells objectAtIndex:indexPath.row];
            ((MyCustomCell *)cell).view = mySwitch;
            break;

        case 1:
            cell = [tableView dequeueReusableCellWithIdentifier:ViewCellIdentifier];
            if (cell == nil)
                cell = [[[MyCustomCell alloc]
                            initWithStyle:UITableViewCellStyleDefault
                            reuseIdentifier:ViewCellIdentifier] autorelease];

            cell.textLabel.text = [arrCells objectAtIndex:indexPath.row];
            ((MyCustomCell *)cell).view = myButton;
            break;

        default:
            cell = [tableView dequeueReusableCellWithIdentifier:CellIdentifier];
            if (cell == nil)
                cell = [[[UITableViewCell alloc]
                            initWithStyle:UITableViewCellStyleDefault
                            reuseIdentifier:CellIdentifier] autorelease];

            cell.textLabel.text = [arrCells objectAtIndex:indexPath.row];
            break;
    }

    return cell;
}

- (void)dealloc {

    [arrCells release];
    [mySwitch release];

    [super dealloc];
}

@end
```

FILES AND NETWORKING

The iPhone runs a slimmed-down version of the Mac OS X operating system, so the file system is similar to its desktop cousin. However, iPhone applications run within a security *sandbox*, a unique area on the iPhone reserved for an application where it can run without affecting the system or any other iPhone applications. So the files and directories you can actually read and write are somewhat limited. Of course, this also means that other applications can't gain access to your application's files!

The iPhone also has some fairly extensive networking capabilities by way of its Wi-Fi, Bluetooth, and 3G connectivity options. In this chapter, you'll learn the classes, methods, and functions used to perform many of the common file and networking tasks encountered as an iPhone developer.

Files

As you learned in Chapter 1, "Objective-C and Cocoa," several Cocoa classes have methods to automatically deal with reading and writing files (**Code Listing 6.1**). Some of these classes are as follows:

◆ UIImage—The imageNamed: method will automatically try to load an image from the resources directory of your application bundle.

◆ NSString—The stringWithContentsOf File: and writeToFile: methods let you load and save strings as files. Additionally, NSString has some other commonly used methods for dealing with file paths.

◆ NSDictionary and NSArray—The dictionaryWithContentsOfFile:, arrayWithContentsOfFile:, and writeToFile: methods allow you to load and save dictionaries and arrays of objects. Note that the objects in your dictionary or array must be property list objects (NSNumber, NSString, NSData, NSArray, or NSDictionary).

◆ NSData—This is normally used when dealing with binary files.

The file system

NSFileManager wraps many of the common actions you will need to perform when dealing with the iPhone file system including creating, deleting, moving, and copying files. You can also use it for getting directory listings, reading and writing file attributes, and more.

Code Listing 6.1 Many common classes have methods to load and save files.

```
- (void)writeStringToDirectory:(NSString *)dir {

    //create filename
    NSString *f = @"somefile.txt";
    NSString *path = [dir stringByAppendingPathComponent:f];

    //create string
    NSString *foo = @"some content";

    //save
    [foo writeToFile:path atomically:YES];

    //read back in and log
    NSString *results = [NSString stringWithContentsOfFile:path];
    NSLog(@"results: %@",results);
}

- (void)writeDictionaryToDirectory:(NSString *)dir
{
    //create file
    NSString *f = @"somefile.txt";
    NSString *path = [dir stringByAppendingPathComponent:f];

    //create dictionary
    NSString *string1 = @"some value";
    NSString *string2 = @"another value";
    NSNumber *num = [NSNumber numberWithInt:12345];
    NSArray *arr = [NSArray arrayWithObjects:
                    @"item1",
                    @"item2",
                    @"item3",nil];
    NSDictionary *dict = [NSDictionary dictionaryWithObjectsAndKeys:
                    string1,@"item1",
                    string2, @"item2",
                    num, @"item3",
                    arr, @"item4", nil];

    //save
    [dict writeToFile:path atomically:YES];

    //read back and log
    NSDictionary *results = [NSDictionary dictionaryWithContentsOfFile:path];
    NSLog(@"results: %@",results);
}
```

- For example, to copy a file from one location to another, you could write this:

```
NSFileManager *fm = [NSFileManager
→ defaultManager];

NSError *error;

BOOL ok = [fm copyItemAtPath:
→ @"somePath" toPath:
→ @"someOtherPath" error:&error];

if (! ok)
    NSLog(@" %@",error.localized
    → Description);
```

- To get an array of filenames for a path, you can use this:

```
NSFileManager *fm = [NSFileManager
→ defaultManager];

NSArray *fileContents =
→ [fm directoryContentsAtPath:@"/"];
```

✔ Tip

- You can read more in the NSFileManager class reference of the developer documentation.

Common directories

The iPhone is quite locked down in regard to which directories you can read and write to, and in practice, you will normally be working with only a couple of directories.

You can retrieve the path of your application by using the NSHomeDirectory() function:

```
NSString *homeDir = NSHomeDirectory();
```

If you log the contents of this directory (**Figure 6.1**) to the console, you'll notice three directories in addition to your application bundle.

- **tmp**—This is the temporary directory, which can also be retrieved using the NSTemporaryDirectory() function:

```
NSString *tempDir =
→ NSTemporaryDirectory();
```

Figure 6.1 The contents of the home directory.

You can use this directory for reading and writing any temporary files you may need in your application. Files in this directory are not guaranteed to continue to exist once you exit your application (they are automatically cleaned out periodically by the system) and are not copied to your computer when you sync your iPhone with iTunes.

◆ **Documents**—This directory is the designated area for your application to read and write files to. Any files written here are copied to your computer when you sync with iTunes. You can retrieve the documents directory by using the following code:

```
NSArray *paths = NSSearchPathFor
→ DirectoriesInDomains(NSDocument
→ Directory, NSUserDomainMask, YES);
NSString *docDir = [paths
→ objectAtIndex:0];
```

◆ **Library**—This directory contains cache and preference files used by NSUserDefaults. Although you can read and write to this directory, you will not normally need to do so.

You can also read files contained within your application bundle, such as images, movies, sounds, or other files that you have added to your project. These will generally be copied into the *resources* directory of the bundle. For example, to get the path of an image named apple.png, you can write the following:

```
NSString *resourcesDir = [[NSBundle
→ mainBundle] resourcePath];
NSString *imageDir = [resourcesDir
→ stringByAppendingPathComponent:
→ @"apple.png"];
```

FILES

✔ **Tip**

■ Although both your application bundle and the home directory can be written to in the iPhone Simulator, they cannot be written to on an actual iPhone. For this reason, you should use the tmp or documents directory if you need to save any files.

Working with files

So far, you've seen some of the classes, methods, and functions you can use when managing files on the iPhone. Now you'll look at an example where being able to load and save an NSDictionary as a file may come in handy. You'll create an application (a simple username and password screen) that populates its user interface from an external settings file. Any changes the user makes to the interface will be saved to the settings file so that they can be restored the next time the application is launched.

One way to do this is to ship your application with a default settings file. When the application launches for the first time, you copy these default settings to the documents directory. It is this copy you then use in your application for loading and saving the user's settings. Since the documents directory is copied to the user's computer each time they sync with iTunes, you know that any changes the user has made will remain safe.

To create an application to load settings from an external file:

1. Create a new view-based application, saving it as SettingsExample.

2. Choose File > New. In the New File dialog box, select the Other category, select Property List, and click Next (**Figure 6.2**).

3. Name the file settings.plist, and click Finish.

4. Select the settings.plist file in the Groups & Files pane to show the file in the property list editor view.

5. Right-click the Root key, and select Add Row (**Figure 6.3**).

Figure 6.2 Creating a property list.

Figure 6.3 Adding a new row to a property list.

Key	Type	Value
▼ Root	Dictionary	(2 items)
username	String	<enter username>
password	String	

Figure 6.4 The completed property list.

Code Listing 6.2 The header file for the Settings example.

```
Code
#import <UIKit/UIKit.h>

@interface SettingsExampleViewController:UIViewController
{
    NSMutableDictionary *dictSettings;
    NSString *settingsFileName;
    UITextField *txtUserName;
    UITextField *txtPassword;
}

@end
```

6. Change the key from New Item to user-name, and leave the type as String.

7. Repeat steps 5-6, adding a second item called password. If you want, you can enter a default value for both keys (**Figure 6.4**).

8. Open the FilesExampleViewController.h file, and create the instance variables you'll use to hold the settings dictionary, filename, and user interface elements (**Code Listing 6.2**).

9. Switch to FilesExampleViewController.m, and create the method getSettings Dictionary:, which will be used to read the settings from the file:

```
NSArray *paths = NSSearchPathFor
→ DirectoriesInDomains(NSDocument
→ Directory, NSUserDomainMask, YES);
NSString *documentsDir = [paths
→ objectAtIndex:0];
NSString *filePath = [documentsDir
→ stringByAppendingPathComponent:
→ settingsFileName];
NSFileManager *fm = [NSFileManager
→ defaultManager];
BOOL exists = [fm fileExistsAtPath:
→ filePath];
```

You first get the user's documents directory and use it to construct the filename for the settings file.

```
NSString *resourcesDir = [[NSBundle
→ mainBundle] resourcePath];
NSString *sourcePath =[resourcesDir
→ stringByAppendingPathComponent:
→ fileName];
[fm copyItemAtPath:sourcePath
→ toPath:filePath error:NULL];
```

continues on next page

FILES

You next check whether the file exists, and if it doesn't, you copy the default settings file (created in step 4) from the application bundle into the documents directory.

```
return [NSDictionary dictionaryWith
→ContentsOfFile:filePath];
```

You then create a dictionary from this file and return it from the method.

10. Create the `createUI` method used to build the user interface.

There is nothing unusual here: You are adding two `UILabels`, two `UITextFields`, and a button to the main view. The text values for the username and password fields are retrieved from the `dictSettings` dictionary.

11. Uncomment and implement the `viewDidLoad` method:

```
settingsFileName = [[NSString
→alloc] initWithString:@"settings.
→plist"];


dictSettings =
→[[NSMutableDictionary alloc]
→initWithDictionary:[self
→settingsDictionary]];
    [self createUI];
```

Here you set the settings filename and retrieve and initialize a dictionary from the file in the documents directory (which will be automatically created if necessary). Then you store the dictionary in an instance variable before creating the user interface.

FILES

12. The final step is to implement the saveClick: method that is called when the user taps the Save button:

```
NSArray *paths = NSSearchPathFor
→ DirectoriesInDomains(NSDocument
→ Directory, NSUserDomainMask,
→ YES);
```

```
NSString *documentsDir = [paths
→ objectAtIndex:0];
```

```
NSString *filePath = [documents
→ Dir stringByAppendingPath
→ Component:settingsFileName];
```

```
[dictSettings setValue:txtUserName.
→ text forKey:@"username"];
```

```
[dictSettings setValue:txtPassword.
→ text forKey:@"password"];
```

```
[dictSettings writeToFile:filePath
→ atomically:NO];
```

This is almost the reverse of the getSettingsDictionary: method. You set the username and password keys of the settings dictionary to the text field values and then write it to the documents directory. **Code Listing 6.3** shows the completed code.

✔ Tip

■ In this example, you saved not only the username but also the user's *password* in the settings file. In a real-world application, you would normally store sensitive information such as passwords in a secure database called the *keychain*. For more information, refer to the *Keychain Services Programming Guide* in the developer documentation.

Code Listing 6.3 The completed code.

```
● ● ●                                   Code
#import "SettingsExampleViewController.h"

@implementation SettingsExampleViewController

- (void)saveClick:(id)sender
{
    NSArray *paths = NSSearchPathForDirectoriesInDomains(NSDocumentDirectory, NSUserDomainMask, YES);
    NSString *documentsDir = [paths objectAtIndex:0];

    NSString *filePath = [documentsDir stringByAppendingPathComponent:settingsFileName];

    [dictSettings setValue:txtUserName.text forKey:@"username"];
    [dictSettings setValue:txtPassword.text forKey:@"password"];

    //save
    [dictSettings writeToFile:filePath atomically:NO];
}
```

(code continues on next page)

Code Listing 6.3 *continued*

```
                                          Code

- (NSDictionary *)getSettingsDictionary {

    NSArray *paths = NSSearchPathForDirectoriesInDomains(NSDocumentDirectory, NSUserDomainMask, YES);
    NSString *documentsDir = [paths objectAtIndex:0];
    NSString *filePath = [documentsDir stringByAppendingPathComponent:settingsFileName];

    //check if file exists in doc dir
    NSFileManager *fm = [NSFileManager defaultManager];
    BOOL exists = [fm fileExistsAtPath:filePath];

    if (! exists)
    {
        NSString *resourcesDir = [[NSBundle mainBundle] resourcePath];
        NSString *sourcePath =[resourcesDir stringByAppendingPathComponent:settingsFileName];
        [fm copyItemAtPath:sourcePath toPath:filePath error:NULL];
    }

    return [NSDictionary dictionaryWithContentsOfFile:filePath];
}

- (void)createUI
{
    UILabel *lblUserName = [[UILabel alloc] initWithFrame:CGRectMake(10,10,100,40)];
    lblUserName.backgroundColor = [UIColor clearColor];
    lblUserName.text = @"Username:";
    [self.view addSubview:lblUserName];
    [lblUserName release];

    txtUserName = [[UITextField alloc] initWithFrame:CGRectMake(115,20,185,24)];
    txtUserName.backgroundColor = [UIColor whiteColor];
    txtUserName.text = [dictSettings objectForKey:@"username"];
    [self.view addSubview:txtUserName];

    UILabel *lblPassword = [[UILabel alloc] initWithFrame:CGRectMake(10,50,100,40)];
    lblPassword.backgroundColor = [UIColor clearColor];
    lblPassword.text = @"Password:";
    [self.view addSubview:lblPassword];
    [lblPassword release];

    txtPassword = [[UITextField alloc] initWithFrame:CGRectMake(115,60,185,24)];
    txtPassword.backgroundColor = [UIColor whiteColor];
    txtPassword.text = [dictSettings valueForKey:@"password"];
    txtPassword.clearsOnBeginEditing = YES;
    txtPassword.secureTextEntry = YES;
    [self.view addSubview:txtPassword];

    UIButton *btnSave = [UIButton buttonWithType:UIButtonTypeRoundedRect];
    btnSave.frame = CGRectMake(200, 100, 100, 34);
    [btnSave setTitle:@"Save" forState:UIControlStateNormal];
    [btnSave addTarget:self action:@selector(saveClick:) forControlEvents:UIControlEventTouchUpInside];
    [self.view addSubview:btnSave];
}

- (void)dealloc {

    [txtUserName release];
    [txtPassword release];
    [settingsFileName release];
    [dictSettings release];

    [super dealloc];
}

@end
```

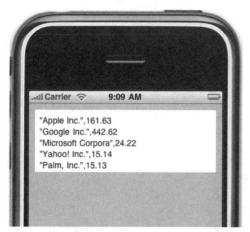

Figure 6.5 Retrieving and displaying stock quotes in an application.

Networking

Now you'll learn how you can accomplish some of the more common networking-related tasks on the iPhone. You'll see how to retrieve content from and send content to web pages. You'll also see how easy it is to work with web pages that require authentication. Finally, you'll use the Game Kit API to create a simple peer-to-peer chat application.

Retrieving content from web pages

The easiest way to get the HTML contents of a web page is by using the `stringWith ContentsOfURL:` method of `NSString`. Next you'll take a look at using this method to retrieve some stock quote data from the Yahoo! finance web page and display it in your application. **Figure 6.5** shows the completed application.

To retrieve stock quotes from a web page:

1. Create a new view-based application, saving it as GetWebContent.

2. Open GetWebContentViewController.h, and add an instance variable to display the web page you will be retrieving:

   `UITextView *resultsView;`

continues on next page

3. Switch to GetWebContentViewController.m, uncomment the `viewDidLoad` method, and add the following code:

```
CGRect resultsFrame = CGRectMake
→ (10,10,300,100);
resultsView = [[UITextView alloc]
→ initWithFrame:resultsFrame];
resultsView.font = [UIFont
→ systemFontOfSize:14.0];
[self.view addSubview:resultsView];
```

You first create a UITextView control that you'll use to display the stock quote information.

```
NSString *symbol = @"AAPL,GOOG,
→ MSFT,YHOO,PALM";
NSString *urlString = [NSString
→ stringWithFormat:@"http://finance.
→ yahoo.com/d/quotes.csv?f=no&s=%@",
→ symbol];
```

You next create a string containing the URL of the Yahoo! finance page. Note how `stringWithFormat:` is used to append the list of stock symbols to the query string.

```
NSURL *url = [NSURL
URLWithString:urlString];
NSString *quotes = [NSString
→ stringWithContentsOfURL:url];

resultsView.text = quotes;
```

Finally, you create an NSURL object and use it to populate a string with the contents of the web page before displaying it in your text view.

Code Listing 6.4 shows the completed code. Notice that there are `NSLog()` statements at the beginning and end of the method. If you examine the console, you will see that the web page content actually takes some time to be downloaded (depending on your Internet connection speed, of course). You may also have noticed that your application was unresponsive while the download was taking place. This is because `stringWithContentsOfURL:` uses a *synchronous* connection, so your application will effectively pause until the download is completed. Worse still, if the page cannot be loaded (either as a result of a bad URL or the server not responding), you won't be told of any errors. You can check this for yourself by changing the URL to an invalid page.

Code Listing 6.4 Retrieving stock quotes from a web page.

```
#import "GetWebContentViewController.h"

@implementation GetWebContentViewController

- (void)viewDidLoad {

    NSLog(@"started");
    CGRect resultsFrame = CGRectMake(10,10,300,100);
    resultsView = [[UITextView alloc] initWithFrame:resultsFrame];
    resultsView.font = [UIFont systemFontOfSize:14.0];
    [self.view addSubview:resultsView];

    NSString *symbol = @"AAPL,GOOG,MSFT,YHOO,PALM";
    NSString *url = @""
    NSString *urlString = [NSString stringWithFormat:@"http://finance.yahoo.com/d/quotes.csv?f=no&s=%@", symbol];
    NSURL *url = [NSURL URLWithString:urlString];
    NSString *quotes = [NSString stringWithContentsOfURL:url];

    resultsView.text = quotes;
    NSLog(@"done");
}

- (void)dealloc {

    [resultsView release];

    [super dealloc];
}

@end
```

Apple provides a more robust way of retrieving web pages—the NSURLConnection class—which allows you to use an *asynchronous* connection as well as deal with situations such as timeouts, server redirects, and errors.

To update the application to use an asynchronous connection:

1. Open GetWebContentViewController.h, and add an instance variable to hold the web page data:

   ```
   NSMutableData *receivedData;
   ```

2. Switch to GetWebContentViewController.m, and modify the viewDidLoad method, replacing the call to stringWithContent OfURL:

   ```
   receivedData=[[NSMutableData alloc]
   → initWithData:nil];


   NSURLRequest *req=[[NSURLRequest
   → alloc] initWithURL:url];
   NSURLConnection *conn =
   → [[NSURLConnection alloc]
   → initWithRequest:req
   → delegate:self];
   ```

   Here you first initialize an instance variable to hold the web page contents as it's received. Next you create an NSURLRequest object, assigning it the same NSURL you used last time, and then you use this NSURLRequest object to create an NSURLConnection object. NSURLConnection asynchronously loads the web page and sends messages to its delegate at various points during the process.

3. Finally, you need to implement the following three delegate methods of `NSURLConnection`:

▲ The `connection:didReceiveData:` delegate method will be called whenever some data is received from the `NSURLConnection`. Here you simply append the data to any that has already been received.

▲ The `connection:didFailWithError:` delegate method will be called if an error occurs. In this example, you display the error, but in a larger application, you might want to clean up your `receivedData` object.

▲ The `connectionDidFinishLoading:` delegate method is called when the `NRURLConnection` has finished loading the web page. You then create a string for the `receivedData` object and display it in the text view as before.

Code Listing 6.5 shows the updated application. If you again put `NSLog()` statements at the beginning and end of the `viewDidLoad` method, you should notice that the time stamp difference is almost zero and that your application starts up and displays the text view even before the stock data has finished downloading. If you also change the URL to an invalid web page, you should now see the error being handled and displayed in an alert view.

Apple recommends that any application that requires an Internet connection should first test for availability of the connection and inform the user if one isn't available. Although the code to perform this type of check is beyond the scope of this book, Apple does provide a sample application with full source code (the "Reachability" example) that shows how this can be done. You can download this application from the "Coding How-Tos" section of the *iPhone Developer Connection* Web site.

NETWORKING

Code Listing 6.5 The code, updated to retrieve stock quotes asynchronously.

```
#import "GetWebContentViewController.h"

@implementation GetWebContentViewController

- (void)connection:(NSURLConnection *)connection didReceiveData:(NSData *)data {

    [receivedData appendData:data];
}

- (void)connection:(NSURLConnection *)connection didFailWithError:(NSError *)error {

    UIAlertView *myAlert = [[UIAlertView alloc] initWithTitle:@"Error"
                                                message:[error localizedDescription]
                                               delegate:nil
                                      cancelButtonTitle:@"OK"
                                      otherButtonTitles:nil];
    [myAlert show];
    [myAlert release];
}

- (void)connectionDidFinishLoading:(NSURLConnection *)connection {

    NSString *quotes = [[NSString alloc]
                        initWithBytes:[receivedData bytes]
                        length:[receivedData length]
                        encoding:NSASCIIStringEncoding];
    resultsView.text = quotes;
    [quotes release];
}

- (void)viewDidLoad {

    NSLog(@"started");

    CGRect resultsFrame = CGRectMake(10,10,300,100);
    resultsView = [[UITextView alloc] initWithFrame:resultsFrame];
    resultsView.font = [UIFont systemFontOfSize:14.0];
    [self.view addSubview:resultsView];

    NSString *symbol = @"AAPL,GOOG,MSFT,YHOO,PALM";
    NSString *urlString = [NSString stringWithFormat:@"http://finance.yahoo.com/d/quotes.csv?f=no&s=%@", symbol];
    NSURL *url = [NSURL URLWithString:urlString];

    receivedData=[[NSMutableData alloc] initWithData:nil];

    NSURLRequest *req=[[NSURLRequest alloc] initWithURL:url];
    NSURLConnection *conn = [[NSURLConnection alloc] initWithRequest:req delegate:self];
    [req release];
    [conn release];

    NSLog(@"done");
}

- (void)dealloc {

    [resultsView release];
    [receivedData release];

    [super dealloc];
}

@end
```

Figure 6.6 Searching Wikipedia and displaying the results.

Code Listing 6.6 The header file for the Wikipedia search application.

```
#import <UIKit/UIKit.h>

@interface PostWebContentViewController : UIViewController {

    NSMutableData *receivedData;
    UIWebView *resultsView;
    NSString *baseURL;
}

@end
```

Sending data to web pages

So far, you've seen how to retrieve data (an HTTP "GET") from a web page, using the query string to pass information to the page. You may, however, want to write an application that simulates the user completing and submitting a form on a web page (usually done with an HTTP "POST").

In this example, you'll create an application that submits a search form to Wikipedia and displays the results in a web view. Note that Wikipedia could also be searched by passing the search criteria on the query string, a technique you've already learned in the "To retrieve stock quotes" exercise earlier in this chapter, so this example is for illustrative purposes only. **Figure 6.6** shows the completed application.

To create an application to search Wikipedia:

1. Create a new view-based application, saving it as PostWebContent.

2. Open PostWebContentController.h, and create some instance variables (**Code Listing 6.6**):

   ```
   NSMutableData *receivedData;
   UIWebView *resultsView;
   NSString *baseURL;
   ```

   Again, the receivedData variable will hold the web content, resultsView will be used to display the resulting HTML, and finally baseURL will be used to correctly resolve any links in the HTML.

continues on next page

3. Switch to PostWebContentController.m, uncomment the `viewDidLoad` method, and add the following code:

```
CGRect resultsFrame = CGRectMake
→ (10,10,300,440);
resultsView = [[UIWebView alloc]
→ initWithFrame:resultsFrame];
[self.view addSubview:resultsView];
```

You first create a web view and add it to your main view. The web view will display the search results.

```
baseURL = @"http://en.wikipedia.
→ org";
NSString *urlString = [baseURL
→ stringByAppendingString:@"/w/
→ index.php"];
NSURL *url = [NSURL URL
→ WithString:urlString];
```

Next construct your URL just as you did before.

```
receivedData=[[NSMutableData alloc]
→ initWithData:nil];
NSMutableURLRequest *req=
→ [[NSMutableURLRequest alloc]
→ initWithURL:url cachePolicy:
→ NSURLRequestReloadIgnoringLocal
→ CacheData timeoutInterval:30.0];
```

Now, initialize an instance variable to hold the content as it's received. This time, however, you create an `NSMutable Request` because you will be setting some properties on the request. You also tell the request to ignore any caching that may be happening and to time out after 30 seconds.

```
[req setHTTPMethod: @"POST"];
[req setHTTPBody:[@"search=iPhone"
→ dataUsingEncoding:NSISOLatin1
→ StringEncoding]];


NSURLConnection *conn =
→ [[NSURLConnection alloc]
→ initWithRequest:req
→ delegate:self];
```

Finally, you set the method of the request to be a POST, set a key-value pair to match the form file contained on the page, and then create an `NSURLConnection` just as you did earlier.

The delegates are implemented in the same way as earlier—only this time you load the resulting HTML into your web view and display the page. Notice that you also implement a fourth delegate, `connection:didReceiveResponse:`. This method is called each time a new response is received, which allows you to handle any page redirects that might happen. In this example, you reset the `receivedData` variable so that you have only the contents of the final page. **Code Listing 6.7** shows the completed code.

Code Listing 6.7 Posting content to a web page.

```
#import "PostWebContentViewController.h"

@implementation PostWebContentViewController

- (void)connection:(NSURLConnection *)connection didReceiveResponse:(NSHTTPURLResponse *)response {

    [receivedData setLength:0];
}

- (void)connection:(NSURLConnection *)connection didReceiveData:(NSData *)data {

    [receivedData appendData:data];
}

- (void)connection:(NSURLConnection *)connection didFailWithError:(NSError *)error {

    UIAlertView *myAlert = [[UIAlertView alloc] initWithTitle:@"Error"
                                                      message:[error localizedDescription]
                                                     delegate:nil
                                            cancelButtonTitle:@"OK"
                                            otherButtonTitles:nil];
    [myAlert show];
    [myAlert release];
}

- (void)connectionDidFinishLoading:(NSURLConnection *)connection {

    NSString *results = [[NSString alloc]
                            initWithBytes:[receivedData bytes]
                                   length:[receivedData length]
                                 encoding:NSASCIIStringEncoding];
    [resultsView loadHTMLString:results baseURL:[NSURL URLWithString:baseURL]];
    [results release];
}

- (void)viewDidLoad {

    CGRect resultsFrame = CGRectMake(10,10,300,440);
    resultsView = [[UIWebView alloc] initWithFrame:resultsFrame];
    [self.view addSubview:resultsView];

    baseURL = @"http://en.wikipedia.org";
    NSString *urlString = [baseURL stringByAppendingString:@"/w/index.php"];
    NSURL *url = [NSURL URLWithString:urlString];
    NSMutableURLRequest *req=[[NSMutableURLRequest alloc]
                                initWithURL:url
                                cachePolicy:NSURLRequestReloadIgnoringLocalCacheData
                            timeoutInterval:30.0];
    receivedData=[[NSMutableData alloc] initWithData:nil];
    [req setHTTPMethod: @"POST"];
    [req setHTTPBody:[@"search=iPhone" dataUsingEncoding:NSISOLatin1StringEncoding]];
    NSURLConnection *conn = [[NSURLConnection alloc] initWithRequest:req delegate:self];
    [req release];
    [conn release];
}

- (void)dealloc {

    [resultsView release];
    [receivedData release];

    [super dealloc];
}
```

NETWORKING

Figure 6.7 Posting a status update to Twitter.

Code Listing 6.8 The header file for the Twitter application.

```
000                    Code
#import <UIKit/UIKit.h>

@interface PostTweetViewController : UIViewController {

    NSMutableData *receivedData;
    UITextField *myTextField;
    UIButton *myButton;
}

@end
```

Responding to HTTP Authentication

So far, you've seen how to get data from and send data to web pages. Next you'll learn how you deal with pages that require authentication by posting a status update to Twitter. **Figure 6.7** shows the completed application.

To create an application to update your status on Twitter:

1. Create a new view-based application, saving it as PostTweet.

2. Open PostTweetViewController.h, and create some instance variables (**Code Listing 6.8**):

   ```
   NSMutableData *receivedData;
   UITextField *myTextField;
   UIButton *myButton;
   ```

   Just as in previous examples, received Data will hold the response from the Twitter server when you post your status update.

3. Switch to PostTweetViewController.m, uncomment the viewDidLoad method, and add the following code:

   ```
   [self createUI];
   ```

   ```
   receivedData=[[NSMutableData alloc]
   → initWithData:nil];
   ```

   You first call a method to create your user interface (a text field for the status update and a button to send the update) and then create the receivedData object.

   continues on next page

4. Implement the `tweetClick:` method:

```
[receivedData setLength:0];

NSString *twitterURL = @"http://
→ twitter.com/statuses/update.xml";
NSURL *url = [NSURL
→ URLWithString:twitterURL];

NSMutableURLRequest *req=
→ [[NSMutableURLRequest alloc]
→ initWithURL:url cachePolicy:NSURL
→ RequestReloadIgnoringLocal
→ CacheData timeoutInterval:30.0];

[req setHTTPMethod: @"POST"];
NSString *twitterBody=[NSString
→ stringWithFormat:@"status=%@",
→ myTextField.text];
[req setHTTPBody:[twitterBody
→ dataUsingEncoding:NSISOLatin1
→ StringEncoding]];

NSURLConnection *conn =
→ [[NSURLConnection alloc]
→ initWithRequest:req
→ delegate:self];
[req release];
[conn release];
```

This is almost the same code as you saw
in the previous exercise. After creating
and populating an NSURL object with the
URL of the Twitter update page, you create a key-value pair containing your text
field's text and post it to the server.

NETWORKING

5. The delegates are implemented just as previously, but this time, since Twitter requires authentication, you also need to implement the `connection:didReceive AuthenticationChallenge:` delegate:

```
NSString *userName = @"";
NSString *userPassword = @"";

if ([chg previousFailureCount] == 0)
{
    NSURLCredential *newCredential;
    newCredential=[NSURLCredential
    ⇥ credentialWithUser:userName
password:userPassword persistence:
⇥ NSURLCredentialPersistenceNone];
    [[chg sender]
useCredential:newCredential
⇥ forAuthenticationChallenge:chg];
}
else
    [[chg sender] cancelAuthentication
    ⇥ Challenge:chg];
```

By looking at the `previousFailureCount`, you can see how many times you have attempted to authenticate and have failed. Assuming you have never attempted to authenticate, you create an `NSURLCredential` object (using your Twitter username and password) and send these using the `useCredential:for AuthenticationChallenge:` method to the connection you created earlier. **Code Listing 6.9** shows the completed code.

In a real-world example, you wouldn't hard-code your username and password like this but would likely store them in the device keychain. Likewise, you would probably try to authenticate several times. In the previous exercise, when the `cancelAuthentication Challenge:` method is called, the `connection: didFailWithError:` delegate can be used to handle the failed authentication.

NETWORKING

Code Listing 6.9 Posting a status update on Twitter.

```
#import "PostTweetViewController.h"

@implementation PostTweetViewController

- (void)connection:(NSURLConnection *)connection didReceiveData:(NSData *)data {

    [receivedData appendData:data];
}

- (void)connection:(NSURLConnection *)connection didFailWithError:(NSError *)error {

    UIAlertView *myAlert = [[UIAlertView alloc] initWithTitle:@"Error"
                                                      message:[error localizedDescription]
                                                     delegate:nil
                                            cancelButtonTitle:@"OK"
                                            otherButtonTitles:nil];
    [myAlert show];
    [myAlert release];
}

- (void)connectionDidFinishLoading:(NSURLConnection *)connection {

    //log response
    NSString *result = [[NSString alloc]
                        initWithBytes:[receivedData bytes]
                               length:[receivedData length]
                             encoding:NSASCIIStringEncoding];
    NSLog(@"%@",result);
    [result release];

    //assume success
    UIAlertView *myAlert = [[UIAlertView alloc] initWithTitle:@"Success"
                                                      message:@"Tweet Posted successfully"
                                                     delegate:nil
                                            cancelButtonTitle:@"OK"
                                            otherButtonTitles:nil];
    [myAlert show];
    [myAlert release];
}

- (void)connection:(NSURLConnection *)connection didReceiveAuthenticationChallenge:(NSURLAuthenticationChallenge *)chg {

    NSString *userName = @"";
    NSString *userPassword = @"";

    if ([chg previousFailureCount] == 0)
    {
        NSURLCredential *newCredential;
        newCredential=[NSURLCredential credentialWithUser:userName
                                                 password:userPassword
                                              persistence:NSURLCredentialPersistenceNone];
        [[chg sender] useCredential:newCredential forAuthenticationChallenge:chg];
    }
    else
        [[chg sender] cancelAuthenticationChallenge:chg];
}
```

(code continues on next page)

NETWORKING

Code Listing 6.9 *continued*

```
- (void)tweetClick:(id)sender
{
    [receivedData setLength:0];

    NSString *twitterURL = @"http://twitter.com/statuses/update.xml";
    NSURL *url = [NSURL URLWithString:twitterURL];

    NSMutableURLRequest *req=[[NSMutableURLRequest alloc]
                             initWithURL:url
                             cachePolicy:NSURLRequestReloadIgnoringLocalCacheData
                             timeoutInterval:30.0];

    [req setHTTPMethod: @"POST"];
    NSString *twitterBody=[NSString stringWithFormat:@"status=%@",myTextField.text];
    [req setHTTPBody:[twitterBody dataUsingEncoding:NSISOLatin1StringEncoding]];

    NSURLConnection *conn = [[NSURLConnection alloc] initWithRequest:req delegate:self];
    [req release];
    [conn release];
}

- (void)createUI {

    CGRect textRect = CGRectMake(10,10,230,32);
    myTextField = [[UITextField alloc] initWithFrame:textRect];
    myTextField.borderStyle = UITextBorderStyleRoundedRect;
    [self.view addSubview:myTextField];

    CGRect buttonRect = CGRectMake(250,10,60,32);
    myButton = [UIButton buttonWithType:UIButtonTypeRoundedRect];
    [myButton setFrame:buttonRect];
    [myButton setTitle:@"Tweet" forState:UIControlStateNormal];
    [myButton addTarget:self action:@selector(tweetClick:) forControlEvents:UIControlEventTouchUpInside];
    [self.view addSubview:myButton];
}

- (void)viewDidLoad {

    [self createUI];

    receivedData=[[NSMutableData alloc] initWithData:nil];
}

- (void)dealloc {

    [myTextField release];
    [receivedData release];
    [super dealloc];
}

@end
```

Using a delegate for authentication works well in situations such as these. If your NSURLConnection request requires authentication, then the delegate method is called—otherwise, it won't be. You don't need to worry about constantly checking to see whether the authentication credentials are still valid on each request.

Notice also how in the connectionDid FinishLoading: delegate the receivedData object is logged to the console. Although this object was not strictly necessary for the example to work, you can use it to parse the Twitter server response and provide some type of meaningful feedback to the user.

Creating peer-to-peer applications

By using the Game Kit API, you can easily create peer-to-peer applications with very little code. All the networking complexity is handled for you, letting you connect devices over Bluetooth without having to do any pairing.

The GKSession class is built on top of the Bonjour networking service and allows you to create both client/server and peer-to-peer connections between devices. In a peer-to-peer scenario, you are notified of the state of the session (such as when a connection is successfully made) via its delegate methods. The GKSession class also handles all the sending and receiving of data between peers.

For selecting which peer to communicate with, you can use the GKPeerPickerController class. This presents a standard UI (**Figure 6.8**) showing you a list of the other peers. It also allows you to accept or decline a peer-to-peer connection request from another iPhone (**Figure 6.9**).

Figure 6.8 The peer picker controller lets you browse for other peers to communicate with.

Figure 6.9 Using the peer picker controller to accept an incoming chat request.

NETWORKING

Figure 6.10 The peer-to-peer chat application.

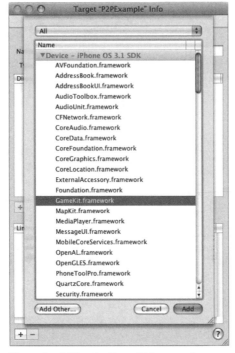

Figure 6.11 Adding the Game Kit framework.

Apple also provides an API to handle voice communication; we won't cover the API here, but you can implement it without too much code. Sample code for building a peer-to-peer voice chat is available in the "Coding How-Tos" section of the *iPhone Developer Connection* Web site.

Although the Game Kit API is geared toward in-game communication and voice, you can use it for other peer-to-peer applications. In this section, you'll use the Game Kit API to see how little code is needed to create a simple peer-to-peer chat application.

Unfortunately, in the current version of the iPhone development tools, the simulator cannot communicate with an iPhone over Bluetooth. This leaves the option of using either two iPhones or two computers both running the simulator. In the example presented here, the code is running in the simulator on two computers. **Figure 6.10** shows the completed application.

To create a peer-to-peer chat application:

1. Create a new view-based application, saving it as P2PExample.

2. In the Groups & Files pane, expand the Targets section, right-click your application target, and select Get Info.

3. Making sure the General tab is selected, click Add (+) at the bottom of the Linked Libraries list, and add GameKit.framework (**Figure 6.11**).

continues on next page

NETWORKING

4. Open P2PExampleViewController.h, include the GameKit.h header, add the GKPeerPickerControllerDelegate and GKSessionDelegate protocol declarations, and create some instance variables (**Code Listing 6.10**):

```
GKPeerPickerController *myPicker;
GKSession *mySession;
UITextView *myTextView;
UITextField *myTextField;
```

You create a peer picker controller that provides an interface to select who to chat with and a session object that will be used to connect and communicate with the other peer. You also create the objects that you'll use to create your user interface.

5. Switch to P2PExampleViewController.m, uncomment the viewDidLoad method, and add the following code:

```
[self createUI];

myPicker = [[GKPeerPickerController
→ alloc] init];

myPicker.connectionTypesMask =
→ GKPeerPickerConnectionTypeNearby;

myPicker.delegate = self;

[myPicker show];
```

You first call a method to create the user interface (a text view for the conversation and a text field and button to send messages). Next you create the peer picker. Setting connectionTypesMask to GKPeerPickerConnectionTypeNearby will make the iPhone use Bluetooth to look for other peers.

Code Listing 6.10 The header file for the peer-to-peer chat application.

```
#import <UIKit/UIKit.h>
#import <GameKit/GameKit.h>

@interface P2PExampleViewController : UIViewController

<GKPeerPickerControllerDelegate, GKSessionDelegate>

{
    GKPeerPickerController *myPicker;
    GKSession *mySession;
    UITextView *myTextView;
    UITextField *myTextField;
}

@end
```

Figure 6.12 Selecting a peer from the peer picker controller.

6. Implement the peer picker delegate method, `peerPickerController:session ForConnectionType:`, which is called when the peer picker is shown:

```
mySession = [[GKSession alloc]
→ initWithSessionID:@"p2pTest"
→ displayName:nil
sessionMode:GKSessionModePeer];
mySession.delegate = self;
return mySession;
```

This method creates and returns a new peer-to-peer session, giving it the ID p2pTest. Any other peers with the same session ID will show up in the peer picker (**Figure 6.12**).

7. You need to implement a delegate method used by your `GKSession` object. The `session:didChangeState:` method is called whenever your session changes state (in this example, when you get a connection to another peer):

```
[mySession setDataReceiveHandler:
→ self withContext:nil];
[myPicker dismiss];
[self sendChatText:@"connected"];
```

Here you tell the session to look in the current object for its receive handler. You also tell the peer picker to hide (since you now have a connection to another peer) and send an initial message to the other iPhone.

continues on next page

NETWORKING

8. Implement the receive handler method
`receiveData:fromPeer:inSession:`
`context:` that was set up in the previous step:

```
NSString *receivedText = [[NSString
→ alloc] initWithData:data
→ encoding:NSUTF8StringEncoding];
NSString *peerName = [[NSString
→ alloc] initWithString:[session
→ displayNameForPeer:peer]];
myTextView.text = [NSString
→ stringWithFormat:@"%@\n[%@]:
→ @",myTextView.text,peerName,
→ receivedText];
```

You create a string from the received data
(the text sent from the other peer), get
the name of the peer, and then append
everything to your text view to show the
conversation.

9. Now that you've written the receive method,
the final step is to implement the send
method (called by the Send button):

```
NSData *sendData = [newText
→ dataUsingEncoding:NSUTF8
→ StringEncoding];
[mySession sendDataToAllPeers:
→ sendData withDataMode:
→ GKSendDataReliable error:nil];
myTextView.text = [NSString
→ stringWithFormat:@"%@\n[ME]:
→ %@",myTextView.text,newText];
```

This is just the reverse of step 8; here
you're creating an `NSData` object from
your message string and sending the data
to the other peer. Again, you append this
text to the text view to show the conversation. **Code Listing 6.11** shows the
completed code.

NETWORKING

Code Listing 6.11 The completed code for the peer-to-peer chat application.

```
#import "P2PExampleViewController.h"

@implementation P2PExampleViewController

- (void)sendChatText:(NSString *)newText {

    NSData *sendData = [newText dataUsingEncoding:NSUTF8StringEncoding];
    [mySession sendDataToAllPeers:sendData withDataMode:GKSendDataReliable error:nil];
    myTextView.text = [NSString stringWithFormat:@"%@\n[ME]: %@",myTextView.text,newText];
}

-(void)buttonClick:(id)sender {

    [self sendChatText:myTextField.text];
    [myTextField setText:@""];
}

- (void)createUI {

    myTextView = [[UITextView alloc] initWithFrame:CGRectMake(10,10,300,180)];
    [myTextView setEditable:NO];
    [self.view addSubview:myTextView];

    myTextField = [[UITextField alloc] initWithFrame:CGRectMake(10,200,230,30)];
    myTextField.borderStyle = UITextBorderStyleRoundedRect;
    [self.view addSubview:myTextField];

    UIButton *myButton = [UIButton buttonWithType:UIButtonTypeRoundedRect];
    [myButton setFrame:CGRectMake(250,200,60,32)];
    [myButton setTitle:@"Send" forState:UIControlStateNormal];
    [myButton addTarget:self action:@selector(buttonClick:) forControlEvents:UIControlEventTouchUpInside];
    [self.view addSubview:myButton];
}

- (void)viewDidLoad {

    [self createUI];

    myPicker  = [[GKPeerPickerController alloc] init];
    myPicker.delegate = self;
    myPicker.connectionTypesMask = GKPeerPickerConnectionTypeNearby;
    //myPicker.connectionTypesMask = GKPeerPickerConnectionTypeNearby | GKPeerPickerConnectionTypeOnline;
    [myPicker show];
}

- (GKSession *)peerPickerController:(GKPeerPickerController *)pck sessionForConnectionType:(GKPeerPickerConnectionType)ct
{
    mySession = [[GKSession alloc] initWithSessionID:@"p2pTest"  displayName:nil sessionMode:GKSessionModePeer];
    mySession.delegate = self;

    return mySession;
}

- (void)session:(GKSession *)session peer:(NSString *)peerID didChangeState:(GKPeerConnectionState)state {

    switch (state) {

        case GKPeerStateConnected:
            [mySession setDataReceiveHandler:self withContext:nil];
            [myPicker dismiss];
            [self sendChatText:@"connected"];
            break;

        case GKPeerStateDisconnected:
            break;
    }
}
```

(code continues on next page)

NETWORKING

Code Listing 6.11 *continued*

```
- (void)receiveData:(NSData *)data fromPeer:(NSString *)peer inSession: (GKSession *)session context:(void *)ctx
{
    NSString *receivedText = [[NSString alloc] initWithData:data encoding:NSUTF8StringEncoding];
    NSString *peerName = [[NSString alloc] initWithString:[session displayNameForPeer:peer]];
    myTextView.text = [NSString stringWithFormat:@"%@\n[%@]: %@",myTextView.text,peerName,receivedText];

    [peerName release];
    [receivedText release];
}

- (void)dealloc {

    [myPicker release];
    [mySession release];

    [super dealloc];
}

@end
```

TOUCHES, SHAKES, AND ORIENTATION

7

The iPhone's primary interface is its large Multi-Touch display. Since it doesn't have a physical keyboard, everything is accomplished via this screen. The iPhone takes things much further than a simple keyboard, however, allowing you to interact with your applications in a very natural and intuitive way. Objects onscreen can be moved, zoomed in or out, and scrolled using simple gestures.

The iPhone can also respond to changes in orientation; it can automatically switch and resize the display to portrait or landscape when you rotate the phone, and it can react to shakes and tilting.

In this chapter you'll see how easy it is to add both single-touch and Multi-Touch support to your applications, including responding to tapping, pinching, rotating, and zooming. You'll learn how you can respond to shake motions before looking at the iPhone's accelerometer and how to control your application UI based on changes in the phone's orientation.

Touch

In the iPhone SDK, all UIKit classes that descend from UIView are what are known as *responder objects*—subclasses of the UIResponder class. Among other things, this class is responsible for providing access to and handling touch and motion events within an iPhone application.

Touch-based events are handled via four main methods:

◆ touchesBegan:withEvent:—Sent at the beginning of a touch life cycle, when the user first touches the screen of the iPhone.

◆ touchesMoved:withEvent:—Sent as the user moves their finger or fingers around on the screen of the iPhone.

◆ touchesEnded:withEvent:—Sent when the user lifts their fingers off the iPhone screen and ends the touch.

◆ touchesCancelled:withEvent:—Sent when the system receives a cancellation event. This can occur in situations such as a low-memory warning or when a phone call is received. Generally, you would use this method to perform any necessary code cleanup for objects and data generated by the other touch methods.

All four of these methods receive a UIEvent object containing UITouch objects for each finger that is interacting with the screen (or, in the case of the touchesEnded:withEvent: method, for each finger that has just been lifted from the screen).

The UITouch object allows you to determine not only *what* is being touched but *when* and *where* it was touched. In the case of movement, it also lets you know where the touched object was and where it was moved.

Code Listing 7.1 The header file of the touch-based application.

```
000                    Code
//
//  TouchExampleViewController.h
//  TouchExample
//

#import <UIKit/UIKit.h>

@interface TouchExampleViewController : UIViewController
{
    UIView *redBox;
}

@end
```

To create a touch-based application:

1. Create a new view-based application, saving it as TouchExample.

2. Open the TouchExampleViewController.h file, and create an instance variable to hold the view you will be controlling by touch (**Code Listing 7.1**).

3. Switch to the TouchExampleView Controller.m file, uncomment the view DidLoad method, and add the following code:

   ```
   float boxSize  = 100.0;
   CGRect redBoxRect = CGRectMake
   → (110,180,boxSize,boxSize);
   redBox = [[UIView alloc]
   → initWithFrame:redBoxRect];
   redBox.backgroundColor =
   → [UIColor redColor];
   [self.view addSubview:redBox];
   ```

   Here you are simply creating a UIView with a red background, setting its dimensions, and adding it to the main.

4. Implement touchesMoved:withEvent: to handle the touch movement:

   ```
   UITouch *touch = [[event touches
   → ForView:redBox] anyObject];
   CGPoint currentPoint = [touch
   → locationInView:self.view];
   ```

   You first retrieve the touch events for the red box view, and then you calculate its location (in relation to its containing view).

   ```
   [touch view].center = currentPoint;
   ```

   Then you set the center of the red box view to the point being touched. **Code Listing 7.2** shows the completed application code.

5. Build and run the application.

   You should be able to move the red box by touching the iPhone's screen.

TOUCH

Code Listing 7.2 The completed touch-based application.

```
#import "TouchExampleViewController.h"

@implementation TouchExampleViewController

- (void)viewDidLoad {

    [super viewDidLoad];

    float boxSize = 100.0;
    CGRect redBoxRect = CGRectMake(110,180,boxSize,boxSize);
    redBox = [[UIView alloc] initWithFrame:redBoxRect];
    redBox.backgroundColor = [UIColor redColor];

    [self.view addSubview:redBox];
}

- (void)touchesMoved:(NSSet *)touches withEvent:(UIEvent *)event {

    UITouch *touch = [[event touchesForView:redBox] anyObject];
    CGPoint currentPoint = [touch locationInView:self.view];

    if (touch.view != self.view)
        [touch view].center = currentPoint;
}

- (void)dealloc {

    [redBox release];
    redBox = nil;

    [super dealloc];
}

@end
```

Code Listing 7.3 The updated header file for the touch-based application.

```
● ● ●                  Code
//
//  TouchExampleViewController.h
//  TouchExample
//

#import <UIKit/UIKit.h>

@interface TouchExampleViewController : UIViewController
{
    UIView *redBox;
    UIView *blueBox;
    UIView *greenBox;
}

@end
```

This simple exercise shows how easy it is to add touch support to applications. Now you'll extend the example to deal with multiple views onscreen, allowing them to be moved around independently of each other. You'll also add a simple zoom animation effect to show which view you are currently touching.

To update the touch-based application:

1. Open TouchExampleViewController.h, and create two more instance variables (**Code Listing 7.3**).

2. Modify the viewDidLoad method to create three different-colored boxes, and add them to the main view.

3. Implement the touchesBegan:withEvent: method:

    ```
    UITouch *touch = [touches
    → anyObject];

    if (touch.view != self.view)
    {…
    ```

    This time, since you have multiple views being touched, you need to check that you are not receiving a touch event from the main, containing view:

    ```
    [self.view bringSubviewToFront:
    → touch.view];
    ```

    You then make sure the view you are touching moves to the front of the screen:

    ```
    float zoom = -25.0;

    CGRect newRect = CGRectInset([touch.
    → view frame], zoom,zoom);


    [UIView beginAnimations:nil
    → context:NULL];

    [UIView setAnimationDuration:0.2];

    [touch.view setFrame:newRect];

    [UIView commitAnimations];
    ```

TOUCH

continues on next page

Next, you create a CGRect that has a frame 25 pixels larger than the touched view and tell the touched view to resize itself. Doing this inside a beginAnimations.. commitAnimations block makes the resize animate nicely.

4. Finally, you implement the touchesEnded: withEvent: method, which is essentially the reverse of the previous step.

Notice that this time you specify a positive value for the CGRectInset function, creating a smaller CGRect. **Code Listing 7.4** shows the updated code.

Code Listing 7.4 The updated touch-based application.

```
#import "TouchExampleViewController.h"

@implementation TouchExampleViewController

- (void)viewDidLoad {

    [super viewDidLoad];

    float boxSize = 100.0;
    CGRect redBoxRect = CGRectMake(0,180,boxSize,boxSize);
    redBox = [[UIView alloc] initWithFrame:redBoxRect];
    redBox.backgroundColor = [UIColor redColor];

    CGRect blueBoxRect = CGRectMake(110,180,boxSize,boxSize);
    blueBox = [[UIView alloc] initWithFrame:blueBoxRect];
    blueBox.backgroundColor = [UIColor blueColor];

    CGRect greenBoxRect = CGRectMake(220,180,boxSize,boxSize);
    greenBox = [[UIView alloc] initWithFrame:greenBoxRect];
    greenBox.backgroundColor = [UIColor greenColor];

    [self.view addSubview:redBox];
    [self.view addSubview:blueBox];
    [self.view addSubview:greenBox];
}

- (void)touchesMoved:(NSSet *)touches withEvent:(UIEvent *)event {

    UITouch *touch = [[event allTouches] anyObject];
    CGPoint currentPoint = [touch locationInView:self.view];

    if (touch.view != self.view)
        [touch view].center = currentPoint;
}
```

(code continues on next page)

Figure 7.1 Moving multiple views by touch.

5. Build and run your application.

Touching a colored box should cause it to come to the front and animate to a larger size (**Figure 7.1**). You can move the box around the screen, and when you let go, it will animate back down to its original size.

Adding tapping support

The `tapCount` property of a `touch` object is the key to adding tap and long-touch support to your applications.

If you revisit the `touchesBegan:withEvent:` method of the previous example and add the following line

```
NSLog(@"tap count: %i",[touch
→ tapCount]);
```

Code Listing 7.4 *continued*

```
- (void)touchesBegan:(NSSet *)touches withEvent:(UIEvent *)event {

    UITouch *touch = [[event allTouches] anyObject];

    if (touch.view != self.view) {
        [self.view bringSubviewToFront:touch.view];

        float zoom = -25.0;
        CGRect newRect = CGRectInset([touch.view frame],zoom,zoom);

        [UIView beginAnimations:nil context:NULL];
        [UIView setAnimationDuration:0.2];
        [touch.view setFrame:newRect];
        [UIView commitAnimations];
    }
}
- (void)touchesEnded:(NSSet *)touches withEvent:(UIEvent *)event {

    UITouch *touch = [[event allTouches] anyObject];
    if (touch.view != self.view) {
        float zoom = 25.0;
        CGRect newRect = CGRectInset([touch.view frame], zoom,zoom);

        [UIView beginAnimations:nil context:NULL];
        [UIView setAnimationDuration:0.2];
        [touch.view setFrame:newRect];
        [UIView commitAnimations];
    }
}
- (void)dealloc {

    [redBox release];
    [blueBox release];
    [greenBox release];

    [super dealloc];
}
@end
```

TOUCH

you can see the tap counts being logged to the console (**Figure 7.2**). There's a problem here, however: Along with double-tap events, you still see events for the single-tap. You need to figure out a way of telling these two apart and ignoring the single-tap events when you double-tap.

Figure 7.2 Logging tap counts to the Debugger Console.

One simple way to do this is to add a small delay to when you actually deal with the tap events, canceling earlier tap events when later tap events occur. This sounds confusing, but it's actually very easy to do.

Other uses for CGRect

In the previous exercise, "To update the touch-based application," you use `CGRectInset` to increase or decrease the size of the `CGRect`. There are many other useful functions that make working with `CGRect`s easier; among them are the following:

`CGRectOffset` creates a rectangle with the origin offset to a source `CGRect`:

```
float offset = 25.0;
CGRect r1 = CGRectMake(100,100,100,100);
CGRect r2 = CGRectOffset(r1,offset,offset);
```

`CGRectIntersectsRect` lets you determine whether two rectangles intersect each other:

```
CGRect r1 = CGRectMake(100,100,100,100);
CGRect r2 = CGRectMake(150,150,100,100);
if (CGRectInstersectsRect(r1,r2)
    NSLog(@"intersecting");
```

`NSStringFromCGRect` is useful for logging `CGRect`s to the console:

```
CGRect r1 = CGRectMake(100,100,100,100);
NSLog(@"rect: %@",NSStringFromCGRect(r1));
```

Likewise, `CGRectFromString` allows you to create a `CGRect` from a string:

```
NSString *r = @"{0,0},{100,100}";
CGRect r1 = CGRectFromString(r);
```

See the `CGGeometry` reference entry in the Apple developer documentation for more details.

To add single-tap and double-tap support:

1. Open TouchExampleViewController.m, and modify the `touchesBegan:withEvent:` method (**Code Listing 7.5**):

`float tapDelay = 0.4;`

This is the amount of time you wait before processing a tap event, which gives you time to check whether it's a single-tap or a double-tap:

`switch ([touch tapCount])`

continues on next page

Code Listing 7.5 Handling double-taps.

```
- (void)touchesBegan:(NSSet *)touches withEvent:(UIEvent *)event {

    UITouch *touch = [[event allTouches] anyObject];

    if (touch.view != self.view)
    {
        float tapDelay = 0.4f;

        switch ([touch tapCount])
        {
            case 1:
                [self performSelector:@selector(singleTap:) withObject:touch.view afterDelay:tapDelay];
                break;

            case 2:
                [NSObject cancelPreviousPerformRequestsWithTarget:self selector:@selector(singleTap:) object:touch.view];
                [self doubleTap:touch.view];
                break;
        }

        [self.view bringSubviewToFront:touch.view];

        float zoom = -25.0;
        CGRect newRect = CGRectInset([touch.view frame], zoom,zoom);

        [UIView beginAnimations:nil context:NULL];
        [UIView setAnimationDuration:0.2];
        [touch.view setFrame:newRect];
        [UIView commitAnimations];
    }
}
```

TOUCH

2. Next you check to see how many taps you have received:

```
case 1:
[self performSelector:@selector
→ (singleTap) withObject:touch.view
→ afterDelay:tapDelay];
```

If you've received a single tap, you make a delayed call to the `singleTap` method:

```
case 2:
[NSObject cancelPreviousPerform
→ RequestsWithTarget:self selector:
→ @selector(singleTap) object:
→ touch.view];

[self doubleTap:touch.view];
```

If you get a double-tap, you first cancel the call to the `singleTap` method before calling `doubleTap`.

✔ Tip

■ Notice how this code could easily be extended to add support for triple or even quadruple taps; however, you may have to increase the value for `tapDelay` to give the user time to perform more than a double-click.

Adding long-touch support

One other useful touch-based interaction is the touch-and-hold, or *long-touch*, effect—as seen on the iPhone home screen when you move applications around or delete them.

Just as in the double-tap example, you make a delayed call to the long-touch method in the `touchesBegan:withEvent:` method; however, this time, since you are effectively dealing with a single-tap only, you cancel the call in the `touchesEnded:withEvent:` method instead.

Figure 7.3 Adding the QuartzCore framework to the project.

Code Listing 7.6 The updated header file.

```
● ● ●              Code
//
//   TouchExampleViewController.h
//   TouchExample
//

#import <UIKit/UIKit.h>
#import <QuartzCore/QuartzCore.h>

@interface TouchExampleViewController : UIViewController
{
    UIView *redBox;
    UIView *blueBox;
    UIView *greenBox;
}

@end
```

Figure 7.4 The simulator showing the animated view.

For bonus points, you'll now make the view "wiggle" just like on the iPhone home screen.

To add long-touch support:

1. In the Groups & Files pane, expand the Targets section, right-click your application target, and select Get Info.

2. Making sure the General tab is selected, click Add (+) at the bottom of the Linked Libraries list, and add QuartzCore.framework (**Figure 7.3**).

3. Open the TouchesExampleViewController.h file, and import the QuartzCore framework (**Code Listing 7.6**).

4. Back in TouchesExampleViewController.m, modify the touchesBegan:withEvent: method:

   ```
   float tapDelay = 1.0f;
   [self performSelector:@selector
   →(startWiggle:) withObject:touch.
   →view afterDelay:tapDelay];
   ```

   Here you set the tap delay to be a slightly larger value than earlier (1 second) before calling the startWiggle: method, passing the view you want to animate.

5. In the touchesEnded:withEvent: method, you make sure to cancel any pending touches, and then you tell the touched view to stop animating.

6. Finally, you implement the startWiggle: and stopWiggle: methods that cause the view to animate.

   Code Listing 7.7 shows the completed code.

7. Build and run the application.

   If you long-touch one of the views, it should start animating (**Figure 7.4**).

TOUCH

Code Listing 7.7 The completed touch-based application.

```
#import "TouchExampleViewController.h"

@implementation TouchExampleViewController

- (void)viewDidLoad {

    [super viewDidLoad];

    float boxSize = 100.0;
    CGRect redBoxRect = CGRectMake(0,180,boxSize,boxSize);
    redBox = [[UIView alloc] initWithFrame:redBoxRect];
    redBox.backgroundColor = [UIColor redColor];

    CGRect blueBoxRect = CGRectMake(110,180,boxSize,boxSize);
    blueBox = [[UIView alloc] initWithFrame:blueBoxRect];
    blueBox.backgroundColor = [UIColor blueColor];

    CGRect greenBoxRect = CGRectMake(220,180,boxSize,boxSize);
    greenBox = [[UIView alloc] initWithFrame:greenBoxRect];
    greenBox.backgroundColor = [UIColor greenColor];

    [self.view addSubview:redBox];
    [self.view addSubview:blueBox];
    [self.view addSubview:greenBox];
}

- (void)startWiggle:(UIView *)theView {

    CALayer *viewLayer = [theView layer];
    CABasicAnimation *anim = [CABasicAnimation animationWithKeyPath:@"transform"];
    anim.duration = 0.1;
    anim.repeatCount = 1e100f;
    anim.autoreverses = YES;
    anim.fromValue = [NSValue valueWithCATransform3D:CATransform3DRotate(viewLayer.transform, -0.1,0.0,0.0,0.5)];
    anim.toValue = [NSValue valueWithCATransform3D:CATransform3DRotate(viewLayer.transform, 0.1,0.0,0.0,0.5)];
    [viewLayer addAnimation:anim forKey:@"wiggle"];
}

- (void)touchesMoved:(NSSet *)touches withEvent:(UIEvent *)event {

    UITouch *touch = [[event allTouches] anyObject];
    CGPoint currentPoint = [touch locationInView:self.view];

    if (touch.view != self.view)
        [touch view].center = currentPoint;

}

- (void)touchesBegan:(NSSet *)touches withEvent:(UIEvent *)event {

    UITouch *touch = [[event allTouches] anyObject];

    if (touch.view != self.view)
    {
        //long-tap support
        float tapDelay = 1.0f;
        [self performSelector:@selector(startWiggle:)
                    withObject:touch.view
                    afterDelay:tapDelay];

        [self.view bringSubviewToFront:touch.view];

        float zoom = -25.0;
        CGRect newRect = CGRectInset([touch.view frame], zoom,zoom);

        [UIView beginAnimations:nil context:NULL];
        [UIView setAnimationDuration:0.2];
        [touch.view setFrame:newRect];
        [UIView commitAnimations];
    }
}
```

(code continues on next page)

TOUCH

Code Listing 7.7 *continued*

```
○ ○ ○                                    Code
- (void)touchesEnded:(NSSet *)touches withEvent:(UIEvent *)event {

    UITouch *touch = [[event allTouches] anyObject];
    if (touch.view != self.view)
    {
        //cancel any pending long-touches
        [NSObject cancelPreviousPerformRequestsWithTarget:self
                                        selector:@selector(startWiggle:)
                                          object:touch.view];

        //make sure we are no longer wiggling
        [self stopWiggle:touch.view];

        [self.view bringSubviewToFront:touch.view];

        float zoom = 25.0;
        CGRect newRect = CGRectInset([touch.view frame], zoom,zoom);

        [UIView beginAnimations:nil context:NULL];
        [UIView setAnimationDuration:0.2];
        [touch.view setFrame:newRect];
        [UIView commitAnimations];
    }
}

- (void)dealloc {

    [redBox release];
    [blueBox release];
    [greenBox release];

    [super dealloc];
}

@end
```

Multi-Touch Gestures

So far you've looked at dealing with single-touch events only. However, the real power of the iPhone becomes apparent once you start thinking about Multi-Touch events. Features such as pinching and zooming can be accomplished only when you use multiple fingers to interact with the display of the iPhone.

You'll now create an application similar to the previous example, but this time you'll have it support Multi-Touch events.

To create an application that supports Multi-Touch gestures:

1. Create a new view-based application, and save it as MultiTouchExample.

2. Open the MultiTouchExampleView Controller.h file, and create an instance variable to hold the Multi-Touch-compliant view (**Code Listing 7.8**).

3. Switch to the MultiTouchExample ViewController.m file, uncomment the viewDidLoad method, and add the following code:

```
float boxSize = 100.0;
CGRect redBoxRect = CGRectMake
→(110,180,boxSize,boxSize);
redBox = [[UIView alloc]
→initWithFrame:redBoxRect];
redBox.backgroundColor =
→[UIColor redColor];
redBox.mutipleTouchEnabled = YES;
[self.view addSubview:redBox];
```

This is just the same code you used in the touch-based application except that this time you've enabled Multi-Touch by setting the multipleTouchEnabled property of the view to YES.

4. Next, back in the `touchesBegan:withEvent:` method, you retrieve the set of touches for the red box view:

```
for (UITouch *touch in [event
→ touchesForView:redBox])
```

Then you log the location `CGPoint` of the touch event to the console. **Code Listing 7.9** show the completed code.

continues on next page

Code Listing 7.8 The header file for the Multi-Touch application.

```
//
// MultiTouchExampleViewController.h
// MultiTouchExample
//

#import <UIKit/UIKit.h>

@interface MultiTouchExampleViewController : UIViewController
{
    UIView *redBox;
}

@end
```

Code Listing 7.9 Logging multiple touches to the console.

```
#import "MultiTouchExampleViewController.h"

@implementation MultiTouchExampleViewController

- (void)viewDidLoad {

    float boxSize = 100.0;
    CGRect redBoxRect = CGRectMake(110,180,boxSize,boxSize);
    redBox = [[UIView alloc] initWithFrame:redBoxRect];
    redBox.backgroundColor = [UIColor redColor];
    redBox.multipleTouchEnabled = YES;

    [self.view addSubview:redBox];
}

- (void)touchesBegan:(NSSet *)touches withEvent:(UIEvent *)event {

    for (UITouch *touch in [event touchesForView:redBox])
        NSLog(@"touch at location: %@",
                NSStringFromCGPoint([touch locationInView:self.view]));
}

- (void)dealloc {
    [super dealloc];
}

@end
```

5. Build and run the application, and try touching the red box view with multiple fingers.

You should see multiple touch events being logged in the console (**Figure 7.5**). If you are using the simulator, you can simulate multiple touches by holding down the Option key. The simulator is limited to only two simultaneous touches.

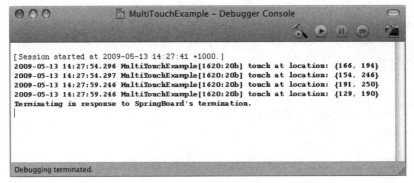

Figure 7.5 Logging touch locations to the Debugger Console.

Figure 7.6 Rotating the view.

Having multiple touches is what gives the iPhone its pinch, rotate, and zoom gestures. You'll now update the application to add this functionality.

To add pinch, rotate, and zoom gestures:

1. Open MultiTouchExampleViewController.m, and modify touchesMoved:withEvent:

```
if ([[event touchesForView:redBox]
→ count] == 1)
{
UITouch *touch  = [[[event
→ touchesForView:redBox] allObjects]
→ objectAtIndex:0];

redBox.transform = transformWith
→ Rotation(redBox.transform,
→ touch,redBox,self.view);
}
```

If there is only a single-touch, you call a function to rotate the view.

```
if ([[event touchesForView:redBox]
→ count] == 2)
{
UITouch *touch1  = [[[event
→ touchesForView:redBox] allObjects]
→ objectAtIndex:0];

UITouch *touch2 = [[[event
→ touchesForView:redBox] allObjects]
→ objectAtIndex:1];

redBox.transform = transformWith
→ Scale(redBox.transform, touch1,
→ touch2);
}
```

If there are two touches you call a function to scale the view. **Code Listing 7.10** shows the completed code.

2. Build and run the application.

   To rotate the red box, use a single finger. To zoom in and out, use two fingers and a zoom or pinch gesture. **Figure 7.6** shows the application after a zoom and a rotation have taken place.

Code Listing 7.10 The updated code for the multi-touch application. You can rotate the view by touching with a single finger and scale by touching with two fingers.

```
#import "MultiTouchExampleViewController.h"

@implementation MultiTouchExampleViewController

- (void)viewDidLoad {

    [super viewDidLoad];

    float boxSize = 100.0;
    CGRect redBoxRect = CGRectMake(110,180,boxSize,boxSize);
    redBox = [[UIView alloc] initWithFrame:redBoxRect];
    redBox.backgroundColor = [UIColor redColor];
    redBox.multipleTouchEnabled = YES;

    [self.view addSubview:redBox];
}

CGFloat distanceBetweenPoints(CGPoint pt1, CGPoint pt2) {
    CGFloat distance;

    CGFloat xDifferenceSquared = pow(pt1.x - pt2.x, 2);
    CGFloat yDifferenceSquared = pow(pt1.y - pt2.y, 2);
    distance = sqrt(xDifferenceSquared + yDifferenceSquared);

    return distance;
}

CGAffineTransform transformWithScale(CGAffineTransform oldTransform,
                                     UITouch *touch1,
                                     UITouch *touch2) {

    CGPoint touch1Location = [touch1 locationInView:nil];
    CGPoint touch1PreviousLocation = [touch1 previousLocationInView:nil];
    CGPoint touch2Location = [touch2 locationInView:nil];
    CGPoint touch2PreviousLocation = [touch2 previousLocationInView:nil];


    // Get distance between points
    CGFloat distance = distanceBetweenPoints(touch1Location,
                                             touch2Location);

    CGFloat prevDistance = distanceBetweenPoints(touch1PreviousLocation,
                                                 touch2PreviousLocation);

    // Figure new scale
    CGFloat scaleRatio = distance / prevDistance;

    CGAffineTransform newTransform = CGAffineTransformScale(oldTransform, scaleRatio, scaleRatio);

    // Return result
    return newTransform;
}

CGAffineTransform transformWithRotation(CGAffineTransform oldTransform,
                                        UITouch *touch,
                                        UIView *view,
                                        id superview) {
    CGPoint pt1 = [touch locationInView:superview];
    CGPoint pt2 = [touch previousLocationInView:superview];
    CGPoint center = view.center;
    CGFloat angle1 = atan2( center.y - pt2.y, center.x - pt2.x );
    CGFloat angle2 = atan2( center.y - pt1.y, center.x - pt1.x );

    CGAffineTransform newTransform = CGAffineTransformRotate(oldTransform, angle2-angle1);

    // Return result
    return newTransform;
}
```

(code continues on next page)

Code Listing 7.10 *continued*

```
- (void)touchesMoved:(NSSet *)touches withEvent:(UIEvent *)event {

    if ([[event touchesForView:redBox] count] == 1)
    {
        UITouch *touch = [[[event touchesForView:redBox] allObjects] objectAtIndex:0];
        redBox.transform = transformWithRotation(redBox.transform,touch,redBox,self.view);
    }

    if ([[event touchesForView:redBox] count] == 2)
    {
        UITouch *touch1 = [[[event touchesForView:redBox] allObjects] objectAtIndex:0];
        UITouch *touch2 = [[[event touchesForView:redBox] allObjects] objectAtIndex:1];
        redBox.transform = transformWithScale(redBox.transform, touch1, touch2);
    }
}

- (void)touchesBegan:(NSSet *)touches withEvent:(UIEvent *)event {

    for (UITouch *touch in [event touchesForView:redBox])
        NSLog(@"touch at location: %@",NSStringFromCGPoint([touch locationInView:self.view]));

}

- (void)dealloc {

    [redBox release];

    [super dealloc];
}

@end
```

The iPhone Accelerometer

The iPhone's accelerometer allows it to automatically detect movement of the phone such as tilting or shaking. The iPhone knows when the phone is rotated between portrait mode and landscape mode, and it's even able to tell whether it is face-up or face-down.

Having access to this information enables you to provide a very rich user experience that can dynamically change. For example, the display can automatically adjust when the phone is rotated, and characters in games can be controlled by simply tilting the phone.

You'll now learn how you go about using the accelerometer in your own applications.

Detecting shakes

Motion events are similar to the touch events described earlier but are much simpler to deal with. An event is generated only when a motion *starts* or *stops*—you can't track individual motions as you can with touch events.

Handling a shake motion is accomplished via three methods:

◆ `motionBegan:withEvent:`—Called when a motion event begins.

◆ `motionEnded:withEvent:`—Called when a motion event ends.

◆ `motionCancelled:withEvent:`—Called if the system thinks the motion is not a shake. Shakes are determined to be approximately a second or so in length.

To create an application that supports shakes:

1. Create a new view-based application, saving it as ShakeExample.

2. Open the ShakeExampleViewController.m file, uncomment the `viewDidAppear:` method, and add the following code:

   `[self becomeFirstResponder];`

   For the view controller to receive motion events, it needs to be the *first responder*—the object at the start of the chain of `UIResponder` subclasses. You also need to implement one more method to make the view controller the first responder:

   ```
   - (BOOL)canBecomeFirstResponder {
   return YES;
   }
   ```

3. Finally, you implement the three methods responsible for handling motion events. **Code Listing 7.11** shows the completed code.

4. Build and run the application.

   If you shake your iPhone, you should see messages being logged to the console. If you are running the application in the simulator, you can generate a shake by pressing Shift+Command+Z.

Code Listing 7.11 The completed code for the shake application.

```
#import "ShakeExampleViewController.h"

@implementation ShakeExampleViewController

-(void)viewDidAppear:(BOOL)animated {

    [self becomeFirstResponder];
    [super viewDidAppear:animated];
}

- (BOOL)canBecomeFirstResponder {

    return YES;
}

- (void)motionBegan:(UIEventSubtype)motion withEvent:(UIEvent *)event {

    if (event.type == UIEventTypeMotion && event.subtype == UIEventSubtypeMotionShake)
        NSLog(@"shake began");
}

- (void)motionEnded:(UIEventSubtype)motion withEvent:(UIEvent *)event {

    if (event.type == UIEventTypeMotion && event.subtype == UIEventSubtypeMotionShake)
        NSLog(@"shake ended");
}

- (void)motionCancelled:(UIEventSubtype)motion withEvent:(UIEvent *)event
{
    NSLog(@"shake cancelled");
}

- (void)didReceiveMemoryWarning {
    // Releases the view if it doesn't have a superview.
    [super didReceiveMemoryWarning];

    // Release any cached data, images, etc that aren't in use.
}

- (void)viewDidUnload {
    // Release any retained subviews of the main view.
    // e.g. self.myOutlet = nil;
}


- (void)dealloc {
    [super dealloc];
}

@end
```

Determining orientation

To determine which way the iPhone is facing, you use the UIDevice singleton and its orientation property. If you register for the UIDeviceOrientationDidChangeNotification notification, you are told not only when the phone is rotated between portrait and landscape modes but also when it's face-up or face-down.

You'll now look at some code to detect a change in orientation. In this simple example, you'll change the background color when the phone orientation changes.

To create an application that detects orientation:

1. Create a new view-based application, and save it as OrientationExample.

2. Open OrientationExampleView Controller.m, and uncomment the view DidLoad method. Add the following code:

    ```
    [[NSNotificationCenter
    → defaultCenter] addObserver:
    → self selector:@selector
    → (noteOrientationChanged:) name:
    → UIDeviceOrientationDidChange
    → Notification object:nil];
    [[UIDevice currentDevice]
    → beginGeneratingDeviceOrientation
    → Notifications];
    ```

    You first add yourself as an observer to the UIDeviceOrientationDidChange Notification notification, which is sent every time the orientation changes. You then tell the iPhone to start generating notifications for orientation changes.

3. Finally, you need to write the code to change the background whenever you receive notification of an orientation change.

    Code Listing 7.12 shows the completed code.

continues on next page

THE iPHONE ACCELEROMETER

4. Build and run the application.

Try rotating your iPhone to see the background change color. If you are running the code in the simulator, you can rotate by pressing Command+left arrow or Command+right arrow.

Code Listing 7.12 Changing the background color in response to a change in orientation.

```
#import "OrientationExampleViewController.h"

@implementation OrientationExampleViewController

-(void)setBackgroundForOrientation:(UIDeviceOrientation)orientation
{
    switch (orientation) {

        case UIDeviceOrientationPortrait:
            [self.view setBackgroundColor:[UIColor brownColor]];
            break;

        case UIDeviceOrientationLandscapeLeft:
            [self.view setBackgroundColor:[UIColor greenColor]];
            break;

        case UIDeviceOrientationLandscapeRight:
            [self.view setBackgroundColor:[UIColor blueColor]];
            break;

        case UIDeviceOrientationFaceUp:
            [self.view setBackgroundColor:[UIColor yellowColor]];
            break;

        case UIDeviceOrientationFaceDown:
            [self.view setBackgroundColor:[UIColor blackColor]];
            break;
    }
}

- (void)noteOrientationChanged:(NSNotification *)aNotification {

    [self setBackgroundForOrientation:[UIDevice currentDevice].orientation];
}

- (void)viewDidLoad {

    [[NSNotificationCenter defaultCenter] addObserver:self
                                  selector:@selector(noteOrientationChanged:)
                                      name:UIDeviceOrientationDidChangeNotification
                                    object:nil];
    [[UIDevice currentDevice] beginGeneratingDeviceOrientationNotifications];
}

- (void)dealloc {

    [[UIDevice currentDevice] endGeneratingDeviceOrientationNotifications];

    [super dealloc];
}

@end
```

Redrawing the interface when the orientation changes

When a user rotates their iPhone between landscape and portrait modes, you are likely to want the application interface to redraw itself. For example, the user might be browsing the Web, and a wider screen would be a more desirable way to view additional content rather than scrolling from side to side.

One way to accomplish this might be to use the `UIDeviceOrientationDidChangeNotification` notification and orientation property of `UIDevice` that you just looked at, manually redrawing the interface each time you detect a change in orientation.

The iPhone SDK offers a much more elegant solution, however: *autorotation*.

Autorotation is handled in your view controller via the method `shouldAutorotateTo InferfaceOrientation`. This method returns a Boolean value indicating whether the current orientation should be autorotated.

To force an application to stay in portrait mode (the default), simply return `NO` from this method. If you want to support all orientations, you can simply return `YES`. Otherwise, you can just inspect the `interfaceOrientation` parameter and determine whether you want to autorotate.

You'll now update the application to use autorotation. You'll draw a box in the center of the screen with some text on it that will automatically rotate when you change the iPhone's orientation. The box will maintain its position in the center of the screen after rotation.

THE IPHONE ACCELEROMETER

To update the application to use autorotation:

1. Open OrientationExampleView Controller.h, and create an instance variable to hold the red box view (**Code Listing 7.13**).

2. Back in OrientationExampleView Controller.m, remove all of the code to change the background of the screen. You can also remove the call to `beginGenerating DeviceOrientationNotifications`. Modify your `viewDidLoad` method to create a box that you will be rotating:

```
float boxSize = 100.0;

redTextBox = [[UITextView alloc]
→ initWithFrame:CGRectMake(110,180,
→ boxSize,boxSize)];

redTextBox.backgroundColor =
→ [UIColor redColor];

redTextBox.textColor = [UIColor
→ whiteColor];

redTextBox.text = @"Hello World";

redTextBox.textAlignment =
→ UITextAlignmentCenter;
```

Nothing special is going on here—you are just creating a `UITextView` and setting its size, text, alignment, background, and text color properties.

Code Listing 7.13 The header file of the autorotation application.

```
#import <UIKit/UIKit.h>

@interface OrientationExampleViewController : UIViewController {

    UITextView *redTextBox;
}

@end
```

The next step is important, however:

```
redTextBox.autoresizingMask =
↪(UIViewAutoresizingFlexible
↪RightMargin

|

UIViewAutoresizingFlexibleLeft
↪Margin    |

UIViewAutoresizingFlexibleTopMargin

|

UIViewAutoresizingFlexibleBottom
↪Margin);
```

When switching between portrait and landscape modes, you want the red box view to keep its position relative to the new orientation. You accomplish this by setting all of its margins to resize automatically—in effect keeping the view in the center of the screen.

3. Finally, uncomment the `shouldAutorotate ToInterfaceOrientation:` method to enable autorotation.

Since you want to support all orientations, you simply return YES from this method. **Code Listing 7.14** shows the updated code.

4. Build and run the application.

Try changing the iPhone between portrait and landscape modes—the red box view will automatically rotate, remaining in the center of the screen. Try removing or commenting out the code that sets the `autoresizingMask` to see the effect on rotating: Although the red box view will still have the same x and y coordinates, the orientation change also changes the width and height of the screen, resulting in the box no longer being drawn at the center of the screen.

Code Listing 7.14 The updated autorotation code. The box in the center of the screen will automatically rotate when the iPhone is switched between portrait and landscape modes.

```
#import "OrientationExampleViewController.h"

@implementation OrientationExampleViewController

- (void)viewDidLoad {

    float boxSize = 100.0;
    redTextBox = [[UITextView alloc] initWithFrame:CGRectMake(110,180,boxSize,boxSize)];
    redTextBox.backgroundColor = [UIColor redColor];
    redTextBox.textColor = [UIColor whiteColor];
    redTextBox.text = @"Hello World!";
    redTextBox.textAlignment = UITextAlignmentCenter;
    redTextBox.autoresizingMask = (UIViewAutoresizingFlexibleRightMargin
                                   |
                                   UIViewAutoresizingFlexibleLeftMargin
                                   |
                                   UIViewAutoresizingFlexibleTopMargin
                                   |
                                   UIViewAutoresizingFlexibleBottomMargin);

    [self.view addSubview:redTextBox];
}

- (BOOL)shouldAutorotateToInterfaceOrientation:(UIInterfaceOrientation)interfaceOrientation
{
    return YES;
}

- (void)dealloc {

    [redTextBox release];

    [super dealloc];
}

@end
```

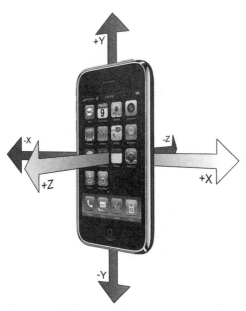

Figure 7.7 The iPhone accelerometer can respond to changes on 3 axes.

Responding to the accelerometer

So far you've looked at how to detect and make your interfaces orient themselves automatically when the user changes their phone from portrait mode to landscape mode.

The iPhone's accelerometer is a lot more powerful than this, however, and is capable of giving you live data for all three dimensions (x, y, and z). This means, for example, you could control onscreen elements simply by tilting the phone in the direction you want.

Accelerometer data is delivered to the applications by the UIAccelerometer single-ton class and a single delegate method, accelerometer:didAccelerate:, which gives you the three axes as UIAcceleration objects. Under normal gravity, each of these will have a value between -1 and +1, with 0 being the middle or "flat" point (**Figure 7.7**). If you increase gravity's effect on the iPhone by moving it rapidly (for instance in a "flick-ing" motion), then these values will increase.

You'll now create an application that allows you to control the red box from the earlier examples simply by tilting the phone.

To create a tilt-sensitive application:

1. Create a new view-based application, and save it as TiltingExample.

2. Open TiltingExampleViewController.h, add the UIAccelerometerDelegate protocol declaration, and create an instance variable to hold the tilt-controlled view (**Code Listing 7.15**).

continues on next page

Code Listing 7.15 The header file for the tilt application.

```
#import <UIKit/UIKit.h>

@interface TiltingExampleViewController : UIViewController <UIAccelerometerDelegate>
{
    UIView *redBox;
}

@end
```

3. Back in TiltingExampleViewController.m, uncomment the `viewDidLoad` method, and set up the accelerometer:

```
[[UIAccelerometer shared
→Accelerometer] setDelegate:self];
[[UIAccelerometer shared
→Accelerometer] setUpdateInterval:
→(1/40.0)];
```

This code tells the accelerometer to deliver events to you every 1/40th of a second.

You then create a red box view and add it to the main view, as in the earlier examples.

4. Next, you need to create a method, `moveBoxWithX:andY:`, to move the red box around on the screen. First add this code:

```
CGPoint boxCenter = redBox.center;
boxCenter.x += xAmount;
boxCenter.y += yAmount;

if (boxCenter.x < 50.0)
    boxCenter.x = 50.0;
if (boxCenter.x > 270.0)
    boxCenter.x = 270.0;

if (boxCenter.y < 50.0)
    boxCenter.y = 50.0;
if (boxCenter.y > 410.0)
    boxCenter.y = 410.0;

redBox.center = boxCenter;
```

This method gets the current center point (a `CGPoint`) of the red box view and increments its x and y values. After a couple of checks to make sure you haven't moved the box view offscreen, you tell the view to move to the new location.

5. The final step is to implement the `UIAccelerometer` delegate method `accelerometer:didAccelerate:`, as shown here:

```
float sensitivity = 25.0f;

float xDistance = acceleration.x *
→ sensitivity;
float yDistance = acceleration.y *
→ -sensitivity;

[self moveBoxWithX:xDistance
→ andY:yDistance];
```

You first set up a variable that will control how far you move by tilting; increasing this value will make the view move faster and/or further when you tilt. You next take the incoming x and y accelerometer values and calculate how many x and y pixels you should move before telling the red box view to move. A small tilt results in small x and y values and thus a small movement. A large tilt results in larger x and y values and so a larger movement. **Code Listing 7.16** shows the completed code.

6. Build and run the application (you will need to install it on an iPhone to test it).

Hold your iPhone so that it is face-up. You should be able to control the red box by tilting the phone.

✔ Tips

■ In the previous exercise, note how you negate the y value. This is because the iPhone coordinate system starts with 0 at the *top* of the screen and the accelerometer at the *bottom* of the screen.

■ You may notice the red box is difficult to keep completely still. You've really created only a very simple example of how to deal with accelerometer data. In reality, you would normally want to implement some type of filter (often called a *low-pass* or *high-pass* filter) to "smooth out" the accelerometer data. Apple provides sample code on the Apple Developer Connection Web site (*http://developer.apple.com*) demonstrating this functionality.

Code Listing 7.16 The completed code for the tilt application.

```
#import "TiltingExampleViewController.h"

@implementation TiltingExampleViewController

- (void)viewDidLoad {

    [super viewDidLoad];

    //setup our accelerometer to update every 1/40th of a second
    [[UIAccelerometer sharedAccelerometer] setUpdateInterval:(1/40.0)];
    [[UIAccelerometer sharedAccelerometer] setDelegate:self];

    //create our red box view
    redBox = [[UIView alloc] initWithFrame:CGRectMake(110,180,100,100)];
    redBox.backgroundColor = [UIColor redColor];

    [self.view addSubview:redBox];
}

-(void)moveBoxWithX:(float)xAmount andY:(float)yAmount  {

    CGPoint boxCenter = redBox.center;

    boxCenter.x += xAmount;
    boxCenter.y += yAmount;

    //don't allow box to go off-screen
    if (boxCenter.x < 50.0)
        boxCenter.x = 50.0;
    if (boxCenter.x > 270.0)
        boxCenter.x = 270.0;

    if (boxCenter.y < 50.0)
        boxCenter.y = 50.0;
    if (boxCenter.y > 410.0)
        boxCenter.y = 410.0;

    redBox.center = boxCenter;
}

- (void)accelerometer:(UIAccelerometer *)accelerometer didAccelerate:(UIAcceleration *)acceleration {

    float sensitivity = 25.0f;
    float xDistance = acceleration.x * sensitivity;
    float yDistance = acceleration.y * -sensitivity;

    [self moveBoxWithX:xDistance andY:yDistance];
}

- (void)dealloc {

    [redBox release];
    redBox = nil;

    [super dealloc];
}
```

LOCATION
AND MAPPING

Having an iPhone means that you need never get lost again. With the iPhone's built-in Global Positioning System (GPS) hardware and some innovative location and mapping software, not only does your iPhone know where you are at any time, but it can also *show* you.

The iPhone uses a technology known as *assisted GPS* to work out where you are. As well as the built-in GPS receiver, the iPhone uses triangulation information from cellular towers and Wi-Fi hot spots to increase the accuracy of the location data it delivers to your applications.

In this chapter, you'll first take a look at Core Location—the framework that lets you quickly and easily find your current location. You'll then look at the Map Kit framework, which enables you to add maps powered by the popular Google Maps engine to your own applications. You'll see how easy it is to perform reverse geocoding to get the address of a location, before finally combining all of these ideas into a mapping application that reproduces much of the functionality of the native Maps application.

About Core Location

Core Location is the framework used to add location awareness to your iPhone applications. It's deceptively simple in its design.

The `CLLocationManager` class and its delegates provide the mechanism by which location information gets delivered to your application. Simply create an instance, optionally set some accuracy properties, and then call the `startUpdatingLocation` method.

`CLLocation` events are generated via the delegate methods of your `CLLocationManager` instance. `CLLocation` objects encapsulate not only geographical coordinates but also information such as speed, altitude, heading, and accuracy.

To make your application location aware:

1. Create a new view-based application, saving it as `CoreLocationExample` (**Figure 8.1**).

2. In the Groups & Files pane, expand the Targets section, right-click your application target, and choose Get Info. Making sure the General tab is selected, click Add (+) at the bottom of the Linked Libraries list, and add CoreLocation. framework (**Figure 8.2**).

3. Open the CoreLocationExample ViewController.h file, import the `CoreLocation` framework, add the `CLLocationManagerDelegate` protocol declaration, and create an instance variable to hold your location manager (**Code Listing 8.1**).

Figure 8.1 Creating a view-based application.

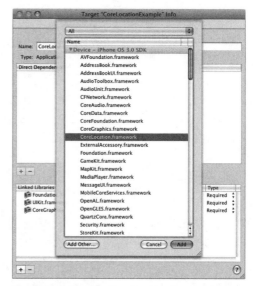

Figure 8.2 Adding the Core Location framework to your project.

4. Switch to the CoreLocationExample ViewController.m file, uncomment the `viewDidLoad` method, and add the following code:

```
lm = [[CLLocationManager alloc]
→ init];

lm.delegate = self;

[lm startUpdatingLocation];
```

You create your `CLLocationManager` instance, setting the delegate to be the view controller (`self`) and then telling the location manager to begin sending location events.

Code Listing 8.2 shows the completed application code.

Code Listing 8.1 The header file for the core location application.

```
#import <UIKit/UIKit.h>
#import <CoreLocation/CoreLocation.h>

@interface CoreLocationExampleViewController : UIViewController <CLLocationManagerDelegate>
{
    CLLocationManager *lm;
}

@end
```

Code Listing 8.2 A bare-bones core location application.

```
#import "CoreLocationExampleViewController.h"

@implementation CoreLocationExampleViewController

- (void)viewDidLoad
{
    [super viewDidLoad];

    lm = [[CLLocationManager alloc] init];
    lm.delegate = self;
    [lm startUpdatingLocation];
}
```

Handling location updates

Believe it or not, that's it—your application is now location aware. However, you still don't have any way of dealing with the information the location manager is giving you. For this you must implement the required delegate methods (recall that you added the `CLLocationManagerDelegate` protocol back in the CLLocationManager.h file).

`CLLocationManager` has just two delegate methods. The first, `locationManager: didUpdateToLocation:fromLocation:`, is called whenever the location manager updates a new location. Both the previous location and the new location are passed unless this is the first location event, in which case `fromLocation:` will be `nil`.

The second delegate method, `location Manager:didFailWithError:`, lets you deal with any errors that have occurred with the location manager trying to retrieve a location value. In this situation, you'd normally want to stop your location manager with a call to `stopUpdatingLocation` in order to save battery power.

Code Listing 8.3 shows the updated Core LocationExampleViewController.m file.

Output is sent to the console (**Figure 8.3**), showing latitude/longitude coordinates, accuracy of the result (in this case plus or minus 100m), your speed, your course or direction, and a time stamp of when the location event occurred.

Code Listing 8.3 The core location application updated to log to the console.

```
#import "CoreLocationExampleViewController.h"

@implementation CoreLocationExampleViewController

- (void)viewDidLoad
{
    [super viewDidLoad];

    lm = [[CLLocationManager alloc] init];
    lm.delegate = self;
    [lm startUpdatingLocation];
}

- (void)locationManager:(CLLocationManager *)manager
    didUpdateToLocation:(CLLocation *)newLoc
         fromLocation:(CLLocation *)oldLoc {

    NSLog(@"location found: %@",newLoc.description);
    [lm stopUpdatingLocation];
}

- (void)locationManager:(CLLocationManager *)manager
        didFailWithError:(NSError *)error {

    NSLog(@"location failed with error: %@",error);
    [lm stopUpdatingLocation];
}

- (void)dealloc {
    [super dealloc];
}

@end
```

Figure 8.3 The Debugger Console displaying location information.

✔ Tips

- Notice how, to preserve battery power, you call `stopUpdatingLocation` on the location manager as soon as you have either a location or an error.

- When the location manager is first started (via `startUpdatingLocation`), it will normally generate a number of location updates in quick succession. These are generally baseline or cached locations that are often inaccurate and can be ignored. You will investigate a technique to handle this situation later in the chapter.

Testing outside the simulator

The navigationally savvy reader may have noticed that when you run the previous example for yourself, the latitude and longitude do not correspond to your own location (that is, unless you are currently working for Apple). When Core Location–based code is run in the iPhone Simulator, it will always report a location of "1 Infinite Loop, Cupertino" (Apple's headquarters).

This obviously makes testing elements such as course and speed impossible in the simulator. Additionally, if you were walking around with your iPhone testing your application, you obviously wouldn't be able to view console output on your computer screen.

From now on, you'll assume the examples in this chapter are running on an actual device rather than in the simulator. You'll add a `UITextView` to your iPhone's main view and write some code to log output to it instead of to the console.

You could just have easily hooked up `UILabel` controls or other, more attractive UI elements—this is just a convenient shortcut that allows you to easily display logging information with minimal effort.

To add logging of location data to the iPhone screen:

1. In CoreLocationExampleViewController.h, create an instance variable to hold your view (**Code Listing 8.4**):

   ```
   UITextView *logView;
   ```

2. Switch to CoreLocationExampleView Controller.m, and create the `logToScreen:` method you will use to log text to the iPhone's screen:

   ```
   CGPoint pt = logView.contentOffset;
   ```

   You first set a variable to hold the `UIView`'s current content position in its scroll view:

   ```
   logView.text = [NSString
   → stringWithFormat:@"%@\n%@",
   → logView.text,output];
   ```

   Next you append the new text and make sure the view scrolls properly if the new text is too large for a single screen:

   ```
   [logView setContentOffset:pt
   → animated:NO];

   [logView scrollRangeToVisible:
   → NSMakeRange([logView.text length],
   → 0)];
   ```

Code Listing 8.4 The updated header file.

```
● ● ●                                                Code
#import <UIKit/UIKit.h>
#import <CoreLocation/CoreLocation.h>

@interface CoreLocationExampleViewController : UIViewController <CLLocationManagerDelegate>
{
    CLLocationManager *lm;
    UITextView *logView;
}

@end
```

location found: <+37.33168900, -122.03073100> +/- 100.00m (speed -1.00 mps / course -1.00) @ 2009-05-05 17:20:03 +1000

Figure 8.4 Logging information is displayed on the iPhone.

3. Update the viewDidLoad method to create and add the new view:

```
logView = [[UITextView alloc]
→ initWithFrame:[self.view bounds]];
logView.editable = NO;
logView.userInteractionEnabled =
→ YES;
[self.view addSubview:logView];
```

4. Finally, to make things work as closely to NSLog() as possible, define the DCLog macro at the top of the file:

```
#define DCLog(format, ...)
→ [self logToScreen:[NSString
→ stringWithFormat:format,
→ ## __VA_ARGS__]];
```

You can now replace calls to NSLog() with a call to DCLog(). Logging information will be displayed on the iPhone's screen (**Figure 8.4**).

Increasing the accuracy

Up to now you may have noticed that the location information you are receiving isn't particularly accurate. This is because the location manager often returns cached or baseline "best-guess" values when it's first started, becoming increasingly accurate over time.

You can do a number of things to filter out these unwanted location events and get a more accurate result.

You've used only the `description` property of the `CLLocation` events so far, but you could use a number of other properties:

- `altitude`—A positive or negative value depending on whether you are above or below sea level

- `coordinate`—A `CLLocationCoordinate` type containing latitude and longitude information

- `course`, `speed`—The direction and speed (in meters) in which the iPhone is traveling

- `horizontalAccuracy`, `verticalAccuracy`—How accurate the coordinate and altitude values are

✔ Tips

- `course` is measured in degrees, with due north being 0, east being 90, south being 180, and west being 270. You probably noticed in the first example that both the course and speed values were `-1.0`. Having only a single location means these values can't be calculated.

- A negative value for `horizontalAccuracy` or `verticalAccuracy` generally indicates that the location event can be ignored.

Adding a timeout

You also want to think about saving iPhone power by timing out and turning off the location manager if you don't receive a valid location within a reasonable amount of time.

To add timeouts to the location manager:

1. In CoreLocationExampleViewController.h, add a new instance variable to hold your timeout:

   ```
   NSTimer *timer;
   ```

2. Switch to CoreLocationExampleViewCon troller.m, and add the following new code to your `viewDidLoad` method:

```
lm.desiredAccuracy =
↳ kCLLocationAccuracyBest;

lm.distanceFilter  =
↳ kCLDistanceFilterNone;
```

This tells the location manager how accurate it should be and how far (in meters) the user must move laterally before a new location event is generated.

You then set up your timer to expire after 1 minute:

```
timer = [NSTimer scheduledTimer
↳ WithTimeInterval:60 target:self
↳ selector:@selector(locationManager
↳ DidTimeout:userInfo:) userInfo:nil
↳ repeats:false];
```

The `desiredAccuracy` code tells the location manager how accurate it should attempt to be when generating location events. Possible values for this property range from "best" to 3km. It's worth noting, however, that although the location manager will attempt to achieve the defined accuracy, it is not guaranteed.

In this example, you're using the most accurate settings for both `desiredAccuracy` and `distanceFilter`. It's important to remember using these settings may take longer to return a location and will have more of an impact on the iPhone battery life.

continues on next page

ABOUT CORE LOCATION

3. Update the location manager delegate to check the age of the location event:

```
  NSTimeInterval eventAge =
→ [newLocation.timestamp
→ timeIntervalSinceNow];
if (abs(eventAge) < 5.0)
```

You are interested only in events that occurred within the last 5 seconds. This will filter out any cached location data.

If an event is new enough, you next check the accuracy:

```
if ([newLocation horizontalAccuracy]
→ > 0.0f && [newLocation
→ horizontalAccuracy] <= 100.0f)
```

which will give only those events that are accurate to within 100m of your actual position (making sure to also ignore negative, invalid values).

Lastly, you stop the location manager and timer and output the result.

4. There are still two more things to do. First you need to handle when a location can't be found:

```
(void)locationManagerDidTimeout:
→ (NSTimer *)aTimer userInfo:(id)
→ userInfo
```

This simply stops the location manager and logs an error to your screen.

Finally, make sure that the timer is stopped if an error occurs by adding the following to the `locationManager:` `didFailWithError:` delegate:

```
[timer invalidate];
```

Code Listing 8.5 shows the completed code.

Code Listing 8.5 The completed core location code.

```
#import "CoreLocationExampleViewController.h"

#define DCLog(format, ...) [self logToScreen:[NSString stringWithFormat:format, ## __VA_ARGS__]];

@implementation CoreLocationExampleViewController

- (void)logToScreen:(NSString *)output {

    CGPoint pt = logView.contentOffset;

    //write text
    logView.text = [NSString stringWithFormat:@"%@\n%@",logView.text,output];

    //tell view to scroll if necessary
    [logView setContentOffset:pt animated:NO];
    [logView scrollRangeToVisible:NSMakeRange([logView.text length], 0)];
}

- (void)viewDidLoad {

    [super viewDidLoad];

    //create logger view
    logView = [[UITextView alloc] initWithFrame:[self.view bounds]];
    logView.editable = NO;
    logView.userInteractionEnabled = YES;
    [self.view addSubview:logView];

    lm = [[CLLocationManager alloc] init];

    lm.delegate = self;

    lm.desiredAccuracy = kCLLocationAccuracyBest; //try to be as accurate as possible
    lm.distanceFilter = kCLDistanceFilterNone;  //report all movement

    timer = [NSTimer scheduledTimerWithTimeInterval:60
                                    target:self
                                  selector:@selector(locationManagerDidTimeout:userInfo:)
                                  userInfo:nil
                                   repeats:false];

    [lm startUpdatingLocation];
}
- (void)locationManager:(CLLocationManager *)manager
    didUpdateToLocation:(CLLocation *)newLocation
           fromLocation:(CLLocation *)oldLocation {

    //how old (in seconds) is the event?
    NSTimeInterval eventAge = [newLocation.timestamp timeIntervalSinceNow];

    //deal with cached locations by ignoring anything older than 5 seconds
    if (abs(eventAge) < 5)
    {
        //only look at locations that are within 100meters
        if ([newLocation horizontalAccuracy] > 0.0f && [newLocation horizontalAccuracy] <= 100.0f)
        {
            //stop the location manager
            [lm stopUpdatingLocation];

            //stop the timer
            [timer invalidate];

            DCLog(@"FINAL location found:\nCoords (%f, %f)\nAlt:%f\nSpeed:%f\nHoriz Accuracy:%f\nVert Accuracy:%f\n\n",
                  newLocation.coordinate.latitude,
                  newLocation.coordinate.longitude,
                  newLocation.speed,
                  newLocation.horizontalAccuracy,
                  newLocation.verticalAccuracy);
```

(code continues on next page)

Code Listing 8.5 *continued*

```
        }
        else
        {
            DCLog(@"APPROX Location found: %@",newLocation.description);
        }
    }
}

- (void)locationManager:(CLLocationManager *)manager
        didFailWithError:(NSError *)error {

    //stop listening to location events
    [lm stopUpdatingLocation];

    //stop the timer
    [timer invalidate];

    DCLog(@"location failed with error: %@",error);
}

- (void)dealloc {

    [logView release];
    [lm release];

    [timer invalidate];
    [super dealloc];
}

@end
```

FINAL location found:
Coords (37.331689, -122.030731)
Altitude:-1.000000
Speed:100.000000
Horiz Accuracy:-1.000000
Vert Accuracy:-0.000000

Figure 8.5 The results of a location search.

Figure 8.5 shows the result of a successful location search. Try running this code on your iPhone—you should see the location events as they arrive (you may need to increase the timeout value if you are indoors), increasing in accuracy over time. Try changing the values for `desiredAccuracy` and `distanceFilter` to see how they affect the results of changing or removing the check for cached locations.

✔ Tips

- Since the location manager works by gradually increasing accuracy and "zeroing in" on a location, it actually may be the case that the first result, although reported as inaccurate, is in fact correct.

- There's always going to be a trade-off between displaying potentially inaccurate information quickly versus making the user have to wait longer for a more accurate result. The code in the previous example is just one approach. Another idea might be to decrease the `desiredAccuracy` level and instead adopt a strategy of counting location events, waiting for a number to arrive before accepting one as valid. The method you choose to use will be determined by your application's requirements.

Accessing the compass

If your iPhone contains a compass, you can receive heading information in much the same way as location updates.

Heading updates are generated by the location manager as `CLHeading` objects, containing attributes for heading values in relation to both magnetic and true north. These attributes are measured in degrees, with `0` representing north and `180` representing south.

ABOUT CORE LOCATION

To check whether the iPhone supports heading updates, you inspect the `headingAvailable` property of the location manager. To start and stop listening to heading events, you call the `startUpdatingHeading` and `stop UpdatingHeading` methods accordingly.

Just as with location updates, heading updates are managed via delegate methods:

◆ `locationManager:didUpdateHeading:`—Called whenever a new heading is received that differs from the previous heading by more than the value specified in the `heading Filter` property.

◆ `locationManagerShouldDisplayHeading Calibration:manager`—Called if your iPhone needs to be calibrated. This will typically happen only with a new iPhone where the compass has never been used. Returning `YES` will cause the compass calibration panel to appear. You can dismiss the panel by calling `dismissHeadingCalibrationDisplay`, or you can prevent it from ever showing by returning `NO` to this method.

In the examples so far, you have concentrated on getting a *single* location as accurately as you can before stopping the location manager. You might want to have a real-world application that updates locations continuously, displaying the course, speed, and heading information as you walk or drive around. You will see an example of this in the "Putting It All Together" section.

Figure 8.6 Adding the Map Kit framework to your project.

Code Listing 8.6 The header file for the map application.

```
●○○                    Code
#import <UIKit/UIKit.h>
#import <MapKit/MapKit.h>

@interface MappingExampleViewController:UIViewController
{
    MKMapView *map;
}

@end
```

About Map Kit

Map Kit, the mapping framework based on the Google Maps engine, gives you the ability to add interactive maps to your applications. Maps can be scrolled and zoomed to any region on the planet and can have pins, or *annotations*, added to the map to display additional information.

To add a map to your application:

1. Create a new view-based application, saving it as MappingExample.

2. In the Groups & Files pane, expand the Targets section, right-click your application target, and select Get Info.

3. Making sure the General tab is selected, click Add (+) at the bottom of the Linked Libraries list, and add MapKit.framework (**Figure 8.6**).

4. Open the MappingExampleView Controller.h file, import the MapKit framework, and create an instance variable to hold your location manager (**Code Listing 8.6**).

continues on next page

ABOUT MAP KIT

5. Switch to the MappingExampleViewController.m file, uncomment the `viewDidLoad` method, and add the following code:

```
map = [[MKMapView alloc]
→ initWithFrame:[self.view bounds]];
[self.view addSubview:map];
```

Code Listing 8.7 shows the updated code.

6. Build and run the application (**Figure 8.7**).

That's it—two lines of code, and you have a map! You should be able to navigate around the map and zoom in/out by using the "pinch" gesture.

Figure 8.7 The application with a full-screen MKMapView.

ABOUT MAP KIT

Code Listing 8.7 The completed code for a bare-bones map application.

```
#import "MappingExampleViewController.h"

@implementation MappingExampleViewController

- (void)viewDidLoad {

    map = [[MKMapView alloc] initWithFrame:[self.view bounds]];
    [self.view addSubview:map];
}

- (void)dealloc {

    [map release];

    [super dealloc];
}
@end
```

Figure 8.8 Displaying the current location on a map.

You'll now update this code to make it a little more interesting.

To show your location on the map:

1. Open MappingExampleViewController.m, and update your `viewDidLoad` method to set the map type to a satellite view and tell it to show the current location—indicated by an animated blue marker:

   ```
   map.mapType = MKMapTypeSatellite;
   map.showsUserLocation = YES;
   ```

   The outer circle on this marker indicates the accuracy of the location data—the wider the circle, the less accurate:

   ```
   CLLocationCoordinate2D coords;
   coords.latitude = 37.331689;
   coords.longitude = -122.030731;
   ```

2. Next you create a variable to hold your map center coordinate, in this case Apple's headquarters:

   ```
   float zoomLevel = 0.018;
   MKCoordinateRegion region =
   ⇥ MKCoordinateRegionMake(coords,
   ⇥ MKCoordinateSpanMake(zoomLevel,
   ⇥ zoomLevel));
   [map setRegion:[map regionThatFits:
   ⇥ region] animated:YES];
   ```

3. To zoom into a map, you need to create an `MKCoordinateRegion`.

   This structure contains not only the coordinates the map should center on but also a *span*, which is comprised of a horizontal and vertical distance determining how much of the map (in degrees) should be shown. A large span creates a zoomed-out view; a small span creates a zoomed-in view (**Figure 8.8**). **Code Listing 8.8** shows the updated `viewDidLoad` method.

Just as with the iPhone's native Maps application, you can display three possible maps with the mapType property:

- MKMapTypeStandard—Shows a normal map containing street and road names. This is the default map type if none is specified.

- MKMapTypeSatellite—Shows a satellite view.

- MKMapTypeHybrid—Shows a combination of the two, in other words, a satellite view with road and street information overlaid.

✔ Tip

- When setting span values, depending on which map type you are using, you may be able to zoom in or out to a greater degree. For example, maps of MKMapTypeSatellite generally contain greater detail and will allow you to zoom in a lot more than MKTypeStandard.

Code Listing 8.8 Updating the code to set and show a location.

```
- (void)viewDidLoad {

    map = [[MKMapView alloc] initWithFrame:[self.view bounds]];

    map.mapType            = MKMapTypeSatellite;
    map.showsUserLocation = YES;

    CLLocationCoordinate2D coords;
    coords.latitude = 37.331689;
    coords.longitude = -122.030731;

    float zoomLevel = 0.0018;
    MKCoordinateRegion region = MKCoordinateRegionMake(coords,
                                        MKCoordinateSpanMake(zoomLevel,zoomLevel));
    [map setRegion:[map regionThatFits:region] animated:YES];

    [self.view addSubview:map];
}
```

Adding annotations

To make your mapping applications richer and more interesting, you will often want to overlay information onto the map, and this is where annotations come in.

Map Kit contains support for adding not only simple "pin" annotations (as seen in the native iPhone Maps application) but also your own custom annotations that can have their own look and feel.

Adding annotations to a map involves a little more work than you've had to do so far.

To add an annotation to your map:

1. Open MappingExampleViewController.h, and add the `MKMapViewDelegate` protocol declaration to the `@interface`:

```
@interface MappingExampleView
→ Controller : UIViewController
→ <MKMapViewDelegate>
```

2. In the MappingExampleViewController.m file, you need to create your own custom class that implements the `MKAnnotation` protocol. At the very least, this class must implement the `coordinate` property.

3. In `viewDidLoad`, set the delegate, and create your annotation by adding the following:

```
customAnnotation *annotation =
→ [[customAnnotation alloc]
→ initWithCoordinate:coords];
annotation.title   = @"The Title";
annotation.subtitle = @"Subtitle";
[map addAnnotation:annotation];
[annotation release];
```

You've removed the `setUserLocation:` line so that you can see your annotation (otherwise, the location marker and annotation will appear in the same place on the map).

continues on next page

4. Finally, implement the mapView:view
ForAnnotation: delegate method to
display the annotation as a pin:

```
MKPinAnnotationView *pinView =
→ (MKPinAnnotationView *) [map
→ dequeueReusableAnnotationViewWith
→ Identifier:annotation.title];
if (pinView == nil)
pinView = [[[MKPinAnnotationView
→ alloc] initWithAnnotation:
→ annotation reuseIdentifier:
→ annotation.title] autorelease];
else
    pinView.annotation = annotation;
```

Code Listing 8.9 shows the updated
code.

Code Listing 8.9 The code updated to add a custom annotation.

```
#import "MappingExampleViewController.h"

@interface customAnnotation: NSObject <MKAnnotation>
{
    CLLocationCoordinate2D coordinate;
    NSString *title;
    NSString *subtitle;
}

@property (nonatomic, readonly) CLLocationCoordinate2D coordinate;
@property (nonatomic,retain) NSString *title;
@property (nonatomic,retain) NSString *subtitle;
- (id)initWithCoordinate:(CLLocationCoordinate2D)coords;

@end
@implementation customAnnotation

@synthesize coordinate,title,subtitle;

- (id)initWithCoordinate:(CLLocationCoordinate2D)coords {

    if (self = [super init])
        coordinate = coords;

    return self;
}

- (void)dealloc
{
    [title release];
    [subtitle release];
    [super dealloc];
}

@end
```

(code continues on next page)

Code Listing 8.9 *continued*

```
@implementation MappingExampleViewController

- (MKAnnotationView *)mapView:(MKMapView *)mapView viewForAnnotation:(id<MKAnnotation>)annotation {

    MKPinAnnotationView *pinView = (MKPinAnnotationView *)[map dequeueReusableAnnotationViewWithIdentifier:annotation.title];
    if (pinView == nil)
        pinView = [[[MKPinAnnotationView alloc] initWithAnnotation:annotation reuseIdentifier:annotation.title] autorelease];
    else
        pinView.annotation = annotation;

    pinView.animatesDrop = YES;
    pinView.canShowCallout = TRUE;

    return pinView;
}

- (void)viewDidLoad {

    map = [[MKMapView alloc] initWithFrame:[self.view bounds]];

    map.mapType          = MKMapTypeSatellite;
    map.delegate = self;

    CLLocationCoordinate2D coords;
    coords.latitude = 37.331689;
    coords.longitude = -122.030731;

    float zoomLevel = 0.0018;
    MKCoordinateRegion region = MKCoordinateRegionMake(coords,
                                        MKCoordinateSpanMake(zoomLevel,zoomLevel));
    [map setRegion:[map regionThatFits:region] animated:YES];

    customAnnotation *annotation = [[customAnnotation alloc] initWithCoordinate:coords];
    annotation.title = @"The title";
    annotation.subtitle = @"Subtitle";
    [map addAnnotation:annotation];
    [annotation release];

    [self.view addSubview:map];
}


- (void)dealloc {

    [map release];
    map = nil;

    [super dealloc];
}
@end
```

The `mapView:viewForAnnotation:` delegate returns an `MKAnnotationView` object. In this example (**Figure 8.9**), you are using the `MKPinAnnotationView` subclass that, as the name suggests, displays annotations as pins. You can, however, return your own subclass if you want a different look and feel for annotations.

You can see the simplest example of this in **Code Listing 8.10**. You set the `image:` property on the base `MKAnnotationView` class. This results in the map shown in **Figure 8.10**.

✔ Tips

- Specifying a reuse queue when creating `MKAnnotationView` objects allows the mapping engine to remove annotations from the map when they move offscreen (for example, if the user zooms or scrolls the map). The annotation is taken out of the queue (also known as *dequeuing*) when it moves back onscreen.

- You can also alter the look and feel of the annotation's callout view (the view that shows up when the user touches the annotation) by overriding `viewForCalloutAccessoryPosition:` in your custom `MKAnnotationView` class.

Figure 8.9 Displaying an annotation on the map.

Code Listing 8.10 Displaying an image as an annotation.

```
- (MKAnnotationView *)mapView:(MKMapView *)mapView viewForAnnotation:(id <MKAnnotation>)annotation {

    MKAnnotationView *aView;
    aView = (MKAnnotationView *) [map dequeueReusableAnnotationViewWithIdentifier:annotation.title];

    if (aView == nil)
        aView = [[[MKAnnotationView alloc]
                    initWithAnnotation:annotation reuseIdentifier:annotation.title] autorelease];
    else
        aView.annotation = annotation;

    [aView setImage:[UIImage imageNamed:@"iPhone.png"]];
    aView.canShowCallout = TRUE;

    return aView;
}
```

Figure 8.10 A custom annotation showing a graphic.

Adding reverse geocoding

Map Kit provides the facility to do lookups on latitude and longitude coordinates to get address information—a process known as *reverse geocoding*. You accomplish this via the MKReverseGeocoder class and its delegate methods.

In the previous example, you created your annotation manually, specifying the coordinates title and subtitle in the viewDidLoad method. You'll now change your code to perform a reverse lookup of your position instead, creating an annotation with your address in its callout view.

To add reverse geocoding:

1. Open MappingExampleViewController.h, and add the MKReverseGeocodeDelegate protocol declaration to the @interface:

   @interface MappingExampleView
   → Controller : UIViewController
   → <MKMapViewDelegate,
   → MKReverseGeocoderDelegate>

   You also create an instance variable to hold your reverse geocoder:

   MKReverseGeocoder *geo;

   Code Listing 8.11 shows the updated code.

continues on next page

Code Listing 8.11 The header file updated to add reverse geocoding.

```
#import <UIKit/UIKit.h>
#import <MapKit/MapKit.h>

@interface MappingExampleViewController : UIViewController <MKMapViewDelegate, MKReverseGeocodeDelegate >
{
    MKMapView *map;
    MKReverseGeocoder *geo;
}

@end
```

2. Back in MappingExampleViewController.m, update the `viewDidLoad` method:

```
geo = [[MKReverseGeocoder alloc]
⇢ initWithCoordinate:coords];
geo.delegate = self;
[geo start];
```

Here you create your geocoder instance, set the delegate, and tell it to start the lookup.

3. Finally, you need to implement the `MKReverseGeocode` delegate methods, adding an annotation if you find an address:

```
[map addAnnotation:placemark];
[geo cancel];
```

and logging a console message on failure:

```
NSLog(@"geo error: %@",error);
[geo cancel];
```

Notice that you cancel the geocoder in both situations. **Code Listing 8.12** shows the completed code. **Figure 8.11** shows your application with the address.

✔ Tip

■ In the `reverseGeocoder:didFindPlace mark:` delegate, you add an `MKPlacemark` as an annotation. This class contains properties to hold location information such as the city or state. Much as in your own custom annotation class earlier, this class implements the `MKAnnotation` protocol, so it can be placed on a map.

Figure 8.11 Displaying the address in an annotation.

Code Listing 8.12 The code updated to perform a reverse-geo lookup and add the address as an annotation to the map.

```objc
#import "MappingExampleViewController.h"

@implementation MappingExampleViewController

- (void)reverseGeocoder:(MKReverseGeocoder *)geocoder didFailWithError:(NSError *)error {

    NSLog(@"reverse geo lookup failed with error: %@",error);
    [geo cancel];
}

- (void)reverseGeocoder:(MKReverseGeocoder *)geocoder didFindPlacemark:(MKPlacemark *)placemark {

    [map addAnnotation:placemark];
    [geo cancel];
}

- (void)viewDidLoad {

    map = [[MKMapView alloc] initWithFrame:[self.view bounds]];

    map.mapType        = MKMapTypeSatellite;
    map.delegate = self;

    CLLocationCoordinate2D coords;
    coords.latitude = 37.331689;
    coords.longitude = -122.030731;

    float zoomLevel = 0.0018;
    MKCoordinateRegion region = MKCoordinateRegionMake(coords,
                                       MKCoordinateSpanMake(zoomLevel,zoomLevel));
    [map setRegion:[map regionThatFits:region] animated:YES];

    geo = [[MKReverseGeocoder alloc] initWithCoordinate:coords];
    geo.delegate = self;
    [geo start];

    [self.view addSubview:map];
}

- (void)dealloc {

    [map release];
    map = nil;

    [super dealloc];
}

@end
```

Putting It All Together

So far you've seen how to get your location, draw and plot a location on a map, and perform reverse geocoding to get the address of a location.

Now you'll combine all of these ideas into a single application that automatically updates as you walk or drive around. You'll also add some fields to show your current address, compass heading, and distance traveled (**Figure 8.12**).

To update your application:

1. As earlier, in the Groups & Files pane, expand the Targets section, right-click the application target, choose Get Info, and add CoreLocation.framework.

2. Open MappingExampleViewController.h, import the Core Location framework header, and add the `CLLocationManager Delegate` protocol. You then add some new instance variables:

   `CLLocationManager *lm;`

   `UITextView *addressView;`

   `UITextView *distanceView;`

   `UITextView *headingView;`

   `CLLocation *startingLocation;`

   `Double previousHeading;`

   The first holds the location manager (as earlier). Then you define a couple of views to display address distance information and the compass heading in your application. Finally, you need somewhere to hold your initial location when calculating the distance traveled as well as a variable to keep track of whether the heading has changed. **Code Listing 8.13** shows the updated code.

Figure 8.12 The final completed core location application.

3. In the MappingExampleViewController.m file, edit your `viewDidLoad` method to add all your new UI elements. You set up the height of your address distance views and heading, and you create a `CGRect` the same size as the main view:

```
float viewHeight = 25.0;
CGRect viewRect = [self.view
→ bounds];
```

You create a `CGRect` for your address view, at the bottom of your main view, and then set the color and alignment. You do the same thing for the distance and heading views, placing them at the top of the main view:

```
CGRect addressViewRect = CGRectMake
→ (viewRect.origin.x,viewRect.size.
→ height-viewHeight,viewRect.size.
→ width,viewHeight);

addressView = [[UITextView alloc]
→ initWithFrame:addressViewRect];

addressView.backgroundColor =
→ [UIColor blackColor];

addressView.textColor      =
→ [UIColor whiteColor];

addressView.textAlignment   =
→ UITextAlignmentCenter;
```

continues on next page

Code Listing 8.13 The final header file code for the core location application.

```
⊖ ○ ○                                    Code
#import <UIKit/UIKit.h>
#import <CoreLocation/CoreLocation.h>
#import <MapKit/MapKit.h>

@interface MappingExampleViewController : UIViewController <MKMapViewDelegate,
                                          MKReverseGeocoderDelegate,
                                          CLLocationManagerDelegate>
{
    MKMapView *map;
    MKReverseGeocoder *geo;
    CLLocationManager *lm;
    UITextView *addressView;
    UITextView *distanceView;
    UITextView *headingView;
    CLLocation *startingLocation;
    double previousHeading;
}

@end
```

You need to adjust the height and y position of the map to make room for the address and distance views:

```
viewRect.size.height -= viewHeight
→ *2;
viewRect.origin.y += viewHeight;
```

The rest of the method is much the same as earlier.

4. Next add a couple of helper methods that are called when you get a new location event. `updateMapViewWithLocation:shouldZoom:` will update your map's position, and `updateGeoCoderWithLocation:` will create a new `MKReverseGeocoder` and `updateHeadingView` whenever a new compass heading is received.

5. Finally, you implement the delegates for the reverse geocoder and location manager, where you update your map and address views whenever you receive a new location.

You also throw up an error dialog box if you fail to get a location. **Code Listing 8.14** shows the completed code.

Code Listing 8.14 The completed core location application code.

```
⊙ ⊙ ⊙                                        Code
#import "MappingExampleViewController.h"

@implementation MappingExampleViewController

- (void)viewDidLoad {

    float viewHeight = 25.0;
    CGRect viewRect = [self.view bounds];

    CGRect addressViewRect = CGRectMake(viewRect.origin.x,viewRect.size.height-viewHeight,viewRect.size.width,viewHeight);
    addressView = [[UITextView alloc] initWithFrame:addressViewRect];
    addressView.backgroundColor = [UIColor blackColor];
    addressView.textColor       = [UIColor whiteColor];
    addressView.textAlignment   = UITextAlignmentCenter;

    CGRect distanceViewRect = CGRectMake(viewRect.origin.x,viewRect.origin.y,viewRect.size.width-50.0,viewHeight);
    distanceView = [[UITextView alloc] initWithFrame:distanceViewRect];
    distanceView.backgroundColor = [UIColor blackColor];
    distanceView.textColor       = [UIColor whiteColor];
    distanceView.textAlignment   = UITextAlignmentCenter;

    CGRect headingViewRect = CGRectMake(viewRect.size.width-50.0,viewRect.origin.y,50.0,viewHeight);
    headingView = [[UITextView alloc] initWithFrame:headingViewRect];
    headingView.backgroundColor = [UIColor blackColor];
    headingView.textColor       = [UIColor whiteColor];
    headingView.textAlignment   = UITextAlignmentCenter;

    //adjust rect to make room for views
    viewRect.size.height -= viewHeight *2;
    viewRect.origin.y += viewHeight;

    //create map and set some properties
    map = [[MKMapView alloc] initWithFrame:viewRect];
    map.mapType           = MKMapTypeSatellite;
    map.showsUserLocation = YES;
    map.delegate          = self;

    //create location manager & set some properties
    lm = [[CLLocationManager alloc] init];
    lm.desiredAccuracy = kCLLocationAccuracyBest; //try to be as accurate as possible
    lm.distanceFilter  = kCLDistanceFilterNone;   //report all movement
    lm.delegate = self;

    //start listening
    [lm startUpdatingLocation];

    //compass?
    if (lm.headingAvailable)
        [lm startUpdatingHeading];

    //add all the subviews to the main view
    [self.view addSubview:addressView];
    [self.view addSubview:map];
    [self.view addSubview:distanceView];
    [self.view addSubview:headingView];
}
- (void)updateMapViewWithLocation:(CLLocation *)location shouldZoom:(BOOL)doZoom {
```

(code continues on next page)

Code Listing 8.14 *continued*

```
        //set zoom quite far so we can see updates frequently
        float zoomLevel = 0.0005;

        //if we haven't drawn map yet, need to set zoom level, otherwise just draw. this maintains any user-adjusted zoom
        if (doZoom) {
            MKCoordinateRegion region = MKCoordinateRegionMake(location.coordinate,
                                        MKCoordinateSpanMake(zoomLevel,zoomLevel));
            [map setRegion:[map regionThatFits:region] animated:TRUE];
        }
        else
            [map setCenterCoordinate:location.coordinate animated:YES];
}

- (void)updateGeoCoderWithLocation:(CLLocation *)location {

        //do reverse-geo lookup
        if (geo) {
            [geo cancel];
            [geo release];
        }

        geo=[[MKReverseGeocoder alloc] initWithCoordinate:location.coordinate];
        geo.delegate=self;
        [geo start];
}

- (void)updateHeadingView
{
        NSString *headingText;
        if (previousHeading < 45.0)
            headingText = @"N";
        if (previousHeading >= 45.0 && previousHeading < 90.0)
            headingText = @"NE";
        if (previousHeading >= 90.0 && previousHeading < 135.0)
            headingText = @"E";
        if (previousHeading >= 135.0 && previousHeading < 180.0)
            headingText = @"SE";
        if (previousHeading >= 180.0 && previousHeading < 225.0)
            headingText = @"S";
        if (previousHeading >= 225.0 && previousHeading < 270.0)
            headingText = @"SW";
        if (previousHeading >= 270.0 && previousHeading < 315.0)
            headingText = @"W";
        if (previousHeading >= 315.0)
            headingText = @"NW";

        headingView.text = headingText;
}

- (void)reverseGeocoder:(MKReverseGeocoder *)geocoder didFindPlacemark:(MKPlacemark *)placemark {

        //update view
        NSString *street = [placemark.addressDictionary objectForKey:@"Street"];
        NSString *city = [placemark.addressDictionary objectForKey:@"City"];
        addressView.text = [NSString stringWithFormat:@"%@, %@",street,city];
}

- (void)reverseGeocoder:(MKReverseGeocoder *)geocoder didFailWithError:(NSError *)error {

        [geo cancel];
}

- (void)locationManager:(CLLocationManager *)mgr didUpdateToLocation:(CLLocation *)newLoc fromLocation:(CLLocation *)oldLoc {

        NSTimeInterval eventAge = [newLoc.timestamp timeIntervalSinceNow];
```

(code continues on next page)

Code Listing 8.14 continued

```
                                                      Code
    //deal with cached locations by ignoring anything older than 5 seconds
    if (abs(eventAge) < 5) {
        //only look at locations that are within 100meters
        if ([newLoc horizontalAccuracy] > 0.0f && [newLoc horizontalAccuracy] <= 100.0f) {
            //is the first location we are recording?
            if (! startingLocation) {
                startingLocation = [newLoc retain];
                [self updateMapViewWithLocation:newLoc shouldZoom:YES];
            }
            else
                [self updateMapViewWithLocation:newLoc shouldZoom:NO];

            //update geocoder and distance view if we've changed location
            if (newLoc.coordinate.latitude != oldLoc.coordinate.latitude
                ||
                newLoc.coordinate.longitude != oldLoc.coordinate.longitude) {
                [self updateGeoCoderWithLocation:newLoc];
                distanceView.text = [NSString stringWithFormat:@"Distance travelled from start: %3.1fm",
                                [newLoc getDistanceFrom:startingLocation]];
            }
        }
    }
}

- (void)locationManager:(CLLocationManager *)manager didFailWithError:(NSError *)error {

    [lm stopUpdatingLocation];
    if (lm.headingAvailable)
        [lm stopUpdatingHeading];

    NSLog(@"an error occurred: %@",error);
}

- (void)locationManager:(CLLocationManager *)manager didUpdateHeading:(CLHeading *)newHeading
{
    if (newHeading.trueHeading != previousHeading) {
        previousHeading = newHeading.trueHeading;
        [self updateHeadingView];
    }
}

- (void)dealloc {

    [map release];

    [lm stopUpdatingLocation];
    [lm release];

    [geo release];

    [addressView release];
    [distanceView release];

    if (startingLocation)
        [startingLocation release];

    [super dealloc];
}

@end
```

Index

Symbols

///!!!: comment type, using in Xcode, 53
///FIXME: comment type, using in Xcode, 53
///MARK: comment type, using in Xcode, 53
///TODO: comment type, using in Xcode, 53
[] (square brackets), using with methods, 4
{} (braces), using with classes, 3
+ (plus) sign, using with class method, 6
<> (brackets), using with classes, 3

A

accelerometer
    creating tilt-sensitive application, 279–282
    detecting shakes, 270
    making tilt-sensitive, 279–282
    responding to, 279–282
action sheet
    versus alert view, 133
    creating, 132–133
actions
    connecting in Interface Builder, 69
    creating manually in Interface Builder, 70–73
    defined, 99
    using in Interface Builder, 62
activity, showing, 128–129
addresses, displaying in annotations, 306
alert view. *See also* views
    versus action sheet, 133
    displaying, 130–131
alloc method, calling, 11
altitude property, using with CLLocation
        event, 290
annotations
    adding to maps, 301–304
    changing callout view for, 304

displaying addresses in, 306
    removing from maps, 304
<app>-Info.plist
    properties file, 40–41
    settings, 81
Apple, registering as developer with, 37
application delegate, using, 78–80
application preferences, 84–85
application settings, overview of, 81
applications
    adding splash screens to, 80
    building in Xcode IDE, 55–57
    copying information between, 96–98
    creating settings page for, 84–85
    creating settings pages for, 84–85
    creating with custom URL scheme, 92–93
    force-quitting, 83
    launching from other applications, 91
    localizing, 89–90
    removing from iPhone Simulator, 61
    running in Xcode IDE, 55–57
    sharing information between, 93–96
archives, using with user preferences, 83
array values, looping through, 23
arrays
    creating, 15, 22–24
    getting lengths of, 22
    removing objects from, 24
    replacing objects in, 24
    sorting, 23
    verifying objects in, 23
arrow keys. *See* keyboard shortcuts
asynchronous connection, updating application
        for, 232–234
autocapitalizationType property, setting for
        keyboard, 146